Lecture Notes of the Institute for Computer Sciences, Social Informatics and Telecommunications Engineering 259

More information about this series at http://www.springer.com/series/8197

Frank Breitinger · Ibrahim Baggili (Eds.)

Digital Forensics and Cyber Crime

10th International EAI Conference, ICDF2C 2018
New Orleans, LA, USA, September 10–12, 2018
Proceedings

 Springer

Editors
Frank Breitinger 🆔
Tagliatela College of Engineering
University of New Haven
West Haven, CT, USA

Ibrahim Baggili 🆔
Tagliatela College of Engineering
University of New Haven
West Haven, CT, USA

ISSN 1867-8211   ISSN 1867-822X   (electronic)
Lecture Notes of the Institute for Computer Sciences, Social Informatics
and Telecommunications Engineering
ISBN 978-3-030-05486-1   ISBN 978-3-030-05487-8   (eBook)
https://doi.org/10.1007/978-3-030-05487-8

Library of Congress Control Number: 2018963584

This Springer imprint is published by the registered company Springer Nature Switzerland AG
The registered company address is: Gewerbestrasse 11, 6330 Cham, Switzerland

Preface

We are delighted to introduce the proceedings of the 10th edition of the 2018 European Alliance for Innovation (EAI) International Conference on Digital Forensics and Cyber Crime (ICDF2C). This conference continues to bridge the gap in the domain, and is truly international and quite visible worldwide. More importantly, this event bridges the gap between industry and researchers.

This year's keynotes are also to be proud of. Our first keynote speaker was Deborah Frincke, the director of research at the National Security Agency (NSA), followed by a pioneer in memory forensics, Golden Richard III from Louisiana State University.

The program was strong and extremely relevant for 2018. One important highlight of the program was a hands-on workshop by Riscure on extracting secrets from encrypted devices using side channel attacks, reverse engineering, fault injection, and the exploitation of weaknesses in secure firmware. Furthermore, the forensic analysis of cryptocurrencies was also a hot topic covered at this event. These topics are becoming ever so important in digital forensics as practitioners are dealing with more devices and applications that are encrypted. The rest of the program covered areas that are of high importance as well; carving and data hiding, Android security and forensics, memory forensic, industry presentations, forensic readiness, hard drive data distribution, and artifact correlation.

Overall, we accepted papers from the following countries and states: Germany, USA (Connecticut, Texas, California, Virginia, Ohio), South Africa, Estonia, Spain, China, and Ireland. The conference further boasted participants from a larger number of countries. The TPC committee accepted only 11 quality double-blind peer-reviewed papers (three were accepted after shepherding), out of 33 submissions (33% acceptance rate), and one short paper. Each paper had an average of four reviews, and best paper awards were selected after review by individuals with no conflict of interest in the selection process.

The conference is now positioned to grow, and we anticipate that next year we will be expanding the event to include topics that go beyond digital forensics.

We are very proud of this year's event, and we hope to continue the success of ICDF2C in the future. We would like to thank everyone who made this conference successful this year, and we look forward to seeing participants at next year's event.

November 2018

Ibrahim Baggili
Frank Breitinger

Organization

Steering Committee

Imrich Chlamtac	Bruno Kessler Professor, University of Trento, Italy
Ibrahim Baggili	University of New Haven, USA
Joshua I. James	DFIRE Labs, Hallym University, South Korea
Frank Breitinger	University of New Haven, USA

Organizing Committee

General Co-chairs

Irfan Ahmed	University of New Orleans, USA
Vassil Roussev	University of New Orleans, USA

TPC Chair and Co-chair

Frank Breitinger	University of New Haven, USA
Mark Scanlon	University College Dublin, Ireland

Local Chair

Minhaz Zibran	University of New Orleans, USA

Workshops Chair

Ibrahim Baggili	University of New Haven, USA

Publicity and Social Media Chair

Hyunguk Yoo	University of New Orleans, USA

Publications Chair

Joshua I. James	DFIRE Labs, Hallym University, South Korea

Web Chair

Manish Bhatt	University of New Orleans, USA

Conference Manager

Radka Pincakova	European Alliance for Innovations

Technical Program Committee

Ashley Podhradsky	Dakota State University, USA
David Lillis	University College Dublin, Ireland
Nhien An Le Khac	University College Dublin, Ireland
Golden Richard	Louisiana State University, USA
Krzysztof Szczypiorski	Warsaw University of Technology, Poland
Kim-Kwang Raymond Choo	The University of Texas at San Antonio, USA
Michael Losavio	University of Louisville, USA
Petr Matousek	Brno University of Technology, Czech Republic
Sebastian Schinzel	Münster University of Applied Sciences, Germany
Richard E. Overill	King's College London, UK
Joshua I. James	Digital Forensic Investigation Research Laboratory
Michael Spreitzenbarth	Siemens CERT
Ibrahim Baggili	University of New Haven, USA
Vik Harichandran	MITRE
Pavel Gladyshev	University College Dublin, Ireland
Virginia Franqueira	University of Derby, UK
Umit Karabiyik	Sam Houston State University, USA
Timothy Vidas	Carnegie Mellon University, USA
Bruce Nikkel	UBS AG
David Dampier	Mississippi State University, USA
Neil Rowe	U.S. Naval Postgraduate School, USA
Alex Nelson	National Institute of Standards and Technology
Harald Baier	CASED
Irfan Ahmed	University of New Orleans, USA
Vassil Roussev	University of New Orleans, USA
David Baker	DFRWS
Frank Adelstein	NFA Digital
Nicole Beebe	University of Texas at San Antonio, USA
Ondrej Rysavy	Brno University of Technology, Czech Republic
Christian Winter	Fraunhofer Gesellschaft
Spiridon Bakiras	Hamad Bin Khalifa University, Qatar
Bradley Schatz	Queensland University of Technology, Australia
Vladimir Vesely	Brno University of Technology, Czech Republic
Stig Mjolsnes	Norwegian University of Science and Technology NTNU, Norway
John Sheppard	Waterford Institute of Technology, Ireland

Contents

Artefact Correlation

Short Paper

Carving and Data Hiding

On Efficiency and Effectiveness of Linear Function Detection Approaches for Memory Carving

Lorenz Liebler[(⊠)] and Harald Baier

da/sec - Biometrics and Internet Security Research Group,
University of Applied Sciences, Darmstadt, Germany
{lorenz.liebler,harald.baier}@h-da.de

Abstract. In the field of unstructured memory analysis, the context-unaware detection of function boundaries leads to meaningful insights. For instance, in the field of binary analysis, those structures yield further inference, e.g., identifying binaries known to be bad. However, recent publications discuss different strategies for the problem of function boundary detection and consider it to be a difficult problem. One of the reasons is that the detection process depends on a quantity of parameters including the used architecture, programming language and compiler parameters. Initially a typical memory carving approach transfers the paradigm of signature-based detection techniques from the mass storage analysis to memory analysis. To automate and generalise the signature matching, signature-based recognition approaches have been extended by machine learning algorithms. Recently a review of function detection approaches claims that the results are possibly biased by large portions of shared code between the used samples. In this work we reassess the application of recently discussed machine learning based function detection approaches. We analyse current approaches in the context of memory carving with respect to both their efficiency and their effectiveness. We show the capabilities of function start identification by reducing the features to vectorised mnemonics. In all this leads to a significant reduction of runtime by keeping a high value of accuracy and a good value of recall.

Keywords: Memory forensics · Carving · Disassembly
Binary analysis

1 Introduction

The analysis of unknown binaries often starts with the examination of function boundaries. Functions are a fundamental structure of binaries and most often an initial starting point for advanced code analysis. As an important structural component of code, they give a schematic representation of the original high level semantics and provide a basis for further inferences. Whereas disassemblers are

F. Breitinger and I. Baggili (Eds.): ICDF2C 2018, LNICST 259, pp. 3–22, 2019.
https://doi.org/10.1007/978-3-030-05487-8_1

capable of reliably decoding the instructions of a binary, the problem of function detection is still an ongoing field of research [1–3,13,14]. Binary analysis research claims that the problem is not yet fully solved. New techniques tend to improve in performance and generalizability, i.e., by the introduction of compiler- or even architecture-agnostic approaches [2,13]. Functions are used to infer the functionality of a given binary and thus, could be used to identify a unknown sample. In more general terms, two binaries that share many similar functions are likely to be similar as well [9]. Summarized, functions could be used to identify, distinguish or interpret unknown code sequences. Beside the field of extended binary analysis, those general tasks are obviously also relevant for other domains of application, where function detection techniques have to consider the present environmental circumstances and constraints.

The examination of process related code fragments is obviously one major benefit of memory based forensically investigations. After successfully reconstructing the running binary out of a process context, steps of binary analysis and reverse engineering are often followed [11]. However, the reconstruction could be hindered by malicious or legitimate changes. Additionally, remaining fragments of already terminated processes are possibly ignored, due to missing structural properties. In case of Linux operating systems the generation of an adequate memory profile could be cumbersome. The continuous development of operating system internals and its related structures require the constant maintenance of interpretive frameworks. Thus, even if the interpretation of operating system related structures is a fundamental component of memory analysis, carving could give a first solid impression or even be a last resort during examination.

In the course of function detection, machine-learning approaches have been proposed, which are trained to recognize signatures located in function prologues or epilogues [3,14]. Static function prologue signature databases have to be maintained over time and the detection performance of those techniques rapidly decreases for highly optimized binaries [4,6]. Machine learning based approaches try to generalize this task and automate the process of signature detection. Beside those signature related approaches, Andriesse et al. [2] introduced an compiler-agnostic approach in the context of extended binary analysis, which is mainly based on structural Control Flow Graphs. Moreover, their research showed significant worrying for all top-tier work on machine learning based approaches, mainly caused by the usage of a biased dataset. The compiler-agnostic approach has been extended by architecture-agnostic detection methods [13].

Considering the function identification process in the field of memory carving, the present conditions exclude most of the extended and agnostic approaches. Those have been proposed in the field of extended binary analysis and require steps of binary lifting, control flow analysis or value set analysis. In the course of memory carving, we further denote suitable function detection approaches as *linear* techniques. Those approaches do not rely on the reconstructability of binaries and could also be used for context-unaware memory analysis.

Contributions: We give an overview of recently discussed function detection techniques in Sect. 2 and categorize them into *linear* and *non-linear* applications. We outline the task of function detection and give insights in two particular machine learning techniques in Sect. 3. As recent publications underline the importance of non-biased data sets for the task of training and evaluation, we first summarize different data sets and the properties of our used set in Sect. 4. The analysis is later used for adapting our proposed models. In Sect. 5 we outline the concrete adaptations to the models and discuss the utilization of mnemonics only. This reduces the overall feature size and improves the runtime performance of the classification. We reassess the capabilities of *linear* function detection in Sect. 6 and emphasize our desired classification goals (i.e., a better performance in terms of recall and classification runtime). Our analysis underlines the applicability by reaching those goals even with significant reduced feature vectors. In contrary to recent publications, we consider runtime performance as an important constraint. We summarize our findings in Sect. 7.

2 Related Work

The enumeration of unknown functions was first established with the generation of signature databases. Signature databases focus on proprietary compilers, as open source compilers create an unhandable diversity of function prologues [4,6]. Especially in case of Linux operating systems, a database lookup of saved signatures during carving a memory image would be not feasible.

In Bao et al. [3] a weighted prefix tree structure was introduced to identify potentially function start addresses. Therefore, they "weight vertices in the prefix tree by computing the ratio of true positives to the sum of true and false positives for each sequence" in a reference data set. The authors additionally introduce an additional step of normalization, which improves precision and recall. The authors created a set of 2,200 Linux and Windows binaries. The executables were generated with different build settings, i.e., the authors used GNU `gcc`, Intel `icc` and Microsoft Visual Studio. In addition, multiple different optimization levels were selected during build time. Their approach, called `Byteweight`, was also integrated into the Binary Analysis Platform (BAP)[1].

In Shin et al. [14] the authors provide an approach for function detection based on artificial neural networks. The paper proposes a function detection technique with the help of Recurrent Neural Networks. In contrast to our work, the approach of [14] was performed without an additional step of disassembling or normalization. The authors point out that the tracking of function calls over large sequences of bytes is not feasible. In fact, recognizing entry and exit patterns by training with fixed-length subsequences is eligible. For training and testing the work is based on the same data set provided by Bao et al.

Andriesse et al. [2] claim that the work of Shin et al. and Bao et al. suffer from significant evaluation bias, as the most of the samples contain of large amounts of similar functions. The authors additionally mention that the viability

---

[1] https://github.com/BinaryAnalysisPlatform/bap (last access 2018-04).

of machine learning for function detection is not yet decided. The publication proposes a compiler-agnostic approach called `Nucleus`, which is mainly based on the examination of advanced control flow analysis and not relies on any signature information. The approach is not applicable in our context, as we want to inspect code fragments in large amounts of data within a sliding window: we have to consider the linear characteristic of our application, which in turn leads us to a signature-based or machine-learning based approach.

Potchik [13] introduced the integration of `Nucleus` in the Binary Ninja Reversing Platform[2] and proposes multiple strategies over multiple analysis passes than just rely on simple heuristics. The author mentions the possible reduction of complexity and scope reduction, by applying the technique with the highest confidence first. Similar to other fields, the approach proposes "a method to interpret the semantics of low-level CPU instructions" by the utilization of value-set analysis. The process of value-set analysis is performed on an extended intermediate language and thus, should be architecture agnostic.

3   Background

We first give a short introduction to the problem of function detection and describe the already introduced condition of *linearity* (Sect. 3.1). For a more detailed and formal explanation of the task of function detection, we refer to previous work [2,3,14]. The already introduced approaches in Sect. 2 are shortly discussed and categorized. We depict two applicable approaches for signature-based function detection and discuss their functionality: Recurrent Neural Networks (RNN) in Sect. 3.2 and Weighted Prefix Tress (WPT) in Sect. 3.3.

3.1   Linear Function Detection

The task of function detection is one of the main disassembly challenges [1]. The problem of function detection (e.g., with the help of static signatures) could be illustrated by the inspection of functions compiled with different optimization levels invoked to the compiler. The function structure and function prologue heavily changes due to optimization and compiler settings. An example could be seen in Fig. 1, which was adopted from [14]. The example shows the remarkable impact by simple adaptations of the compiler flags. Most of the instructions in the function prologues of `mul_inv` heavily differ from each other. The process of function detection itself is most often divided into subtasks. We stick to similar notation of previous work and refer to those publications [2,3,14].

The subtasks of function detection could be differentiated into *function start detection* and *function end detection*. The problem of *function boundary detection* is a superset of *function start* and *function end detection*. In the course of this work, we mainly focus on the task of function start detection. We borrowed most of the following definitions from Shin et al., where C defines a given code base of

---

[2] https://binary.ninja/ (last access 2018-04).

Listing 1.1: Original C Source

```c
int mul_inv(int a, int b) {
  int b0 = b, t, q;
  int x0 = 0, x1 = 1;
  if (b == 1) return 1;
  while (a > 1) {
    q=a/b, t=b, b=a%b, a=t;
    t=x0, x0=x1-q*x0, x1=t;
  }
  if (x1 < 0) x1 += b0;
  return x1;
}
```

Listing 1.2: gcc -O0

```asm
<mul_inv>:
push  %rbp
mov   %rsp,%rbp
mov   %edi,-0x24(%rbp)
mov   %esi,-0x28(%rbp)
mov   -0x28(%rbp),%eax
...
```

Listing 1.3: gcc -O3

```asm
<mul_inv>:
cmp   $0x1,%esi
mov   %edi,%eax
je    400878
cmp   $0x1,%edi
jle   400878
mov   %esi,%ecx
mov   $0x1,%r8d
xor   %edi,%edi
...
```

Fig. 1. Adopted example from [14] with a function written in C and compiled with two different levels of optimization (gcc 4.9.1).

a binary, which consists of several functions $f_1, \ldots, f_n \in F$. A function $f_x \in F$ consists of a sequence of instructions I, with $i_y \in I$. The task of detection could be simplified into three basic tasks for a given target function f_t:

1. **Function start:** The first instruction of $i_s \in I$ of $f_t \in F$ within C.
2. **Function end:** The last instruction of $i_e \in I$ of a $f_t \in F$ within C.
3. **Function boundaries:** The tuple of instructions, which define the boundaries of a function, i.e., determine $(i_s, i_e) \in I$ of $f_t \in F$ within C.

The scope of function detection normally sticks to disciplines of analysing stripped binaries in the context of reverse engineering, malware analysis or code reuse detection. However, most of these applications are not limited in their form of application and are not underlying any time constraints. As we transfer the function detection problem to the field of context-unaware domains, we have to consider the constraints of *linear* processing. A concrete field of application is the examination of function boundaries in the domain of unstructured and context-unaware memory analysis. As previous publications showed fundamental improvements in the case of compiler- and architecture-agnostic techniques, we emphasize the motivation behind signature-related techniques, as we could not rely on features like binary lifting, intermediate representations or control flow analysis. Our goal is the integration of a function start identification approach, which works on an instruction buffer within a single sliding window pass. So we refine the problem of function detection to be a *linear function detection* problem. This leads to the evaluation of signature-based approaches.

Shown in Table 1, different approaches have been suggested. In this work we focus on signature-related (Sig.) and linear approaches (Lin.). The approach of Shin et al. [14] is based on Bi-directional Networks, which are not applicable in our context. Those networks require the presence of a complete binary at application time. The lookup of signature databases on for Linux operating systems was already mentioned as impracticable. As we try to carve functions out of a memory, we could not rely on the recreation of a previously detected process.

Table 1. Overview of different approaches in the context of carving memory.

Approach	Sig.	Lin.	Comment
Guilfanov [6]	✓	✓	Impractical for diversity of Linux systems
Bao et al. [3]	✓	✓	Weighted Prefix Trees are applicable
Shin et al. [14]	✓	-	Bi-directional RNN not applicable
Andriesse et al. [2]	✗	✗	Process-context recreation needed
Potchik [13]	✗	✗	Process-context recreation needed

3.2 Recurrent Neural Networks

The authors of [14] provide a detailed overview of the different characteristics of Recurrent Neural Networks. Beside the work of [14], we refer to [12] and [8] for a detailed introduction. We outline differences between our approach and the approach of Shin et al. [14] later: The specific settings, hyperparameters and implementation details of our model are described in Sect. 5.

The processing of sequences with Recurrent Neural Networks is a promising strategy for many different fields. In contrast to feedforward neural networks, the cells keep different states of previously processed input and consider sequences which have an explicit or implicit temporal relation. A sample x_t of a sequence is additionally labeled with its corresponding time step t of appearance. Where a corresponding target y_t of labeled data also shares this temporal notation. The basic architecture of those nets could strongly vary for different fields of application. In Fig. 2 a simplified and unfolded model is shown, which takes multiple input vectors over time and outputs a single vector after several time steps. The term unfolding denotes the unfolding of the cyclic characteristic, by displaying each timestep. Each of the edges in between the columns span adjacent time steps. The model in Fig. 2 depicts a many to one relation.

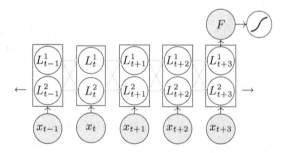

Fig. 2. Simplified RNN model with two LSTM-layers, where the model represents a many to one structure. The final state is processed by a Fully Connected Layer F and a sigmoid layer, which outputs a probability.

Long Short-Term Memory (LSTM): Training Recurrent Neural Networks bares several pitfalls. Namely, the problems of vanishing and exploding gradients. There are different extensions of RNNs which try to consider those issues, one of those specimens are LSTM based Networks [5,8]. Those networks replace traditional nodes in the hidden layers with memory cells (see Fig. 3). Each cell consists of an input node (g) and internal state (c). The memory cells contain self-connected recurrent edges, to avoid vanishing or exploding gradients across many time steps. Those edges are named gates, where each of the LSTM cells has a forget gate (f), an input gate (i) and an output gate (o). A multiplication node ($\prod$) is used to connect those components with each other. The final memory cell reaches an intermediate state between long-term and short-term memory of classic RNNs. Those types of cells outperform simple RNNs in case of long-range dependencies [12]. The original work of Shin et al. is based on Bi-directional RNNs. The authors mention that those models are applicable in the context of having access to the entire binary at once. As we discuss the applicability of RNNs in the context of linear processing large amounts raw data, we have to consider the temporal component and focus on a LSTM based model.

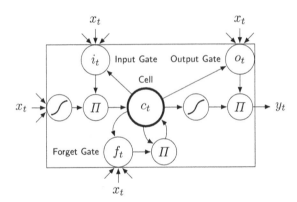

Fig. 3. LSTM Memory cell proposed by [5], which extends the model of [8] with additional forget gates (f_t).

Training and Classification: There are different strategies for training and updating a neural model. The predominant algorithm for training is backpropagation, which is based on the chain rule. The algorithm updates the weights of the model by calculating the derivative of the loss function for each parameter in the network and adjusts the values by the determined gradient descent. However, the problem is a NP-hard Problem and different heuristics try to avoid stucking in a local minimum. A common strategy for training is stochastic gradient descent (SGD) using mini-batches. In the course of RNNs with time-related connections between each time step, the process of training is often denoted as backpropagation through time (BPTT) [12]. Bao et al. [3] proposed a flipped order of prologues during processing to support the training phase. Additionally, the work shows a better performance for bidirectional structures than unidirectional structures like LSTM. Each model was trained with 100.000 randomly-extracted 1000-byte chunks. A one-hot encoding converts a byte into a $\mathbb{R}^{256}$ vector.

3.3   Weighted Prefix Tress

Bao et al. [3] introduced the application of weighted prefix trees for the task of binary function detection, called `Byteweight`. The approach uses a weighted prefix tree, and matches binary fragments with the signatures previously learned. The path from the root node to the leaf node represents a byte sequence of instructions. Inside the tree, the weights are adapted to the previously processed ground truth. In the original implementation an additional step of value-set analysis and control flow recovery process is proposed for boundary detection.

Byteweight: Similar to this work and the work of Shin et al. [14], Byteweight focuses on the task of function start identification. More formally, the authors denote the problem as simple classification problem, where the goal is to label each byte of a binary as either function start or not. Their approach was demonstrated on raw byte sequences and previously disassembled sequences. The reference corpus is compiled with labelled function start addresses. In contrary to raw bytes, the usage of normalized disassembled instructions showed a better performance in case of precision and recall. The authors proposed a twofold normalization: immediate number normalization and `call-jump` instruction normalization. In Fig. 4 an overview of the normalized prefix tree is given. A given sequence of bytes or instructions is classified by inspecting the corresponding terminal node in the tree. As soon as the stored value exceeds a previous defined threshold t, the sequence is considered as a function start. We do not consider subsequent steps of advanced control flow graph recovery as proposed by the authors.

Training and Classification: A corpus of input binaries is used during the learning phase. The maximum sequence length l defines the upper bound of the resulting trie height. The first l elements are used for training, where elements

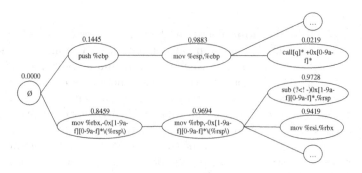

Fig. 4. Example of normalized prefix tree proposed by Bao et al. [3].

could be disassembled instructions or the raw bytes itself. The likelihood that
a sequence of elements corresponds to a function start (i.e., represented as a
specific path in the trie) is saved in each corresponding node as specific weight.
Considering the example in Fig. 4, the instruction `push %ebp` were truly function
starts in 14.45% of all cases. The weights of a prefix are lowered if they do not
correspond to a function start. As described in Eq. 1, the weight of a specific
node W_n is the ratio between positive function starts (T_+) and all matches
$(T_+ + T_-)$. The classification of an input sequence is performed by matching the
given elements against the tree. The weight of the last matching terminal node,
describes the final weight of a sequence and is compared to t. For the process
of training and classification, the authors proposed an input size of $l = 10$
consecutive instructions and a threshold of $t = 0.5$.

$$W_n = \frac{T_+}{T_+ + T_-}. \tag{1}$$

4 Training and Evaluation Data Sets

In recent publications, different sources of ground truth binaries have been proposed and criticized. In this paragraph we give a short overview of the different
sources and outline some details of capacity and source. As we focus on the
domain of Linux executable binaries, we formally introduce ELF binaries contained in different test suites. A comprehensive overview of the different test
suites is given in Table 2 which have been public available[3,4,5] at the time of
writing.

Table 2. Overview of different evaluation datasets [13].

Source	System			Description (ELF, Linux)
	WIN	LIN	OSX	
Byteweight	✓	✓	✗	ELFs (129): `coreutils`, `binutils` and `findutils`; used by Bao et al. [3] and Shin et al. [14]
Nucleus	✓	✓	✗	ELFs (521): real-world applications and the SPEC CPU2006 Benchmark Suite; see Table 3 for details
CGC Corpus	✓	✓	✓	ELF binaries of custom-made programs specifically designed to contain vulnerabilities

---

[3] https://github.com/Vector35/function_detection_test_suite (last access 2018-04).
[4] https://github.com/trailofbits/cb-multios (last access 2018-04).
[5] http://security.ece.cmu.edu/byteweight/ (last access 2018-04).

As already outlined in the introduction, the work of Bao et al. [3] and Shin et al. [14] are criticized by Andriesse et al. [2] for using a biased data set, with a large amount of overlapping and similar functions. Andriesse et al. [1] outlined that the average binary in their SPEC-based test suite contains less than 1% of shared functions, not considering bootstrap functions. We base our analysis on the data set introduced by Andriesse et al. [1] and perform a detailed examination of the function structures in the following paragraphs.

The `Nucleus` data set consists of approximately 4.2 GiB precompiled ELF files and its corresponding ground truth assembly structure. The process of data set generation depends on some major parameters: operating system, instruction set architecture, language, compiler and optimization level. The 521 binaries consist of the SPEC CPU2006 Benchmark Suite and some real-world application written in C and C++. The samples are compiled for x86 and x64 with five different optimization levels (O0-O3 and Os). The set contains dynamically and statically linked binaries, where some of them are stripped and some are equipped with symbols. For further details on the construction of the ground truth we refer to [1]. An overview of the binaries is given in Table 3. In the following paragraphs we give a detailed introduction of the data set. Therefore, we focus on three properties of our used data set: *Function Sizes*, *Function Prologue Distribution* and *Mnemonic Distribution*. As already described in the introduction, the examination of the underlying code structure should give us additionally insights for better design and parameter decisions.

Table 3. `Nucleus` - ELF ground truth obtained by [1] (gcc-510, llvm-370).

Samples	Arch		Compiler		Language		Optimization				
	32	64	gcc	llvm	C	C++	O0	O1	O2	O3	OS
SPEC	✓	✓	✓	✓	✓	✓	✓	✓	✓	✓	✓
glibc	✗	✓	✓	✗	✗	✗	✗	✗	✗	✗	✗
Server	✓	✓	✓	✓	✗	✗	✗	✗	✗	✗	✗
Count	200	321	321	200	360	140	100	100	100	100	100

Function Sizes: The examination of the frequencies of different function sizes is required for further analysis and inferences. The function size defines the possible size of extracted features, before a single feature vector overlaps with a subsequent function start. In addition, the function size gives better insights into the possible dimension of further function prologues examinations. We examined the function size (in bytes) of the different binaries. As could be seen in Fig. 5, the function sizes vary for different compiler and optimization levels. The median function size illustrates that in every language, compiler and optimization setting, the amount of small functions (i.e., smaller than 200 Bytes) is significant. The average value of function sizes outlines the presence of large functions, where in all settings the average size is always lower than 800 Bytes.

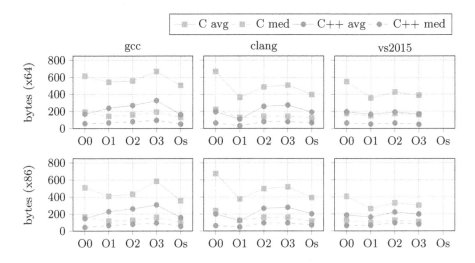

Fig. 5. Average and median function size in bytes.

Function Prologue Distribution: To gain a better understanding of the function detection problem with the help of signature-based detection mechanisms, we examined the present ground truth set and the distribution of common function prologues. We extracted the functions of each binary and aggregated them into a comprehensive set. Figure 6 illustrates the population of function prologues by comparing the ratio η between distinct function prologues ρ_d to the overall amount of function prologues ρ for a specific language, compiler and optimization level (for further details see Eq. 2).

$$\eta = \frac{\#\,\text{distinct function prologues}}{\#\,\text{function prologues}} = \frac{\rho_d}{\rho} \qquad (2)$$

We discriminate the function prologues by its consisting number of instructions i, which are considered and which have been decoded to a single mnemonic. The plot underlines the common axiom that function prologues strongly vary for different compilers, languages and optimization levels. The plot visualizes the impact on the diversity of the prologue instructions in dependency to the selected optimization levels and helps to argue about an appropriate input size.

With the x86 instruction set an instruction could have variable-length, where one instruction could vary between one and fifteen bytes. For further details we refer to the Intel Instruction manual[6]. Considering the previous examination of function sizes and the median value of 200 Bytes per function, we do not expect all instructions of a prologue sequence to reach the maximum amount of fifteen bytes. It is clear that a large chosen amount of input mnemonics raises the diversity the model has to deal with, but also increases the possible classification quality. Considering the plots in Fig. 6, the diversity significantly increases

---

[6] https://software.intel.com/en-us/articles/intel-sdm (last access 2018-04).

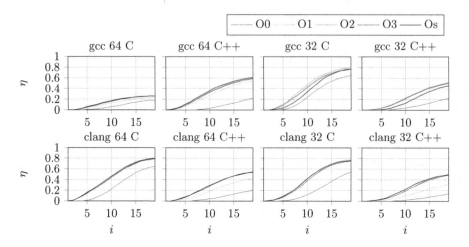

Fig. 6. Illustration of distinct function prologues; η denotes fraction of distinct function prologues to the number of all functions for i instructions (mnemonic).

for several settings, even after a considerable short amount of consecutive prologue instructions. For example, inspecting `clang-32-C` without optimization (i.e., `O0`), approximately 40% of all function prologues of 10 consecutive instructions represent a distinct instruction sequence. Figure 6 also underlines that non-optimized binaries (`O0`) often share the same beginning instructions (mnemonic).

Mnemonic Distribution: We use the ground truth of assembly files to determine the distribution of mnemonics in the used set. Additionally, we extract the bigrams of mnemonics, which could be often found in the course of assembly based code and similarity analysis. The following values give us an initial overview of the mnemonics distribution. For details see Table 4. Roughly spoken it is an overview of the instruction distribution of already decoded byte sequences. We splitted the set of assemblies by its architecture and determined the *total* amount of unigrams and bigrams. In our case a unigram consists of a single mnemonic. The *total* amount of occurring mnemonics also represents the total amount of occurring instructions. The column of *distinct* values describes the set of all occurring mnemonics. The columns *max, mean* and *min* describe the assignment of the *total* amount of instructions to each *distinct* occuring unigram or bigram. In detail, *the most frequently occurred mnemonic* in the set of

Table 4. Overview of unigram and bigram mnemonic counts.

	32 bit (200 files)				64 bit (321 files)			
	Total	Distinct	Max	Mean	Total	Distinct	Max	Mean
Unigrams	35,232 k	322	11,714 k	1531	61,441 k	436	21,627 k	1859
Bigrams	35,232 k	11632	5,889 k	17	61,441 k	16059	10,360 k	28

32 bit files, namely `mov`, represents 11,714,270 instructions. Thus, `mov` represents approximately 33.25% of all instructions in the course of 32 bit files.

5   Linear Function Detection

In this Section we discuss concrete adaptations and realizations of linear function detection techniques. Beside the reassessing of machine learning-based approaches we aim for a reduction of the used feature sizes to improve the theoretically runtime performance. Therefore, we introduce an additional step of approximate disassembling by the usage of an approximate disassembler [10]. In previous work the created pipelines are partially based on the processing of features on a byte-level. The input sequences for training and evaluation are one-hot encoded into $\mathbb{R}^{256}$. As our approach is based on integerized mnemonics, the distinct occurring mnemonics define our underlying vocabulary size.

We first describe the general pipeline and the used set for training and evaluation (Sect. 5.1). We explicitly address the problem of imbalanced classes, i.e., the ratio between function starts and general offsets. Afterwards, we introduce the proposed models and concrete adaptations (Sects. 5.2 and 5.3).

5.1   General Pipeline of Feature Extraction

In Fig. 7 an overview of the single steps of feature extraction is given. We only considered allocable code sections (i.e., .text) of the used ground truth ELFs [1]. Thus, we filtered all offsets which are known to be data ❶.

Similar to Bao et al. [3] and contrary to Shin et al. [14] we propose a layer of disassembling for further feature extraction ❷. We additionally reduce the used vectors to mnemonics only. We decode the raw byte sequences into an approximate disassembly with an integerized mnemonic for each instruction. Beside the reduction of variances in the underlying byte structure, this additionally reduces the overall amount of data which needs to be processed and saved. The classification is not performed at each byte offset, but rather at every instruction offset. Thus, we reduce the overall vector input size and therefore the runtime performance.

As we have to deal with an heavily imbalanced set of classes, we first determine the positive (function beginnings) and negative classes (code offsets) for each file ❸. For each class, we created vectors of N_{max} consecutive instructions at each instruction offset, represented by a single and integerized mnemonic. Considering the function prologue distribution in Sect. 4, most of the displayed distributions showed tendencies to stabilize after the first 20 instructions. The future vector size should also consider the determined average and median function sizes, as we try to avoid feature vectors which overlap into subsequent functions. Where Shin et al. proposed the processing of 1000-byte chunks for RNN-based classification and Bao et al. suggested the usage of 10 consecutive instructions for the creation of Weighted-Prefix-Trees, we considered a maximum vector size of $N_{max} = 20$ mnemonics for creating our data set. This empowers us to vary different input sizes during different model evaluation passes.

We created two sets for both classes and performed an additional step of deduplication for each class over the whole set. This results in two sets of distinct feature vectors ❹. In Table 5 an overview of the imbalanced distribution of classes is given. We also examined possible overlaps between each class, i.e., vectors of mnemonics which occur in the positive T_+ and negative class T_-. This is obviously caused by the strong reduction to mnemonic feature vectors. We relabel the negative classes of $T_+ \cap T_-$ to provoke false positives. We outline this decision in Sect. 6. The two distinct features have been shuffled before and splitted into a training and test set ❺. In the case of RNN based training, we additionally added an step of oversampling T_+ and undersampling T_- ❻.

Table 5. Overview of class distribution, i.e., number of distinct function starts (T_+) and distinct inner function offsets (T_-) for all used 64 bit binaries.

Set	T_-	T_+	$T_+ \cup T_-$	$T_+ \cap T_-$
Count	18,575,407	207,714	18,779,238	3,883

5.2   RNN Model Adaptation

In the following subsection, we describe the final model settings for our linear RNN-based classification. The basic steps of processing are displayed in Fig. 8. The extracted and integerized mnemonics are transformed into a one-hot encoding and fed into the RNN for further processing. This pipeline is consistent for all further training and evaluation steps performed on our RNN settings.

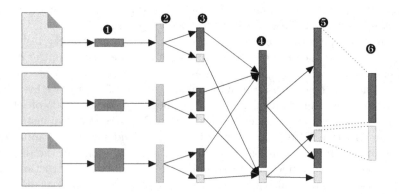

Fig. 7. Simplified overview of the general pipeline of feature extraction.

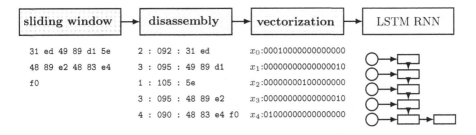

Fig. 8. The general processing pipeline during RNN-based classification.

Input Vectors: We are not expecting to train with an input time series larger than 20. In particular, we try to avoid long series for classification, to minimize the impact on runtime performance later. After the examination of distinct function prologues shown in Fig. 6, we varied the input vector size between 16 and 20 consecutive and integerized instructions. For the final model, we depicted the vector size of instructions as $N_i = 16$. Similar to Shin et al. we reversed the order of our input vectors, which showed a significant improvement in nearly all of our evaluations. Summarized, the network expects a reversed one-hot encoded input vector $x_t \in \mathbb{R}^K$ for each decoded instruction i_t, where K describes the current size of the vocabulary.

Hidden Cells and Layers: As already described in Sect. 3, we use Long Short-Term Memory cells for creating our RNN model. In detail, we use a two-layered model with a different number of hidden cells. To reduce the complexity we use LSTM in contrary to bi-directional RNNs as suggested by Shin et al.. We initially compared two-layered RNNs with one-layered models. In most of the cases a two-layered model improved the accuracy, which made us to perform all of the further proceedings with a two-layered model. We vary the number of hidden cells in the subsequent evaluation between 32 and 512 for our two-layered setting. We finally choose the amount of $N_h = 256$ hidden cells.

Training and Optimization: Similar to Shin et al. [14] we performed our steps of optimization by the usage of *stochastic gradient descent*. We tried different concepts of gradient adaptation and initially used *RMSProp* for optimization with different initial learning rates. In the further proceedings of the evaluation, we switched to *AdamOptimizer* which showed a similar performance. The gradients were updated with the help of mini-batches, where the size of the batches was also varied during evaluation and performance tuning. After several manual test runs, we set the final batch size to $N_b = 2048$.

Dropout: We reduced the risk of overfitting our models by adding an intermediate Dropout layer. A Dropout step randomly turns off activations of neurons between our two LSTM layers. The Dropout is not applied on the recurrent connections itself [7]. A defined value of $N_d = 0.75$. sets the probability if a connection is *not* deactivated. We keep this value for all of our trained models.

Output Layer: For a binary classification of the function starts we process the output of the final LSTM state by a fully connected layer. The final layer of the setup is a sigmoid layer, which is used for transforming our output into a binary classification. A single probability is generated with the help of an additional *sigmoid cross entropy* layer or *weighted cross entropy* layer. With the usage of a *weighted cross entropy* layer, we could additionally set the focus on improving our final recall or precision rate.

Training and Sampling: To handle the heavily imbalanced ground truth, we performed an additional step of oversampling the positive and undersampling the negative class. Those steps had an remarkable influence on the performance in case of precision and recall. During training we randomly selected the half of the negative class member (inner function offsets) and oversampled the positive class members (function starts) to an even amount.

5.3   Weighted Prefix Tree Adaptation

The major adaptation in case of our proposed Weighted-Prefix-Tree model, is the utilization of single mnemonic representatives instead of raw bytes or normalized disassembly instructions. The basic steps of processing are displayed in Fig. 9. We selected different lengths for trie creation up to $l_{max} = 20$ instructions. The mentioned vocabulary size K (see Sect. 4) gives us the theoretical upper bound for the possible trie size. The implementation of evaluation was realized with Python, not yet considering runtime in first case. We depict an initial threshold value of $t = 0.5$ and $l = 10$, which was proposed by Bao et al. [3].

Tree Pruning: Similar to the original approach we additionally performed a step of tree pruning. In detail, we deleted all intermediate nodes with no negative counts ($T_- = 0$) and thus, all first occurring intermediate nodes with $W_i = 1$ are transformed to terminal nodes. This reduces the overall tree size from approximately 1.9 million nodes to 264,834 nodes.

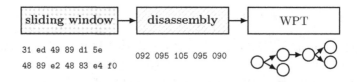

Fig. 9. The general processing pipeline during WPT-based classification.

6   Evaluation

In this section, we discuss the different evaluations of our proposed models. We inspect the time of creation and training our models, without considering the pass of feature extraction (Sect. 6.1). Afterwards, we examine the performance in terms of accuracy, precision and recall for both models (Sect. 6.2). Finally, we discuss in detail the possible application of weighted prefix trees (Sect. 6.3). Our evaluation aims to answer the following questions:

1. Could we use only mnemonics for the task of function start identification?
2. Which of the considered linear techniques is better suited for our context?

Classification Goals: We consider our models for the fast identification of function starts in large portions of raw data. As described in Sect. 5.1, the reduction of our proposed features leads to overlapping class members. We relabelled those members to positive members and further treat recall more important than precision: we accept higher values of false positives by lower values false negatives with a constant high value of true negatives. We propose an additional step of classification for lowering the value of false positives afterwards.

Methodology: To argue if our models generalise the task of function detection, we performed a 10 fold validation by dividing our set of *distinct* integerized mnemonic vectors into ten equally sized sub-sets. We used nine of those subsets for training and one for evaluation. In the case of WPT-based training, we repeated this task 10 times. In our current evaluation we focus on 64 bit ELF binaries of the Linux operating system. Our used test set consists of nearly 1.9 million unique vectors with approximately 20 k positive cases. The set of training consisted of 16 million negative and nearly 190k positive class members.

6.1   Training Performance

First, we examine the general runtime performance in case of model creation and training. Both models have been fed with the already prepared integerized mnemonic vectors and a maximum length of 20. In the case of our RNN model, we already cropped the initial feature vectors to a maximum size of 16.

As already described in Fig. 8, in case of training our proposed RNN the processing began with the reversing of the input vector and the one-hot encoding. Considering those steps, the training of our model took approximately 2.5 hours for one epoch. As we trained our model for 10 to 20 epochs, the process most often took *several days* on a machine with 64 cores and more than 256 GiB of RAM. We utilized Tensorflow and implemented our model in Python.

In contrary, the creation of the weighted prefix tree was performed on an ordinary Laptop with Intel Core i5 2x 2,2 GHz Processor and 8 GiB RAM. The time of building the initial tree, calculating the final weights, pruning the tree and performing an additional step of lookup took approximately *180 s* in total. Our current prototype implementation was realized in Python.

Table 6. Performance of the function start identification for x86-64 ELF binaries. (*:average values of 10-fold cross validation)

Model	Accuracy	Precision	Recall	Population	TP	TN	FP	FN
WPT*	0.9943	0.7532	0.7233	1,878,311	15,023	1,852,616	4,924	5,747
RNN	0.9861	0.4300	0.7674	1,878,016	15,940	1,836,117	21,128	4,831

6.2 Function Start Identification

For our final models, we used the in Sects. 5.2 and 5.3 described settings. As could be seen in Table 6 the application of our RNN performs similar to our proposed WPT. In both cases we gain a high value of accuracy with lower values of precision and recall. However, the results of the WPT clearly outperforms the RNN in case of precision. As already described in Sect. 5.2, the adaptation of the underlying RNN model could influence the classification in terms of focusing on better values of recall or precision. However, in contrary to our WPT implementation, the adaptation of those RNN parameters must be done before the training of the model. The WPT approach empowers to influence the value of recall by parametrizing the lookup, which is more flexible than approaching the perfect parameters by multiple time consuming training passes.

6.3 Examination of WPT

As the previous evaluations underlined, we achieved similar or better classification capabilities in less training time by the utilization of our WPT model. For the WPT model, we could additionally adapt the classification goal during a lookup pass. This leads to a detailed examination of our WPT model.

To improve the quality of WPT-based classification, we examined the different parameters and their influence on the overall classification task. In detail, we varied different parameters, like the maximum sequence length l and the threshold t. In addition, we introduce a third parameter m, which denotes the minimum required length of a matching sequence inside the tree. After the inspection of the Prologue Distributions in Sect. 4, we selected a range from 0 to 18 (instructions) for the parameters m and l. Respecting our classification goal, we focus on runtime performance by accepting a higher amount of false positives instead of false negatives. Inspecting the classification in Table 7, we could argue that the reduction of false negatives could be achieved by increasing the considered vector size l. The processing time for the nearly 1.9 million test vectors was approximately 12 s for all of the parameter variations. We should mention that during

Table 7. WPT classification by varying different parameters t, l and m.

t	$m\backslash l$	Accuracy			Precision			Recall			Time (sec.)		
		10	14	18	10	14	18	10	14	18	10	14	18
0.6	0	0.9944	0.9944	0.9944	0.7867	0.7666	0.7589	0.6829	0.7222	0.7278	11.043	11.134	11.152
	4	0.9944	0.9944	0.9944	0.7889	0.7685	0.7608	0.6793	0.7186	0.7243	11.063	11.163	11.154
	8	0.9933	0.9933	0.9933	0.8203	0.7893	0.7785	0.5067	0.5460	0.5517	11.066	11.135	11.371
0.5	0	0.9937	0.9936	0.9934	0.7098	0.6868	0.6786	0.7385	0.7743	0.7800	11.408	11.853	11.871
	4	0.9937	0.9936	0.9935	0.7127	0.6893	0.6810	0.7359	0.7718	0.7775	11.429	11.084	11.564
	8	0.9930	0.9928	0.9927	0.7504	0.7147	0.7029	0.5542	0.5901	0.5957	11.587	11.556	11.422
0.4	0	0.9932	0.9929	0.9928	0.6686	0.6476	0.6415	0.7691	0.7974	0.8024	11.316	11.481	11.881
	4	0.9933	0.9930	0.9929	0.6752	0.6535	0.6472	0.7648	0.7931	0.7981	11.804	11.653	11.326
	8	0.9929	0.9926	0.9925	0.7283	0.6931	0.6835	0.5749	0.6032	0.6082	11.326	11.908	11.950
0.3	0	0.9917	0.9913	0.9912	0.5942	0.5757	0.5707	0.8046	0.8314	0.8361	11.297	11.418	11.539
	4	0.9920	0.9916	0.9915	0.6072	0.5875	0.5821	0.8001	0.8268	0.8315	11.505	11.430	11.414
	8	0.9924	0.9920	0.9919	0.6758	0.6414	0.6327	0.6064	0.6332	0.6379	11.055	11.135	11.277

our initial implementation we did not focus on any runtime optimizations, which could be further improved.

7   Conclusion

In this paper, we inspected the capabilities of linear function detection and underlined the need of signature-based detection methods in the course of memory carving. After performing a detailed analysis of our underlying ground truth, we introduced several considerations and model adaptations. The main adaptation of our approach is the utilization of mnemonics only.

Our analysed models showed good classification results in term of accuracy, where we achieved for RNN and WPT based models a value of accuracy above 98%. The utilization of menmonic-based weighted prefix trees showed good capabilities for our considered context of application. The application of WPT performs the classification of 1.9 million offsets in 12 s and reaches with simple parameter adaptations an acceptable value of recall beyond 80%.

Considering the mentioned techniques within multiple steps of classification, our proposed WPT could be used for the fast identification of possible function starts and drastically reduces the amount of offsets which need to be reclassified.

Acknowledgement. This work was supported by the German Federal Ministry of Education and Research (BMBF) as well as by the Hessen State Ministry for Higher Education, Research and the Arts (HMWK) within CRISP (www.crisp-da.de).

References

1. Andriesse, D., Chen, X., van der Veen, V., Slowinska, A., Bos, H.: An in-depth analysis of disassembly on full-scale x86/x64 binaries. In: USENIX Security Symposium (2016)
2. Andriesse, D., Slowinska, A., Bos, H.: Compiler-agnostic function detection in binaries. In: IEEE European Symposium on Security and Privacy (2017)
3. Bao, T., Burket, J., Woo, M., Turner, R., Brumley, D.: Byteweight: learning to recognize functions in binary code. In: USENIX (2014)
4. Eagle, C.: The IDA Pro Book: The Unofficial Guide to the World's Most Popular Disassembler. No Starch Press, San Francisco (2008). ISBN 1593271786, 9781593271787
5. Gers, F.A., Schmidhuber, J., Cummins, F.: Learning to Forget: Continual Prediction with LSTM (1999)
6. Guilfanov, I.: IDA Fast Library Identification and Recognition Technology (Flirt Technology): In-depth (2012)
7. Hinton, G.E., Srivastava, N., Krizhevsky, A., Sutskever, I., Salakhutdinov, R.R.: Improving neural networks by preventing co-adaptation of feature detectors. arXiv preprint arXiv:1207.0580 (2012)
8. Hochreiter, S., Schmidhuber, J.: Long short-term memory. Neural Comput. **9**(8), 1735–1780 (1997)

9. Jin, W., et al.: Binary function clustering using semantic hashes. In: 2012 11th International Conference on Machine Learning and Applications (ICMLA), vol. 1, pp. 386–391. IEEE (2012)

10. Liebler, L., Baier, H.: Approxis: a fast, robust, lightweight and approximate disassembler considered in the field of memory forensics. In: Matoušek, P., Schmiedecker, M. (eds.) ICDF2C 2017. LNICST, vol. 216, pp. 158–172. Springer, Cham (2018). https://doi.org/10.1007/978-3-319-73697-6_12

11. Ligh, M.H., Case, A., Levy, J., Walters, A.: The Art of Memory Forensics: Detecting Malware and Threats in Windows, Linux, and Mac Memory. Wiley, US (2014)

12. Lipton, Z.C., Berkowitz, J., Elkan, C.: A critical review of recurrent neural networks for sequence learning. arXiv preprint arXiv:1506.00019 (2015)

13. Potchik, B.: Architecture agnostic function detection in binaries. https://binary.ninja/2017/11/06/architecture-agnostic-function-detection-in-binaries.html

14. Shin, E.C.R., Song, D., Moazzezi, R.: Recognizing functions in binaries with neural networks. In: USENIX Security Symposium, pp. 611–626 (2015)

fishy - A Framework for Implementing Filesystem-Based Data Hiding Techniques

Thomas Göbel$^{(\boxtimes)}$ and Harald Baier

da/sec - Biometrics and Internet Security Research Group,
Hochschule Darmstadt, Darmstadt, Germany
{thomas.goebel,harald.baier}@h-da.de

Abstract. The term anti-forensics refers to any attempt to hinder or
even prevent the digital forensics process. Common attempts are to hide,
delete or alter digital information and thereby threaten the forensic investigation. A prominent anti-forensic paradigm is hiding data on different
abstraction layers, e.g., the filesystem layer. In modern filesystems, private data can be hidden in many places, taking advantage of the structural and conceptual characteristics of each filesystem. In most cases,
however, the source code and the theoretical approach of a particular
hiding technique is not accessible and thus maintainability and reproducibility of the anti-forensic tool is not guaranteed. In this paper, we
present *fishy*, a framework designed to implement and analyze different
filesystem-based data hiding techniques. *fishy* is implemented in Python
and collects various common exploitation methods that make use of
existing data structures on the filesystem layer. Currently, the framework is able to hide data within ext4, FAT and NTFS filesystems using
different hiding techniques and thus serves as a toolkit of established
anti-forensic methods on the filesystem layer. *fishy* was built to support
the exploration and collection of various hiding techniques and ensure
the reproducibility and expandability with its publicly available source
code. The construction of a modular framework played an important role
in the design phase. In addition to the description of the actual framework, its current state, its use, and its easy expandability, we also present
some hiding techniques for various filesystems and discuss possible future
extensions of our framework.

Keywords: Anti-forensics · Anti-anti-forensics · Digital forensics
Data hiding · File system analysis · ext4 · NTFS · FAT

1 Introduction

Since there are new cyber attacks and threats on a daily basis, the topic *anti-
forensics* is now an important part of digital forensics. As cybercrime increases
and attacks become more frequent and sophisticated, research in the field of anti-
forensics is becoming increasingly relevant. In order to gather reliable evidence

F. Breitinger and I. Baggili (Eds.): ICDF2C 2018, LNICST 259, pp. 23–42, 2019.
https://doi.org/10.1007/978-3-030-05487-8_2

during a digital forensic investigation, it is important to know about appropriate countermeasures and mitigation strategies against anti-forensic methods, techniques and tools. Current data hiding approaches vary from encryption techniques on different abstraction layers, various steganography types, data contraception methods, hard disk and filesystem manipulation, to network-based data hiding [1].

In recent years, various taxonomies have been presented that categorize and summarize known anti-forensic techniques and methods [2–4]. The most recent taxonomy was proposed by Conlan et al. [1]. Their extended taxonomy distinguishes between hiding techniques on the hard disk layer and hiding techniques on the filesystem layer. In fact, a prominent anti-forensic paradigm is hiding data on different abstraction layers, e.g., the filesystem layer. As an example of potential hiding places in the filesystem, the authors mention alternate data streams and slack spaces.

Various proof of concept implementations and tools for different hiding techniques have been released in the past. These are known to the forensic community[1]. However, in most cases the authorship of the previously published tools is unknown and the source code or the documentation of the tools is inaccessible. For this reason, the maintenance of existing anti-forensic projects and the reproducibility of the source code of available tools are not guaranteed. Moreover, the theoretical approaches of potential hiding techniques in the filesystems are often not published. In addition, there is usually a separate tool for each hiding technique that can only be used with a specific filesystem (e.g., the anti-forensic tool called *slacker* can only conceal data within NTFS slack space). A common anti-forensic toolkit that collects various hiding techniques is missing so far. Furthermore, many of the existing tools are obsolete as they relate to old filesystems, such as ext2.

The aforementioned problems make research in the field of anti-forensics considerably more difficult. The inconsistent provision of the tools not only prevents the validation, reproducibility and further development of the hiding approaches themselves, but also the possible evaluation of existing forensic suites. The importance of digital forensic tool testing in order to get authentic, accurate and reliable evidence is obvious and well known to the members of the digital forensic community [4]. If the forensic software is unable to detect hidden data on the medium for some reason, this could cause courts to render judgments based on inaccurate or incomplete evidence [5]. This scenario gives an attacker the opportunity to exploit the weakness of forensic software to hide relevant evidence [6].

1.1   Contribution

The practical, uniform and publicly available implementation of multiple hiding techniques is advantageous for a later evaluation of forensic software components.

---

[1] http://www.forensicswiki.org/wiki/Anti-forensic_techniques#Generic_Data_Hiding (last accessed 2018-05-10).

Therefore, we want to introduce our Python-implemented toolkit and framework called *fishy* - filesystem hiding techniques in Python. While [7] presents the current state of the framework and already implemented hiding techniques, this paper focuses on the framework architecture, the usage of the framework, and instructions on how to add further hiding techniques. In this paper, we also publish the link that refers to our GitHub repository, which includes the full source code of the framework[2].

The toolkit is intended to introduce people to the concept of established anti-forensic methods associated with data hiding on the filesystem layer. *fishy* is able to obfuscate arbitrary data in a way that conventional file access methods cannot recognize the concealed content. The new framework allows the digital forensic community to implement, categorize and test filesystem-based data hiding techniques. Since the framework is open source, it can be extended by anyone and at any time with additional hiding techniques. The modular structure of the framework allows us (i) to easily implement further custom hiding techniques, (ii) to manipulate multiple filesystem types with one and the same framework, and (iii) to add compatibility for additional modern filesystems (e.g., APFS, Btrfs, ReFS, or XFS) in the future without having to change the basic functions of the framework. Currently, *fishy* supports the most popular filesystems: ext4, FAT and NTFS. The toolkit provides a command line interface that can be used to hide data. Furthermore, the already implemented hiding techniques can be used in other projects by importing *fishy* as a library, e.g., to analyze whether existing hiding techniques are recognized by common forensic software.

To the best of our knowledge, there is currently no actively maintained toolkit for filesystem-based data hiding techniques, other than *fishy*. As *fishy* aims to provide an easy to use framework for creating new hiding techniques, this project might be useful for security researchers and members of the digital forensic community who are concerned with security issues and data hiding attacks.

In addition to a detailed description of the actual framework architecture, we present some exemplary hiding techniques and demonstrate in detail how the framework can be used and how additional hiding techniques can be integrated.

1.2   Structure of the Paper

The rest of this paper is organized as follows: Sect. 2 presents some related work, especially relevant information about anti-digital forensics and previously published tools that allow to manipulate or hide data within filesystems. In Sect. 3, we explain in detail the core design principles and the modular structure of our framework. Section 4 gives some background information about the manipulated filesystem data structures and a brief explanation of all the hiding techniques that have been implemented so far. In addition, other hiding techniques, which are currently under development, are mentioned. Section 5 shows how to use the framework by explaining the typical command structure and the integration of new hiding techniques into the existing framework. Further technical details

---

[2] https://github.com/dasec/fishy/.

can be found within the module reference in our GitHub repository. It documents the most important modules and classes, which you might use, if you want to integrate *fishy* into your own projects. In Sect. 6, we evaluate the current state of our implementation and present limitations of the framework. Section 7 concludes the paper and presents further tasks that supplement the work done so far.

2   Related Work

In this section, we review related work with respect to anti-forensics in general and previously published data hiding methods and tools for various filesystems in particular.

2.1   Anti-Forensics

Well known definitions for the term anti-forensics were proposed by Rogers [2] and Harris [3]. The most recent contribution in the field of anti-forensics is a paper provided by Conlan et al. [1]. The authors summarized previous definitions and defined the term anti-forensics as "any attempts to alter, disrupt, negate, or in any way interfere with scientifically valid forensic investigations". To better distinguish different anti-forensic techniques, Rogers [2] subdivided them into the following four categories: (i) data hiding, (ii) artifact wiping, (iii) trail obfuscation, and (iv) attacks against the computer forensic process and tools. Conlan et al. [1] expand Rogers' widely accepted taxonomy by a fifth category: (v) possible indications of anti-digital forensic activity, and came up with a more comprehensive and up-to-date taxonomy. Now that a variety of anti-forensic techniques are known, the authors additionally subdivide the five categories into several subcategories. This allows a more precise categorization of new anti-forensics techniques. Hiding techniques, as presented in this paper, can be assigned to the *data hiding* category and, in particular, to its subcategory *filesystem manipulation*.

2.2   Hiding Data in Filesystems

Hiding data in filesystem metadata was carried out by Anderson et al. [8] along with the development of a steganographic filesystem. This resulted in StegFS [9], a steganographic filesystem based on ext2, which allowed people to deny the existence of hidden data. Meanwhile, many other hiding places are known which make it possible to conceal sensitive data without affecting the actual function of the filesystem. In addition to the well-known hiding places, such as file slack or alternate data streams [10], hiding places in less popular filesystem structures can be used to hide data, such as the slack space of several block bitmaps or inode bitmaps [11]. Likewise, existing data structures, such as timestamps [12,23], or reserved areas for future filesystem extensions, such as reserved group descriptor table blocks [13], may be used to hide arbitrary data.

In digital forensic investigations, the knowledge of these, at first glance inconspicuous, hiding places definitely plays a decisive role in securing all incriminating digital traces. There are a few papers that deal with different filesystem hiding methods and countermeasures. Our list of existing publications indicates which filesystem is discussed in the respective paper. Eckstein et al. [14] show how to hide data in file and directory slack space or reserved inodes in ext3 and in alternate data streams in NTFS. Piper et al. [15] show how to hide data in the partition boot sector, in reserved portions of the superblock and in redundant superblocks of ext2/ext3 filesystems. Grugq [16] demonstrates further hiding places in ext2, such as the manipulation of directory entries and the utilization of reserved space in superblocks, group descriptors and inodes. Huebner et al. [17] present various approaches to hide data in metadata files of NTFS, e.g., in the $BadClus file, the $DATA attribute and the $Boot file. Krenhuber et al. [18] show how to hide data in NTFS using file slack, faked bad clusters, additional cluster allocation and alternate data streams. Other methods for ext filesystems, such as file slack, the mount procedure and extended file attributes, are shown. Berghel et al. [19] present approaches to conceal data using the slack space of various ext2/ext3 data structures, such as superblocks, group descriptor tables and directory entries. The authors also discuss some hiding places for NTFS, for instance the $Bitmap file, additional $FILE attributes or MFT entries.

It should be mentioned here that many of the existing publications on this topic are outdated and there are only a few recent contributions. A slightly newer work analyzes the most important filesystem data structures of ext4 in a digital forensic way [13]. Several potential data hiding places in ext4 are mentioned (e.g., group descriptor growth blocks, data structures in uninitialized block groups and Htree nodes), but not explored any further. The most recent publication in this field presents, analyzes and evaluates various anti-forensic techniques for ext4 and verifies whether previously mentioned hiding techniques still work in ext4 since most of them were developed for ext2/ext3 [11]. Unfortunately, this paper only discusses ext4 and does not focus on NTFS.

2.3   Available Data Hiding Tools

In our literature research on existing tools for filesystem-based data hiding techniques we found only a few working tools. None of these provide a consistent interface with support for multiple filesystems and various hiding techniques. For most of them it seems that development has been stopped. It is also noticeable that the data set provided by Conlan et al. [1], which collects 308 anti-forensic tools in total, only includes two tools (*bmap* and *slacker*) in its subcategory *filesystem manipulation*.

Three filesystem-based data hiding tools, that seem to be used more often, are *bmap*, *slacker.exe* and *FragFS* [21,22]. *bmap* is a Linux tool for hiding data in the NTFS slack space. However, this project seems to have no official website or any trustworthy repository, i.e., development of the tool probably stopped. Sources can only be found on some questionable websites[3]. *slacker.exe* is also a tool for hiding data in NTFS slack space, but is built for Windows. It was developed by Bishop Fox and integrated into the Metasploit framework under the name *Metasploit Anti-Forensic Investigation Arsenal (MAFIA)* along with some other anti-forensic tools (e.g., *Timestomp* - a tool to manipule NTFS timestamps)[4]. However, the tool is currently not available for download. *FragFS* is able to hide data within the last 8 bytes of an MFT entry in the NTFS Master File Table [20]. Available download links were not found here either.

In addition, several anti-forensics tools have been developed in the past for the ext filesystem [16]. Most of them, however, are outdated because they were originally developed for ext2 instead of the current version ext4. First, *Rune FS*[5] was able to hide data by taking advantage of a bug in the Coroner's Toolkit. Second, *Waffen FS* adds an ext3 journal to an ext2 filesystem and conceals up to 32 MB of data. Third, *KY FS* manipulates a directory entry as if the entry is not used to, subsequently, hide data in the directory entry. Fourth, *Data Mule FS* is able to conceal about 1 MiB data in a 1 GiB large ext2 image using all reserved areas in superblocks, group descriptors and inodes.

Two newer tools can hide data within timestamps. *Timestamp-Magic* [23] conceals data within the nanoseconds part of multiple timestamps in the inode table of an ext4 filesystem. *TOMS* [12] demonstrates a similar approach using the filename attribute of MFT entries in NTFS.

When reviewing existing tools it is noticeable that, with a few exceptions, the source code of the tools is often no longer publicly available. In addition, many of the tools were originally developed for earlier filesystem versions and development has been discontinued in the meantime. *fishy* allows a consistent implementation of hiding techniques that will facilitate the reproducibility and evaluation of forensic software in the future.

3   Framework Architecture

The following section explains in detail the basic architecture and the modular structure of the *fishy* framework. The depicted architecture overview gives an introduction to *fishys'* core design principles and structures. The key modules and classes someone might use to integrate *fishy* into their own projects are mentioned here. The command structure and its use are described in Sect. 5.

In the design process, we made sure that the architecture is as modular as possible. Different layers allow to encapsulate functionalities. The flowchart diagram in Fig. 1 represents the logical procedure of using a hiding technique. What we can see in the flowchart diagram is that the `Command Line Interface (CLI)` parses the given command line parameters and calls the appropriate `Hiding Technique Wrapper`. The `Hiding Technique Wrapper` then checks

[3] https://packetstormsecurity.com/files/17642/bmap-1.0.17.tar.gz.html (last accessed 2018-05-10).
[4] http://www.bishopfox.com/resources/tools/other-free-tools/mafia/ (last accessed 2018-05-10).
[5] http://index-of.es/Linux/R/runefs.tar.gz (last accessed 2018-05-10).

for the filesystem type of the given filesystem image and calls the respective
`Hiding Technique` implementation for this filesystem. The modular structure
of the framework is clearly visible here by treating the three different filesystems
already implemented (ext4, FAT and NTFS) separately. In case of calling the
write method, the `Hiding Technique` implementation returns metadata needed
to restore the hidden data later. Currently, this metadata is written to the disk,
using a simple JSON data structure. As future work it is considered to hide the
metadata itself in the filesystem with a suitable hiding technique.

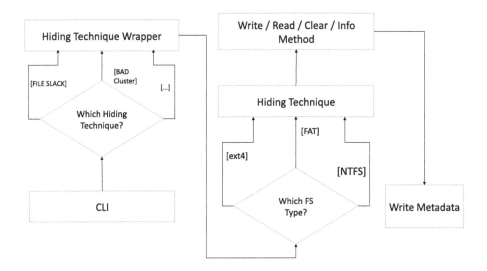

Fig. 1. Overview of the modular framework structure of *fishy*.

The command line argument parsing part is implemented in the *cli.py* module. `Hiding Techniques Wrapper` are located in the root module. They adopt
converting input data into streams, casting/reading/writing hiding technique
specific metadata and calling the appropriate methods of those hiding technique specific implementations. To detect the filesystem type of a given image,
the `Hiding Technique Wrapper` use the *filesystem_detector* function which uses
filesystem detection methods implemented in the particular filesystem module.
Several filesystem specific `Hiding Technique` implementations provide at least
a write, read and clear method to (i) hide data in the filesystem, (ii) to read
or restore hidden content, and (iii) to delete previously hidden data. `Hiding
Technique` implementations use either *pytsk3*[6] to gather information of the given
filesystem or use custom filesystem parsers which are then located within the
particular filesystem package.

---

[6] Python bindings for The Sleuth Kit: https://github.com/py4n6/pytsk (last accessed
2018-05-14).

3.1 Command Line Interface

As depicted in Fig. 1, the CLI module takes care of parsing the command line arguments and, depending on the given subcommand, calls the appropriate Hiding Technique Wrapper. The CLI thus forms the user interface of our toolkit.

Each hiding technique is accessible with a special subcommand, which itself defines further options. The CLI must be able to read data, that the user wants to hide, either from stdin or from a file. Previously hidden data that the user wants to recover is returned to either stdout or a specified file. If reading data from a file, the CLI is in charge of turning the content into a buffered stream, on which the hiding technique operates in the subsequent process.

3.2 Hiding Technique Wrapper

Each type of hiding technique has its own wrapper. This Hiding Technique Wrapper gets called by the CLI and subsequently calls the filesystem specific Hiding Technique, based on the filesystem type. As previously mentioned, to detect the filesystem type, the *filesystem_detector* function is called.

In order to find the correct offset of hidden data, read and clear methods of the hiding techniques require some metadata, which is gathered during a write operation. For this reason, the Hiding Technique Wrapper is responsible for reading and writing metadata files and providing hiding technique specific metadata objects for read and write methods. If the user wants to restore previously hidden data and store the information in a file instead of putting it to stdout, the Hiding Technique Wrapper is responsible for writing that file.

3.3 Hiding Technique

Multiple Hiding Technique implementations do the real work of this toolkit. Every Hiding Technique must at least offer a write, read and clear method in order to conceal new data and to restore or to delete hidden content. These methods must operate on streams only to ensure high reusability and reduce boilerplate code. All hiding techniques in the framework are called by the Hiding Technique Wrapper. The clear method must overwrite all hidden data with zeros and leave the filesystem in a consistent state. If an error occurs during the write process, i.e., while the private data is hidden, already written data must be deleted before exiting the program.

To get the required information about the current filesystem, hiding techniques use either the *pytsk3* library or a filesystem parser implementation located in the appropriate filesystem package.

If a hiding technique relies on some specific metadata (e.g., the exact offset of a MFT entry in NTFS) to restore hidden data, it must implement a hiding technique specific metadata class. This specific metadata class is used during the write process to store all information that is necessary for the recovery of the hidden data. The write method must return this metadata instance, so that the *Hiding Technique Wrapper* can serialize it and pass it to the read and clear methods.

Hiding techniques may implement further methods that are relevant for the hiding procedure, such as sub-methods that are relevant to actually hide the data in the right place or to split larger data into smaller parts to hide them in multiple data structures.

3.4   Filesystem Detector

The *filesystem_detector* is a simple wrapper function to unify calls to the filesystem specific detection functions, which are implemented in the corresponding filesystem package.

3.5   Metadata Handling

To be able to restore hidden data, most hiding techniques need some additional information. These information are stored in a JSON metadata file. The main-metadata class called *fishy.metadata* provides functions to read and write metadata files and to automatically decrypt or encrypt the metadata if a password is provided. The main purpose of this class is to ensure that all metadata files have a similar reasonable data structure. The program can thus recognize at an early point that, for example, the user is using a wrong hiding technique to restore hidden data.

When implementing a new hiding technique, this technique must also implement its own hiding technique-specific metadata class. The hiding technique itself therefore defines which data will be stored later during the hiding process. The write method then returns this hiding technique-specific metadata class which then gets serialized and stored in the main-metadata class.

4   Implemented Hiding Techniques and Current Work

An overview of all currently implemented hiding techniques in the framework, and hiding techniques that are stilfHides arbitrary data in l in development or are about to be added in the near future, is given in Table 1. Already finished hiding techniques are marked with the ✓ symbol, hiding techniques that are still in progress are marked with the ✗ symbol. The - symbol addresses hiding techniques which are filesystem specific, i.e., the respective data structure is missing in other filesystems. The table also includes a brief explanation of each implemented hiding technique. Moreover, all hiding techniques are briefly evaluated for their gained capacity, stability and their detection probability. *Capacity* addresses, how much data can be hidden by using the respective hiding technique, since an attacker is interested in storing a reasonable amount of data. *Detection probability* means the difficulty of finding the concealed artifacts, i.e., the likelihood that a forensic investigator discovers hidden data. For example, the default filesystem check or the standard GUI filesystem interface should not

Table 1. Overview of currently implemented **Hiding Techniques** (function call based on the respective subcommand) and work in progress of the framework *fishy* for different filesystems (**FS**) and our rating according to available *Capacity* (**C**), *Detection probability* (**D**) and *Stability* (**S**) (○=low; ◐=medium; ●=high).

Hiding Technique (Subcommand)	FS FAT	FS NTFS	FS EXT4	Description	C	D	S
fileslack	✓	✓	✓	Exploitation of File Slack	●	◐	○
mftslack	-	✓	-	Exploitation of MFT Entry Slack	●	●	○
ads	-	✗	-	Use of Alternate Data Streams	●	●	◐
addcluster	✓	✓	✗	Additional Cluster/Block Allocation	●	◐	○
badcluster	✓	✓	✗	Bad Cluster/Block Allocation	●	◐	●
reserved_gdt_blocks	-	-	✓	Exploitation of reserved GDT Blocks	●	●	◐
superblock_slack	-	-	✓	Exploitation of Superblock Slack	◐	●	●
superblock_reserved	-	-	✗	Use of reserved space in Superblocks	○	◐	●
superblock_backups	-	-	✗	Exploitation of Superblock Backups	◐	◐	●
osd2	-	-	✓	Use of unused Inode Field osd2	○	◐	●
obso_faddr	-	-	✓	Use of unused Inode Field obso_faddr	○	◐	●
nanoseconds	-	✗	✓	Use of Nanoseconds Timestamp Part	◐	○	●
bootsector	✗	✗	✗	Exploitation of Partition Bootsector	○	●	●
null_dir_entries	-	-	✗	Exploitation of Directory Entries	●	◐	○
gdt_slack	-	-	✗	Exploitation of GDT Slack Space	◐	●	◐
groupdescr_reserved	-	-	✗	Use of reserved space in Group-Desc.	○	◐	●
gdt_backups	-	-	✗	Exploitation of GDT Backup Copies	●	◐	◐
blockbitmap_slack	-	-	✗	Exploitation of Block Bitmap Slack	○	●	●
inodebitmap_slack	-	-	✗	Exploitation of Inode Bitmap Slack	○	●	●
inode_slack	-	-	✗	Exploitation of Inode Record Slack	●	◐	◐
inode_reserved	-	-	✗	Use of reserved space in Inode Struct	●	◐	●
uninit_datastructure	-	-	✗	Exploitation of Data Structures in Uninitialized Block Groups	●	◐	○

disclose hidden data. *Stability* describes whether hidden data remains in the filesystem without complications, i.e., the possibility of data being overwritten is low.

As shown in Table 1, the development of many other hiding techniques is still in progress right now, for example the transfer of the nanosecond hiding approach to the NTFS filesystem [12]. Besides, a major focus is on the integration of additional ext4 hiding techniques, as a recent work by Göbel and Baier [11] reveals many interesting hiding techniques for this filesystem. Nevertheless, the integration of the upcoming Windows filesystem ReFS and the upcoming Linux filesystem Btrfs, as well as some completely new hiding techniques are considered as future tasks. Members of the forensic community are also invited to add further filesystems and new hiding techniques to our framework.

We now present the manipulated filesystem data structures and give a brief explanation of each hiding technique that has been implemented so far.

4.1   File Slack

If a file is smaller than the cluster or block size of the filesystem, writing this file will result in some unusable space, which starts at the end of the file and ends at the end of the cluster/block. The remaining space can be used to hide data and is in general called File Slack [24, p. 187].

Most filesystem implementations of FAT and NTFS pad the RAM Slack with zeros, nowadays. This padding behavior must be honored by our implementation, as non-zero values in this area would be suspicious to any observer.

In case of ext4 filesystems, most implementations pad the complete File Slack with zeros, making the distinction between RAM and Drive Slack unnecessary but also making the detection of hidden data more likely. Our implementation for ext4 therefore calculates the end of a file on the filesystem and writes data into the following File Slack until no data is left or the end of the current block is reached.

4.2   MFT Entry Slack

The Master File Table contains the necessary metadata for every file and directory stored in a NTFS partition. An MFT entry does not have to fill up all of its allocated bytes, which often leads to some unused space at the end of an entry. The MFT entry slack is an suitable place to hide data inconspicuously.

NTFS uses a concept called Fixup [24, p. 253] for important data structures, such as the MFT, in order to detect damaged sectors and corrupt data structures. When an MFT entry is written to the disk, the last two bytes of each sector are replaced with a signature value. To avoid damaging the MFT, it is important to not overwrite the last two bytes of each sector when hiding data in the MFT entry slack. Besides this measure, the framework is able to write a copy of the hidden data in $MFT to corresponding entries in $MFTMirr to avoid detection by a simple `chkdsk` [24, p. 219].

4.3   Bad Cluster Allocation

If a sector or a cluster of sectors is damaged, read and write operations would lead to faulty data. Therefore the filesystem marks the affected area as bad clusters.

The filesystem saves the addresses for future reference and won't allocate them to a file or directory anymore. By marking some actually free cluster or blocks as faulty ones, we can reserve them to hide data in them.

In NTFS, affected areas are saved in an MFT file entry called $BadClus, the entries in this file will be ignored. In FAT, clusters are marked as bad in the File Allocation Table. In ext4, there is a list of bad blocks in the reserved inode 1 [24, p. 183, p. 225, p. 293].

4.4   Additional Cluster Allocation

Clusters are either unallocated or allocated to a file. By allocating an additional, actually unallocated, cluster to a file, the filesystem does not attempt to allocate or write data to that cluster, so that data can be hidden in that cluster [17].

If the file the cluster is allocated to grows in size and exceeds the boundary of its originally allocated clusters, the file will grow into the additionally allocated cluster and overwrite the hidden data. For this reason, a file that is unlikely to grow should be preferred as a carrier to hide data.

4.5   Reserved Group Descriptor Table Blocks

Reserved GDT blocks of an ext4 filesystem are not used until the filesystem is extended and group descriptors are written to this location. The reserved GDT blocks are located behind the group descriptors and are repeated in each backup copy. The number of copies varies depending on the sparse_super flag, which limits the copies of the reserved GDT blocks to block groups whose group number is either 0 or a power of 3, 5, or 7 [13].

Since the GDT growth blocks are really big reserved areas, this hiding method is quite obvious. Therefore our implementation skips the primary reserved GDT blocks before embedding some data. This prevents e2fsck from noticing these flaws in the filesystem. A big advantage of this technique is the high capacity. On the other hand, hidden data is overwritten in the case of a filesystem extension.

4.6   Superblock Slack

Depending on the block size, there is an acceptable amount of slack space behind the actual content of the Superblock which is repeated multiple times across the ext4 filesystem. The amount of copies of the Superblock depends on the sparse_super flag, i.e., less space to hide data if the flag is set [19].

The hiding technique collects all block numbers of the Superblock copies from each block group, taking the sparse_super flag into account. Data then gets written to the slack space of each of these blocks, considering the filesystem block size. This hiding technique benefits from the Superblock's characteristics, resulting in a safe storage because this data structure does not get overwritten. But as with all slack space hiding methods, hidden data is easy to find.

4.7   osd2, obso_faddr

The osd2 hiding technique uses the last two bytes of the 12 byte osd2 field, which is located at 0x74 in each inode of an ext4 filesystem. This field only uses 10 bytes at max, depending on the tag being either *linux2*, *hurd2* or *masix2* [25].

To hide data, the method writes data directly to the two bytes in the osd2 field in each inode, which address is taken from the inode table, until there is either no inode or no data left. Available space is small, but hidden data might be tough to find since data is distributed over several inodes across the filesystem.

The obso_faddr field in each inode at 0x70 is an obsolete fragment address field of 32bit length. This technique works accordingly to the osd2 technique, has the same advantages and flaws but can hide twice the data.

4.8   Nanosecond Timestamps

Modern filesystems like NTFS or ext4 support nanosecond precise timestamps. As shown in [12,23], hiding data in nanosecond timestamps is feasible. In ext4, four extra 32-bit fields i_[c|m|a|cr]time_extra were added to the existing inode structure. The lower 2 bits are used to extend the Unix epoch, the upper 30 bits are used for nanoseconds. Therefore, our implementation only uses the upper 30 bits of the nanosecond timestamps.

Data hidden by this technique is difficult to find. Common file explorers, as well as Autopsy, do not support nanosecond accuracy. Linux commands like stat [file] or debugfs -R 'stat <inode>' [image] are able to parse nanosecond timestamps, but this does not offer concrete information about hidden data. Furthermore, tests have shown that the Sleuthkit's istat command does not take the extra epoch bits into account and therefore timestamps beyond 2038 (Unix Epoch time overflow) are not decoded properly.

5   Use of the Framework

In this section we present how to use the framework and how to integrate new hiding techniques into the existing architecture. If the paper is accepted, theres is also an official module reference including the exact documentation of the most important modules and classes that might be helpful if *fishy* is integrated into other projects.

5.1   Using the CLI Interface

This section will give beginners a first introduction to the *fishy* command structure to better understand how to work with the toolkit. As we have already seen in Table 1, the CLI groups all hiding techniques into specific subcommands. Each subcommand provides specific information about how it is used via the --help switch. Additionally to the subcommands above, there are the following informational subcommands available:

fattools. Provides relevant meta information about a FAT filesystem, such as sector size, sectors per cluster or the offset to the data region. This command also shows the entries of the file allocation table or current files in a directory.

```
# Get some meta information about the FAT filesystem
$ fishy -d testfs-fat32.dd fattools -i
FAT Type:                                FAT32
Sector Size:                             512
Sectors per Cluster:                     8
Sectors per FAT:                         3904
FAT Count:                               2
Dataregion Start Byte:                   4014080
Free Data Clusters (FS Info):            499075
Recently Allocated Data Cluster (FS Info): 8
Root Directory Cluster:                  2
FAT Mirrored:                            False
Active FAT:                              0
Sector of Bootsector Copy:               6
[...]
```

metadata. Displays the information stored in a metadata file which is created while writing information into the filesystem and are required to restore those information or to wipe hidden content. The first example shows the information that is stored when hiding data in the FAT file slack: (i) the cluster ID with hidden slack space data, (ii) the byte offset to the hidden content starting from cluster ID, and (iii) the length of the data which was written to file slack. The second example shows the information that is stored when hiding data in the MFT entry slack: (i) offset to the MFT slack space, (ii) length of data which was written to file slack, and (iii) sector address of MFT_Mirror when an additional copy of the hidden data is stored in the MFT_Mirror. In addition, the metadata file is password protected in the second case.

```
# Parse a given metadata file
$ fishy metadata -m metadata1.json
Version: 2
Module Identifier: fat-file-slack
Stored Files:
  File_ID: 0
  Filename: 0
  Associated File Metadata:
    {'clusters': [[12, 512, 11]]}

$ fishy -p password metadata -m metadata2.json
Version: 2
Module Identifier: ntfs-mft-slack
Stored Files:
  File_ID: 0
  Filename: secret.txt
  Associated File Metadata:
    {'addrs': [[16792, 11, 5116312]]}
```

The following subsections give some more examples how to use the subcommands of selected hiding techniques in the framework. Since space is limited here, not all techniques can be shown. However, the command structure of all hiding techniques behaves similarly.

fileslack. Hides arbitrary data in the file slack. Provides methods to read (-r), write (-w) and wipe (-c) the file slack of files and directories in ext4, FAT and NTFS filesystems. In addition, we can use the info switch (-i) to check the available slack space of a file in advance.

```
# Write data into slack space of a file (here: testfile.txt)
$ echo "TOP SECRET" | fishy -d testfs-fat32.dd fileslack -d testfile.txt
-m metadata.json -w

# Read hidden data from slack space
$ fishy -d testfs-fat32.dd fileslack -m metadata.json -r
TOP SECRET

# Wipe slack space
$ fishy -d testfs-fat32.dd fileslack -m metadata.json -c

# Show information about slack space of a file (size of testfile.txt: 5 Bytes)
$ fishy -d testfs-fat32.dd fileslack -d testfile.txt -i
File: testfile.txt
   Occupied in last cluster: 5
   Ram Slack:                507
   File Slack:               3584
```

addcluster. Additional cluster allocation where data can be hidden. Provides methods to read, write and wipe additional clusters for a file in FAT and NTFS.

```
# Allocate additional clusters for a file (myfile.txt) and hide data in it
$ echo "TOP SECRET" | fishy -d testfs-fat12.dd addcluster -d myfile.txt
-m metadata.json -w

# Read hidden data from additionally allocated clusters
$ fishy -d testfs-fat12.dd addcluster -m metadata.json -r
TOP SECRET

# Clean up additionally allocated clusters
$ fishy -d testfs-fat12.dd addcluster -m metadata.json -c
```

mftslack. Exploitation of MFT entry slack. Provides methods to read, write and wipe the MFT entries slack space in a NTFS filesystem. The info switch prints further information about the available slack space of each MFT entry (suppressed here because of its length).

```
# Writes the contents of secret.txt (TOP SECRET) into MFT slack space
# and additionally into MFT_Mirror slack space when --domirr is set
$ fishy -d testfs-ntfs.dd mftslack -m metadata.json --domirr -w secret.txt

# Read hidden data from MFT slack space
$ fishy -d testfs-ntfs.dd mftslack -m metadata.json -r
TOP SECRET

# Wipe MFT slack space
$ fishy -d testfs-ntfs.dd mftslack -m metadata.json -c

# Display information about the MFT slack
$ fishy -d testfs-ntfs.dd mftslack -i
```

reserved_gdt_blocks. Exploitation of reserved GDT blocks. Provides methods to read, write and wipe the space reserved for a future file system extension. The info switch summarizes all available bytes of different reserved GDT blocks in all block groups starting from block group 1 since hidden data in block group 0 causes file system check errors. Furthermore, already used space is shown.

```
# Writes the contents of secret.txt (TOP SECRET) into reserved GDT Blocks
$ fishy -d testfs-ext4.dd reserved_gdt_blocks -m metadata.json -w secret.txt

# Read hidden data from reserved GDT Blocks
$ fishy -d testfs-ext4.dd reserved_gdt_blocks -m metadata.json -r
TOP SECRET

# Clean up reserved GDT Blocks
$ fishy -d testfs-ext4.dd reserved_gdt_blocks -m metadata.json -c

# Show relevant information about reserved GDT blocks
$ fishy -d testfs-ext4.dd reserved_gdt_blocks -i
Block size: 1024
Total hiding space in reserved GDT blocks: 1048576 Bytes
Used: 1024 Bytes
```

As we can see, the framework understands the same command switches regardless of which hiding technique or filesystem is currently in use. For all other hiding techniques the same command structure applies, which is why we do not have to introduce all hiding techniques here. Achieving such behavior was one of the goals of the basic design principles of the framework.

5.2 Integration of New Hiding Techniques

This section shows how additional hiding techniques can be integrated into the existing project structure. This can also be understood as a call to the forensic community to add self-developed hiding techniques to the framework. In order to implement a new hiding technique, one can follow the following five steps:

1. Following the repository structure via the folder 'fishy' to the folder 'wrapper', where we first create a new wrapper module for each hiding technique to be added. As already mentioned in Sect. 3, this wrapper module handles the filesystem specific hiding technique calls and fulfills the main-metadata handling. If, for example, another file system has already implemented this type of hiding technique, no new wrapper module needs to be created.
2. Only the CLI module knows about a new wrapper module, not the filesystem specific hiding technique module (bottom-up approach). Therefore, we first need to integrate the new hiding technique wrapper to the CLI module.
3. All currently implemented hiding techniques are located either in the ext4, fat or ntfs submodule. Please notice that further file systems can be added in the future. To add a new hiding technique implementation, we create a new file with an appropriate module name in the respective filesystem subfolder. A simple example would be fishy/ext4/nanoseconds.py. The filesystem specific implementation must then be added to the existing wrapper module.

4. A metadata class within the new hiding technique implementation is created. This class holds hiding technique-dependent metadata to correctly recover hidden data after write operations. The write method must return an instance of this class, which then will be written to the metadata file.
5. At least one `write`, `read` and `clear` method is implemented within the new hiding technique. The `info` method is optional. Additional internal helper methods can be implemented as needed. In order to keep the actual hiding technique implementation reusable and simple, we only operate on streams.

6   Evaluation

The practical usability of the framework has already been demonstrated in Sect. 5. Some of the results of our evaluation have already been included in Table 1. It offers an overview about the possible capacity gain of each hiding technique. It also contains a founded rating of its stability. Lastly, we evaluated the detection probability of each technique. The scenario we examined was whether a common filesystem check would detect inconsistencies and point to a modification. Accordingly, we used the standard OS filesystem check utilities to perform the evaluation: `fsck.ext4` for ext4, `fsck.fat` for FAT and `chkdsk` for NTFS.

To test the currently implemented hiding techniques several unit test have already been created. These can be found in the *'tests'* folder of our *fishy* repository. Existing unit tests can be executed by running `pytest`.

Using the `create_testfs.sh` script, it is possible to create prepared filesystem images for all supported filesystem types. These images already include files, which get copied from `utils/fs-files/`. The script has other options, which will be useful when writing unit tests. The created filesystems are intended to be used by unit tests and for developing a new hiding technique. To create a set of test images, we simply run $ `./create_testfs.sh -t all`. The script is capable of handling branches to generate multiple images with a different file structure. These are especially useful for writing unit tests that expect a certain file structure on the tested filesystem.

6.1   Limitations

fishy still has limitations that are important to mention. First, *fishy* is currently only tested on Linux. Other operating systems may provide different functions to access low level devices.

Although it is possible to hide multiple different files on the filesystem, *fishy* is currently not capable of handling this situation. So, it is up to the user to avoid overwritten data. The CLI is limited to store only one file per call and does not consider other files already written to disk. A simple workaround would be to store multiple files in a zip file before embedding them into the filesystem. However, as a long-term solution, it is better to integrate the functionality of checking whether some data is already hidden and in case to add new content to the previously hidden data.

Currently, *fishy* does not encrypt the data it hides. If the user actually needs encryption, it is up to him to encrypt his data before using the framework. Since tracing unencrypted data with forensic tools is relatively easy, regardless of the hiding technique used (e.g., with file carving), the integration of an additional encryption layer will definitely be considered as a future task. The same applies to data integrity functionality. Since most hiding techniques are not stable, for example if data is hidden in slack spaces where the associated files might change at any time, some data integrity methods would be useful to at least detect whether the hidden data has been damaged in the meantime. Therefore, some redundant information could be added to the original file before the content is actually hidden in the data structure. Depending on the amount of redundant information, data can be recovered, even if some parts are missing.

Manipulating specific data structures in ext4 causes the original metadata checksums to no longer match the new content of the data structures. Therefore, we need to repair the metadata checksums to exactly match the new content, otherwise this could raise suspicions during a forensic investigation. In ext4, the filesystem check tool `e2fsck` can be used to repair inconsistencies, such as wrong metadata checksums. The filesystem check repairs all inconsistencies and another forced filesystem check does not give any further warnings afterwards. However, it would be more convenient to integrate the metadata checksum calculation into the framework to no longer rely on a workaround.

7   Conclusion and Future Work

This paper introduced a new framework called *fishy*, developed in Python. Currently, the implementation contains interfaces for three popular filesystems: ext4, FAT and NFTS. The current state of the framework provides enough functionality to hide data within the supported filesystems and to recover it afterwards. In contrast to previously released tools, we focused on the consistent implementation of different hiding techniques and their long-term reproducibility. The reproducibility and expandability of the framework as well as its modular structure allow the integration of additional hiding techniques and other modern filesystems in the near future (e.g., APFS, Btrfs, ReFS, or XFS).

However, the framework still has a lot of potential for future enhancements and improvements. This section gives a brief overview of some future tasks that complement the work done so far. The filesystem auto detection for FAT and NTFS is currently performed by checking an ASCII string in the boot sector. In order to increase the reliability of *fishy*, it could be reimplemented by using the detection methods that are already realized in regular filesystem implementations. Hidden data can be further obfuscated by filesystem independent approaches like data encryption and steganography. In its current state, *fishy* does not provide on the fly data encryption and has not implemented data integrity methods. Currently, *fishy* produces a metadata file for each hiding operation. Although the metadata file can be encrypted, it is visible through traditional data access methods and gives unwanted hints to hidden data. As a workaround, the metadata file itself could be hidden using an appropriate hiding technique. As a future work, we also consider to automate the evaluation of the hiding approaches against respective filesystem checks as well as the evaluation of forensic suites. Through the integration of *fishy* as an open source library into forensic suites we can analyze whether common filesystem checks recognize hidden data or not. Furthermore, the integration of the CRC32C algorithm into the framework is considered since it is used to calculate metadata checksums within kernel code of ext4 filesystems. Finally, the introduction of multi-data support is another future task. This would greatly enhance the regular use of this toolkit.

Acknowledgments. This work was supported by the German Federal Ministry of Education and Research (BMBF) within the funding program Forschung an Fachhochschulen (contract number: 13FH019IB6) as well as by the Hessen State Ministry for Higher Education, Research and the Arts (HMWK) within CRISP (www.crisp-da.de). In addition, we would like to thank all participating students of the bachelor module Project System Development, who played a major role in the implementation of the framework.

References

1. Conlan, K., Baggili, I., Breitinger, F.: Anti-forensics: Furthering digital forensic science through a new extended, granular taxonomy. Digit. Investig. **18**, 66–75 (2016)
2. Rogers, M.: Anti-Forensics, presented at Lockheed Martin, San Diego, 15 September 2005. www.researchgate.net/profile/Marcus_Rogers/publication/268290676_Anti-Forensics_Anti-Forensics/links/575969a908aec91374a3656c.pdf. Accessed 12 May 2018
3. Harris, R.: Arriving at an anti-forensics consensus: Examining how to define and control the anti-forensics problem. Digit. Investig. **3**, 44–49 (2006)
4. Wundram, M., Freiling, F.C., Moch, C.: Anti-forensics: The next step in digital forensics tool testing. IT Security Incident Management and IT Forensics (IMF), pp. 83–97 (2013)
5. Ridder, C.K.: Evidentiary implications of potential security weaknesses in forensic software. Int. J. Digit. Crime Forensics (IJDCF) **1**(3), 80–91 (2009)
6. Newsham, T., Palmer, C., Stamos, A., Burns, J.: Breaking forensics software: weaknesses in critical evidence collection. In: Proceedings of the 2007 Black Hat Conference. Citeseer (2007)
7. Kailus, A.V., Hecht, C., Göbel, T., Liebler, L.: fishy - Ein Framework zur Umsetzung von Verstecktechniken in Dateisystemen. D.A.CH Security 2018, syssec Verlag (2018)
8. Anderson, R., Needham, R., Shamir, A.: The steganographic file system. In: Aucsmith, D. (ed.) IH 1998. LNCS, vol. 1525, pp. 73–82. Springer, Heidelberg (1998). https://doi.org/10.1007/3-540-49380-8_6
9. McDonald, A.D., Kuhn, M.G.: StegFS: a steganographic file system for Linux. In: Pfitzmann, A. (ed.) IH 1999. LNCS, vol. 1768, pp. 463–477. Springer, Heidelberg (2000). https://doi.org/10.1007/10719724_32

10. Piper, S., Davis, M., Shenoi, S.: Countering hostile forensic techniques. In: Olivier, M.S., Shenoi, S. (eds.) Advances in Digital Forensics II. IFIP AICT, vol. 222, pp. 79–90. Springer, Boston, MA (2006). https://doi.org/10.1007/0-387-36891-4_7

11. Göbel, Thomas, Baier, Harald: Anti-forensic capacity and detection rating of hidden data in the Ext4 filesystem. In: Peterson, G., Shenoi, S. (eds.) Advances in Digital Forensics XIV. IFIP AICT, vol. 532, pp. 87–110. Springer, Cham (2018). https://doi.org/10.1007/978-3-319-99277-8_6

12. Neuner, S., Voyiatzis, A.G., Schmiedecker, M., Brunthaler, S., Katzenbeisser, S., Weippl, E.R.: Time is on my side: steganography in filesystem metadata. Digit. Investig. **18**, 76–86 (2016)

13. Fairbanks, K.D.: An analysis of Ext4 for digital forensics. Digit. Investig. **9**, 118–130 (2012)

14. Eckstein, K., Jahnke, M.: Data hiding in journaling file systems. In: Proceedings of the 5th Annual Digital Forensic Research Workshop (DFRWS) (2005)

15. Piper, S., Davis, M., Manes, G., Shenoi, S.: Detecting Hidden Data in Ext2/Ext3 File Systems. In: Pollitt, M., Shenoi, S. (eds.) Advances in Digital Forensics. ITI-FIP, vol. 194, pp. 245–256. Springer, Boston, MA (2006). https://doi.org/10.1007/0-387-31163-7_20

16. Grugq, T.: The art of defiling: defeating forensic analysis. In: Blackhat Briefings, Las Vegas, NV (2005)

17. Huebner, E., Bem, D., Wee, C.K.: Data hiding in the NTFS file system. Digit. Investig. **3**, 211–226 (2006)

18. Krenhuber, A., Niederschick, A.: Forensic and Anti-Forensic on modern Computer Systems. Johannes Kepler Universitaet, Linz (2007)

19. Berghel, H., Hoelzer, D., Sthultz, M.: Data hiding tactics for windows and unix file systems. In: Advances in Computers, vol. 74, pp. 1–17 (2008)

20. Thompson, I., Monroe, M.: FragFS: an advanced data hiding technique. In: Black-Hat Federal, January 2018. http://www.blackhat.com/presentations/bh-federal-06/BH-Fed-06-Thompson/BH-Fed-06-Thompson-up.pdf. Accessed 12 May 2018

21. Forster, J.C., Liu, V.: catch me, if you can... In: BlackHat Briefings (2005). http://www.blackhat.com/presentations/bh-usa-05/bh-us-05-foster-liu-update.pdf. Accessed 12 May 2018

22. Garfinkel, S.: Anti-forensics: techniques, detection and countermeasures. In: 2nd International Conference on i-Warfare and Security, pp. 77–84 (2007)

23. Göbel, T., Baier, H.: Anti-forensics in ext4: On secrecy and usability of timestamp-based data hiding. Digit. Investig. **24**, 111–120 (2018)

24. Carrier, B.: File System Forensic Analysis. Addison-Wesley Professional, Boston (2005)

25. Wong, D.J.: Ext4 Disk Layout, Ext4 Wiki (2016). https://ext4.wiki.kernel.org/index.php/Ext4_Disk_Layout. Accessed 12 May 2018

Android

If I Had a Million Cryptos: Cryptowallet Application Analysis and a Trojan Proof-of-Concept

Trevor Haigh, Frank Breitinger$^{(\boxtimes)}$, and Ibrahim Baggili

Cyber Forensics Research and Education Group (UNHcFREG),
Tagliatela College of Engineering University of New Haven,
West Haven, CT 06516, USA
thaig1@unh.newhaven.edu, {FBreitinger,IBaggili}@newhaven.edu

Abstract. Cryptocurrencies have gained wide adoption by enthusiasts and investors. In this work, we examine seven different Android cryptowallet applications for forensic artifacts, but we also assess their security against tampering and reverse engineering. Some of the biggest benefits of cryptocurrency is its security and relative anonymity. For this reason it is vital that wallet applications share the same properties. Our work, however, indicates that this is not the case. Five of the seven applications we tested do not implement basic security measures against reverse engineering. Three of the applications stored sensitive information, like wallet private keys, insecurely and one was able to be decrypted with some effort. One of the applications did not require root access to retrieve the data. We were also able to implement a proof-of-concept trojan which exemplifies how a malicious actor may exploit the lack of security in these applications and exfiltrate user data and cryptocurrency.

Keywords: Cryptowallet · Cryptocurrency · Bitcoin · Coinbase
Android

1 Introduction

The popularity of cryptocurrencies like Bitcoin and Ethereum exploded in 2017; more and more people are buying into digital currencies. Managing digital currencies requires software to buy, sell and transfer digital coins. This software is commonly known as a cryptowallet and is available for all major mobile platforms or online. Similar to a bank account, it is essential that these wallets are secure which is not always the case. For instance, in December 2017 "thieves stole potentially millions of dollars in bitcoin in a hacking attack on a cryptocurrency company [named NiceHash]. The hack affected NiceHash's payment system, and the entire contents of the company's bitcoin wallet was stolen" [14]. While this is certainly one of the more significant incidents that has happened

F. Breitinger and I. Baggili (Eds.): ICDF2C 2018, LNICST 259, pp. 45–65, 2019.
https://doi.org/10.1007/978-3-030-05487-8_3

with approximately $60 million dollars stolen, there are other examples, e.g., "an unidentified thief has reportedly stolen more than $400,000 in Stellar Lumens after hacking the digital wallet provider BlackWallet" [10]. Another 5 hacks are highlighted by [7].

Besides online cryptowallets, there are also offline applications that one can install on personal devices. For instance, ikream.com[1] lists 5 crypowallets for Mac OS X: Electrum, Exodus, Jaxx, Coinbase and Trezor. Most of these applications also have a Windows version and are available for Android as well as iOS.

In this paper we examine seven cryptowallet applications for Android – Coinbase, Bitcoin Wallet, Xapo, Mycelium, Bitpay, and Coinpayments. The goal of this research is to discover forensic artifacts created by applications through the analysis of persistent data stored on the device as well as through application analysis (source code analysis) of each application. Our work provides the following contributions:

- The robustness assessments showed that several application use outdated security practices and thus are not protected against reverse engineering and tampering.
- The artifact analysis showed that several applications store sensitive information (e.g., private keys) as well as unencrypted data (e.g., passwords) on the device.
- We describe a proof-of-concept Trojan attack that exploits weaknesses found in one of the applications.

The structure of this paper is as follows: The upcoming Sect. 2 discusses previous and related work. The methodology is presented in Sect. 3. The heart of this paper is Sect. 4 which presents our findings followed by Sect. 5 which presents the proof-of-concept trojan. The last sections highlight future work and conclude the paper.

2   Related Work

In the related work section we first briefly present the technologies behind Cryptocurrency followed by the state of the art of Android artifact acquisition in Sect. 2.2. In Sect. 2.3 we summarize the literature for reverse engineering Android applications. The last section briefly discusses cryptowallet analysis.

2.1   Blockchain Technology

The blockchain is a decentralized, public ledger of all transactions that have been executed [17]. Because of its distributed and public nature, users do not have to put trust in a third-party (e.g. a bank). Anyone can download the entire

---

[1] https://www.ikream.com/2018/01/5-best-bitcoin-wallet-mac-os-x-26068 (last accessed 2018-05-08).

blockchain and sites like https://blockchain.info/ allow people to search the Bitcoin blockchain for specific transactions.

Blockchain relies on encryption in order to function where transactions are performed using public/private key pairs to verify if they are authorized by the owner of the wallet [13]. The biggest security challenge of a wallet application is how the keys are managed. If private keys are stored insecurely, then attackers can obtain them and thus steal all of the currency associated with that wallet. Because of this, wallet applications are almost always the focus of attacks rather than the blockchain itself. In fact, it is practically impossible to attack the blockchain directly because in order to steal one Bitcoin, its entire history would have to be rewritten on the publicly viewable blockchain [18].

The way wallets are managed differs depending on the wallet itself. Some applications (e.g., Bitcoin Wallet[2]) store the information only on the physical device. If the device is lost or damaged, there is no way to recover any currency associated with these wallets (in this case it is highly recommended to have backups). Other applications transfer the information to online servers, like Coinbase[3]. In this case, users access their wallets via a username and password created for the application. Another approach is seen in applications like Electrum[4] which stores the wallet on the device but then allows for the recovery of the wallet via a series of random words that was used to generate the keys.

2.2 Android Artifact Acquisition

Much research has been conducted on Android artifact analysis and therefore we selected some from different application categories to provide an overview. For instance, [20] focused on the analysis for social media applications like oovoo and was able to show that many do not use encryption. They were able to recover images as well as messages. [9] and [12] focused on GPS geodata from various applications on an Android device and demonstrated that applications like Waze provide a lot of helpful information for investigators. Other work focused on extracting media files from encrypted vault applications [21] where the Authors found significant vulnerabilities in 16 Vault applications.

While applications are very different, the approach for obtaining data the researchers took was similar. In referenced work, the researchers created logical copies of the data using the Android Debug Bridge[5] (ADB). ADB is a command line tool for Android that allows for the transfer of files to and from a connected Android device to a forensic workstation via a USB connection or Wi-Fi (workstation and Android device need to be on the same Wi-Fi). The data that can be pulled with ADB is limited by the permission level. For instance, for an unrooted phone, one can only access files viewable by the user, such as Documents, Downloads, or files in external storage. To access application specific data, ADB must

---

[2] https://wallet.bitcoin.com/ (last accessed 2018-05-08).

[3] https://www.coinbase.com/?locale=en-US (last accessed 2018-05-08).

[4] https://electrum.org/ (last accessed 2018-05-08).

[5] https://developer.android.com/studio/command-line/adb.html (last accessed 2018-05-08).

have root access (the phone needs to be rooted). Thus, having root access is generally required to access all (most useful) data, such as application folders or stored preference files. While there are many methods to obtain root access on a device, such as those described by [8], they vary wildly depending on the device, Android version, and carrier. Generally, newer devices are becoming more and more difficult to obtain root access on.

Another method to obtain application data without root permission is to backup the application data using ADB. The backup can then be decompressed and analyzed on the forensic workstation [4]. This method still requires physical access to the device, though, in order to obtain the backup and application developers can prevent their application data from being backed up via a flag in the application's manifest file.

While most methods, like ADB, utilize software to recover artifacts, there are also hardware solutions. For instance, one solution is to use specialized equipment to detach the flash memory chip from the device's PCB [6]. Naturally, this is a much more invasive process and the device is very unlikely to be restored to its original condition.

2.3   Reverse Engineering Android Applications

Reverse engineering of Android Applications can be done both statically and dynamically. Most work is done by statically analyzing application code. This is an easier process to automate as it does not require an environment in which the application has to execute in. [1] proposed an automated static analyzer that inspects seemingly harmless applications for malicious functions.

Static analysis is usually performed using tools such as Apktool[6] and Dex2Jar[7] to decompile the code into Smali or Java, respectively. Smali is an 'assembly-like' language for Dalvik, Android's Java VM implementation. In most cases the translation from dex to Java is not always perfect so an understanding of Smali is necessary to get full knowledge of the code.

The smali code and other files (such as the manifest or shared preferences) can be modified to change the operation of the application. Many third party application markets contain legitimate applications that were modified to add malware or advertisements [22]. Static analysis can be used to detect these modified applications. [16] presented a machine learning algorithm that uses static analysis to classify Android applications and detect malware.

Dynamic analysis is performed by running the application on the device and hooking into the process with a debugging tool, such as Android Studio[8] with the smalidea plugin[9]. Dynamic analysis has the advantage of being able to set breakpoints within the code as well as view/manipulate variable values. The downside is that not all code paths may execute. Some applications may

---

[6] https://ibotpeaches.github.io/Apktool/ (last accessed 2018-05-08).

[7] https://sourceforge.net/projects/dex2jar/ (last accessed 2018-05-08).

[8] https://developer.android.com/studio/index.html (last accessed 2018-05-08).

[9] https://github.com/JesusFreke/smali/wiki/smalidea (last accessed 2018-05-08).

also employ methods to hinder dynamic analysis attempts [15] and change their behavior accordingly. Unlike static analysis, dynamic analysis is more difficult to automate; some sample tools that support the automation of dynamic analysis are TaintDroid [5] or Crowdroid [2]. However, in many cases dynamic analysis still has to largely be conducted manually for each application.

2.4 Cryptowallet Application Analysis

Most research into the analysis of cryptowallet applications has been performed on the desktop (Windows) environment. [3] analyzed a machine running two wallet applications as well as a Bitcoin mining application and was able to recover evidentiary artifacts linking Bitcoind transactions to that machine. Similarly, [19] analyzed the process memory of two other wallet applications and were able to, in certain cases, recover private keys and seeds allowing seizure of funds from the wallets.

Limited research has been conducted regarding cryptowallet applications in the mobile space. [11] checked for forensic artifacts in four different applications for Android and iPhone, Android being the most relevant as far as this paper is concerned. The applications were tested on both an emulator and a physical device. They discovered some forensic artifacts leftover from cryptocurrency transactions made with those wallet applications. Cryptocurrency has exploded since this research was completed, so there are many new applications that have become popular and were not examined in the previous work. Furthermore, the researcher was also solely focused on finding forensic evidence of the wallets rather than also evaluating the security of the applications.

3 Methodology

This section discusses how each application was chosen as well as which methods were used to analyze the applications and their data. For testing, we utilized a Samsung Galaxy S3 Active running Android version 4.4 (KitKat) and a laptop running Linux to retrieve and analyze the data. There was no particular reason for the device except that we possessed jail-broken devices. Initially, the device was running Android version 5.0, however it had to be downgraded to 4.4 in order to obtain root level access on that particular model. As of writing, Android version 4.4 still has over a 10% market share[10]. Furthermore, our research focused on the applications rather than the operating system, thus we deemed it acceptable.

3.1 Application Setup

For this work, we focused on the Android operating system. Next, we chose applications based on the number of downloads. As a result, we analyzed the seven applications listed in Table 1.

---

[10] https://developer.android.com/about/dashboards/ (last accessed 2018-05-08).

Table 1: Chosen Android cryptocurrency applications ordered by number of downloads.

	Application	Package Name	Downloads	Version
1	Coinbase	com.coinbase.android	5m+	5.0.5
2	Binance	com.binance.dev	1m+	1.4.5.0
3	Bitcoin Wallet	de.schildbach.wallet	1m+	6.23
4	Xapo	com.xapo	1m+	4.4.1
5	Mycelium	com.mycelium.wallet	500k+	2.9.12.2
6	Bitpay	com.bitpay.wallet	100k+	3.15.2
7	Coinpayments	net.coinpayments.coinpaymentsapp	50k+	1.0.0.6

After downloading, each application was executed and set up. Note, all applications were installed in parallel. While most applications did not require to create a user account and manage the wallet locally, Coinbase and Xapo forced us to register an account as information is stored online.

3.2   Data Acquisition

Before acquiring the data from the phone, we started each application and performed basic setup operations such as creating an account for applications that required it or setting up passcodes to access the wallet. Next, we utilized ADB to download the data (the APK file and the Application data folder) for each application.

APK File is the application itself and can be found in `/data/app/<package_name>` (where `<package_name>` is the package name of the application as listed in Table 1). The application is important because it contains the compiled source code and other resources. We needed the APK file in order to perform code decompilation and analysis.

Data Folders can be found in `/data/data/<package_name>`. This folder is created for each application and is usually only accessible by the application itself. Inside the folder one can find items such as settings files and databases. Any existing artifacts would most likely be found in these folders.

Note, to gain access to these folders and to pull the data, the phone has to be rooted. In order to automate the process we created a Python script that utilized monkeyrunner[11] and ADB to pull the data folders for each application. Monkeyrunner is an API that allows a program to control an Android device or emulator. By using monkeyrunner, we were able to automate performing

---

[11] https://developer.android.com/studio/test/monkeyrunner/index.html
(last accessed 2018-05-08).

shell commands on the Android device. The process of pulling the data was accomplished in two steps.

Step 1: The data is copied from /data/data to /sdcard/data using the command   su -c cp -R /data/data/<package_name> /sdcard/data/ <package_name>. This is done because 'sdcard' can be accessed without root access, unlike 'data'.

Step 2: The data is pulled from the device using the Python script in Listing 5 in Appendix A. As shown, the command adb pull /sdcard/data/ <package_name> is run using the subprocess package. The command copies the data folders from the device to the forensic workstation. After completion, the script cleans up by deleting /sdcard/data/<package_name>.

3.3 Creating Transactions

In order to populate the applications with artifacts, transactions were performed for/from each application. Specifically, we purchased 0.01255964 BTC ($100 worth at the time of purchase) and passed it from one application to another. This ensured that each application has at least one incoming and one outgoing transaction logged.

3.4 Analysis

After extracting the data from the device, we analyzed both the artifacts and the application source code where the primary focus was on the artifacts. Code analysis was done to assess the general security of the applications.

Artifact Analysis was performed manually on the files extracted from the device. Notable files were XML preference files and database files where we especially focused on XML files (viewed using a text editor) and the SQLite database files (viewed using a SQLite database browser[12]). When analyzing the extracted data, we focused on finding the following items:

Wallet Private Keys are probably the most sensitive and critical artifacts managed by these applications as the entire purpose of the application is to manage and store the private key(s) securely. Finding the private key is essentially the 'golden ticket' as it can be used to siphon all funds from the wallet. Therefore, being able to obtain the private keys is a sure sign of an insecure application.

Wallet Seed is similar to the private keys in that they both lead to direct control of the wallet. Many wallet managers use a list of words, or seed, to generate the key pair. This exists as a recovery mechanism and the idea is that a user would write down the list of words in a secure place and use them to recover the wallet by generating the key pair again. Because of this, if we are able to obtain the wallet seed, we could recover the wallet ourselves and control the funds.

---

[12] http://sqlitebrowser.org (last accessed 2018-05-08).

Transaction History can be important from a forensic investigation point of view. While the blockchain is public, it may be difficult to find exactly where the transactions related to the suspect are located. Being able to pull transaction history directly from the wallet application, without needing the login credentials could be a great boon in an investigation. For this reason, we focused on trying to pull as much transaction information as possible.

Application-specific data including passwords, PINs, etc. should be managed securely in any application, especially in ones that manage money. An application could store and manage the keys securely but if they store the user's login credentials in plaintext, for example, then we can simply use that to log into an account, barring any two-factor authentication.

Code Analysis was performed to assess the general security/resilience of the applications by looking for common reverse engineering countermeasures. Specifically, we looked for the following three properties:

Code obfuscation is the act of purposely making your code difficult to read and understand. For Android applications this means renaming class and variable names by 1–3 letter names (e.g., 'aaa', 'aab', etc.) which is always done using software. For instance, Google's Android Studio has built-in options to obfuscate code using Proguard[13,14]. There are also commercial obfuscation tools that such as Dexguard[15] that come with more capabilities.
Code obfuscation is important as it slows down reverse engineering attempts. Heavily obfuscated code is difficult and time-consuming to navigate (and can even break some code analysis tools). It should be noted that obfuscation does not inherently prevent reverse engineering, and security through obscurity is generally not a tactic that should be relied on. Code obfuscation was tested by decompiling each application using JEB[16] and viewing the code.

Signature verification is a method of ensuring an application has not been tampered by a third party. Before Android applications are installed on a device, they must be cryptographically signed by a developer. Any modifications made to the application would also change the signature (assuming the attacker does not have access to the developer's private key). A common security practice is to verify that the installed application's signature matches the signature of the release version and disallow any operations if it does not. Without this step, applications are vulnerable to modifications with malicious code. An example of this is provided in Sect. 5 where we created a modified version of Coinbase that steals users' credentials.
Signature verification was tested by decompiling each application with Apktool, recompiling it, and signing it with our own key. The recompiled application was then installed on the device using ADB and executed to ensure it

[13] https://www.guardsquare.com/en/proguard (last accessed 2018-05-08).
[14] Note, Proguard is mostly used to minimize and optimize code and offers minimal protection against reverse engineering.
[15] https://www.guardsquare.com/en/dexguard (last accessed 2018-05-08).
[16] https://www.pnfsoftware.com (last accessed 2018-05-08).

functions normally. Since we do not have access to the developers' keys, our signed APKs will have a different signature than the official versions.

Installer verification ensures that the application was installed from a legitimate source. When installed, each application records the package name of the application that installed it (e.g., com.android.vending is the package name for the Google Play Store). Because a malicious version of the application could not be installed from the Google Play Store, it must be installed from another source. Assuming the legitimate version is only distributed on the Play Store, the application can be made to only function if the Google Play Store is its installer. This security method is generally uncommon as it prevents the 'sideloading' of applications which may be a legitimate method of obtaining the application.

The installer verification was tested the same way as 'signature verification', by redeploying the application to the phone and executing it. Any installer verification should fail as the applications' installer was ADB and not the Play Store.

3.5 Manipulation of an Application

The smali code of an application can be edited to perform a wide array of actions such as removing a pay wall or enabling additional features. A more nefarious option is to include malware in the application that sends user information to a remote server. Without any of the security methods mentioned above, an altered application would function normally and the user would be unaware of the malware on their device. To illustrate how an attack like this works, we constructed a proof-of-concept trojan version of Coinbase.

Note, the biggest challenge of these types of attacks is actually distributing the malware. Without the developer's private key, an attacker cannot upload a malicious version of the application to the Play Store (all applications need to be signed). If this signature is not valid, then Google will reject the upload. Thus, the only way to get malware installed is by social engineering users into 'side-loading'[17] the application which was not part of this research paper.

4 Findings

In this section, we discuss findings for each application as well as assessing whether they implement any of the security features mentioned previously.

4.1 Coinbase

Coinbase the most popular application we analyzed with over 5 million downloads which uses the cloud; keeps most of the wallet data, including the private

---

[17] Side-loading is installing an application directly rather than through a market. This usually requires an additional option to be enabled on the device before the OS will allow the installation.

keys, on their servers. This means that the security of the wallet is primarily dependent on their server security, rather than the physical device storage.

Focusing on the application revealed that Coinbase is not obfuscated. This made modifying the code quite trivial as we show later in our trojan proof of concept (see Sect. 5). The application also does not implement any signature or installer verification which allowed us to resign the APK, install it with ADB, and run it without any issues. Additional findings:

Plaintext Password was found in the shared_prefs XML file which contains various options and preferences for the application. The account password only seems to exist in the preferences if the account is created on the device. If the application is uninstalled and reinstalled, or one signs in to an existing account rather than creating a new one, then the password is no longer shown.
PIN Enabled is a boolean variable that also exists in the shared preferences. This is critical as changing the value from 'true' to 'false' disables the PIN. However, it requires a text editor with root access installed on the device, so it may not be a practical attack vector.
Transaction and Account Databases were found containing data items such as transaction amounts, account ids, and account balances. After performing some transactions, the database was populated with plaintext data so even if you cannot get into the account, you can still view the full transaction history. Note, this information is also stored in the blockchain but would require an investigator to know the public key of the wallet (or the transaction ID).

4.2 Binance

Like Coinbase, Binance does not store sensitive information on the device but on their servers, e.g., Binance users can access their wallets from any device through their website or mobile application. Unlike Coinbase, though, Binance does not store any transaction information on the physical device. This was confirmed by testing the application without Internet access. It fails to retrieve any transaction history or wallet information indicating that the information is pulled from the server on the fly rather than stored on the local device.

Code wise, Binance is obfuscated using Proguard. The application verifies its signature and crashes when trying to open an incorrectly signed version. There is no installer verification.

4.3 Bitcoin Wallet

Bitcoin Wallet is built on Bitcoinj[18], an open source, Java Bitcoin implementation that aids the creation and management of Bitcoin wallets. Bitcoinj uses Google's protocol buffer to serialize the wallet data. Thus, it is trivial to read the wallet data using custom or pre-existing software, e.g., wallet-tool. Furthermore, Bitcoinj includes tools to dump wallet data which we utilized to view the data.

---

[18] https://bitcoinj.github.io/ (last accessed 2018-05-08).

By using Bitcoinj's *wallet-tool*, we were able to find the private keys and seed associated with Bitcoin wallet as well as the complete transaction history. Note, Bitcoinj does have the option of encrypting the wallet with a password, but Bitcoin Wallet does not implement this feature.

4.4 Mycelium

Mycelium stores its transaction data in a SQLite database. Unfortunately traditional SQLBrowsers were fruitless as most of the data is stored in binary. However, the structure of the table looks like it is storing key-value pairs, i.e., a table with two columns where one is the key (*tkey* in the following) and two is the value. To pull out the data from the database, we implemented a Python script and converted the data into different encodings (e.g., string, hex) until we realized that most of the data in the value column is encrypted. To identify what was stored in the database, we analyzed the code that stores/reads from the database and following it backwards until the *tkey* for the desired value was found. Our analysis revealed that besides encrypted data, it also contains unencrypted data. For instance, the transaction ID was found in cleartext which can be used to look up the transaction on a Bitcoin blockchain explorer. Additionally, we found that AES encryption was used.

An overview of the encryption process is depicted in Fig. 1. Mycelium uses a randomly generated encryption key named *ekey* to encrypted sensitive strings (e.g., wallet master seed, private keys). The encrypted information is stored in the database. The *ekey* is then encrypted using *kkey* and stored in the database. While normally *kkey* should be generated from a user password, the developers use a hardcoded string to generate this key.

Using this method, we determined that the *tkey* for the *ekey* was a single byte ('00'). It was also the first entry in the table. We continued using this method to find that the table contained other sensitive information, e.g., private keys or wallet master seed.

In order to decipher the data, we modified the open-source code to decrypt the data. In detail: we created a Java project using Mycelium's encryption classes as well as the class for handling master seed creation. Our own class was then created which reads from the SQLite database and called the necessary Mycelium functions to generate the default encryption key and decrypt the data. The MasterSeed class has a function to generate a seed from the bytes decrypted from the database. The resulting object contained the seed words which could be used to recreate the wallet on another device.

It is noteworthy that the application has a method of preventing this attack, by generating the key encryption key with a user-provided password rather than one generated from a hardcoded string. This password feature exists in the code, but is not used in the current official version of the application. Once this changes, it will be impossible to decrypt the content (if the user has a strong password that hinder bruteforce attacks).

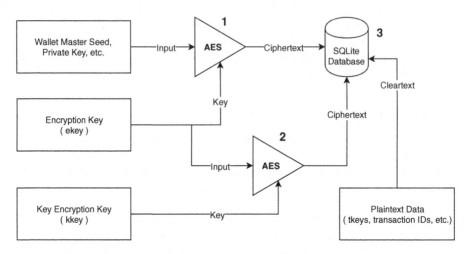

Fig. 1: Current work flow for storing information in mycelium.

4.5 Xapo

Like Coinbase and Binance, Xapo also stores the wallet private keys in the cloud and not on the physical device. It does, however, store a plaintext database containing transaction information, much like Coinbase.

As far as the code goes, Xapo was obfuscated to the point where Apktool could not decompile it without errors. JEB was able to view the code, but was not able to write the files without error. Because of this, we could not recompile and resign the application to check for signature verification.

4.6 Bitpay

Bitpay differs from the other applications mentioned so far in that it was developed using Cordova. Cordova is a platform that allows for the development of mobile applications using JavaScript and HTML. The weakness of this platform is that the source code is included in the APK file so it can be viewed by simply unzipping the APK file; no particular software needed. The source code is not obfuscated and also does not implement any signature or installer verifications. Furthermore, we found the following artifacts in Bitpay's data folders:

Wallet Keys were found in a file `com.bitpay.wallet/files/profile`. This file also contained many key pairs including API keys, request keys, and AES encryption keys. In reality, only the wallet private key is needed to steal funds, but all of the other keys exemplify the lack of security implemented by this application.

Transaction History was found in the file `com.bitpay.wallet/files/ txsHistory -<wallet-id>`. This file contained transaction information including the transaction id, amount, address of the sender, and time of the transaction.

4.7   Coinpayments

Besides Bitpay, Coinpayments was also developed using Cordova and suffers from the same weakness. Furthermore, Coinpayments allows the user to backup the application data which can be used by someone with physical access to the device to access the application data by backing it up and decompressing it on a forensic workstation[19]. Note, this procedure does not require root access. The following artifacts were found in Coinpayments' data folders:

API Public/Private key pair found in a database in `net.coinpayments.` `coinpaymentsapp/app_webview/databases/file__0`. With access to these keys, it may be possible to send requests as the user and transfer funds from their wallet.

Passcode in plaintext is found in the same database as the public/private key pair. This passcode is used to access the application and with it, an attacker/investigator could enter the application and control the funds in the wallet.

4.8   Summary

To summarize, Bitcoin Wallet, Coinpayments, and Bitpay show a complete lack of basic security practices such as encrypting sensitive wallet or application data. It is also noteworthy that 6 of the 7 applications store transaction history on the device, even if they store other wallet data on their servers. Based on our findings, we rank the applications from most to least secure[20]:

1. *Binance* does not store any information on the physical device. Application code is obfuscated and signature verification is performed.
2. *Xapo* does not store wallet private keys, but does store transaction history. The code is heavily obfuscated and even crashes Apktool when trying to disassemble it.
3. *Mycelium* stores all the data on the device, but it is encrypted. It is currently possible to decrypt the data, however a potential solution for this exists in the code; it is just not implemented.
4. *Coinbase* does not store wallet private keys on the device but it does store the transaction history. There is also a specific scenario where a plaintext password can be obtained.
5. *Bitcoin Wallet* also to obtain all wallet information, including private keys, by using an open source tool to dump the wallet data. It is possible to make this more secure by requiring a password to dump private keys but that is not implemented.
6. *Bitpay* provides next to no security as wallet keys are stored in plaintext. Transaction history for the wallet can also be found.

---

[19] https://nelenkov.blogspot.ca/2012/06/unpacking-android-backups.html (last accessed 2018-05-08).

[20] When ranking these applications, server-side security is not considered. This research was only concerned with what data, if any, is present on the physical device.

```
private void login() {
    if (!Utils.isConnectedOrConnecting(((Context)this))) {
        Utils.showMessage(((Context)this), 0x7F0801B0, 1);
    }
    else {
        this.showProgress(true);
        this.mReferrerId = PreferenceManager.
getDefaultSharedPreferences(((Context)this)).getString("
referral", null);
        this.getAuthTypeForLogin(this.mEmailView.getText().
toString(), this.mPasswordView.getText().toString(), this.
m2faToken, this.mReferrerId, new AuthCallback() {

    ...
```

Listing 1: Application code that handles the user's email and password.

7. *Coinpayments* stores wallet keys in plaintext. Additionally, even if the user locks the application with a passcode, that passcode is stored in a plaintext database and easily retrieved.

5   Trojan Proof-of-Concept

To illustrate how an insecure reverse engineered wallet may be exploited, we constructed a proof-of-concept trojan for Coinbase that steals user login credentials. This type of attack does not only apply to Coinbase and in many cases the same code used in this attack may be used for other applications. This section details how the trojan was created.

Locating the Data to Steal. The purpose of this trojan is to steal the users' data and upload it to a remote server. In the case of Coinbase, the ideal data to steal would be the user's e-mail and password associated with the application. Coinbase does not store the wallet private keys on the local device but rather on the Coinbase servers. Because of this, the most useful data to an attacker is the user's login information. With this, an attacker gains full access to the user's account and thus can steal the cryptocurrency in the wallet. It should be noted that Coinbase offers two-factor authentication which may prevent an attacker from logging into the account. This additional security is opted-into, so not all users will have it enabled. Even if two-factor authentication is enabled, other user data may be exfiltrated such as the user's credit card details.

To locate where the e-mail and password is used in the code, we decompiled the application to the base smali code. We used JEB for this, however, it can be conducted with free tools mentioned earlier in this paper such as Apktool and Dex2Jar. With no code obfuscation, locating the relevant code was straight forward. The class titled 'LoginActivity' handles the login process. In this class we found a login() method which pulls the e-mail and password from the GUI and submits it to the authentication method. We chose this location to insert our code to steal the user's credentials. The advantage of this location is that the application already does the job of acquiring data from the GUI so all we have to do is copy the values and send them to our remote server.

Listing 1 shows the code in the application that steals the user's e-mail and password from the GUI. This snippet shows how tools like JEB and Dex2Jar

```
.class public Lcom/coinbase/android/signin/uploader;
.super Ljava/lang/Object;

.implements Ljava/lang/Runnable;

.field public urlstring:Ljava/lang/String;

.method public constructor <init >(Ljava/lang/String;)V
    .locals 3
    invoke-direct {p0}, Ljava/lang/Object;-><init >()V

    iput-object p1, p0, Lcom/coinbase/android/signin/uploader
    ;->urlstring:Ljava/lang/String;

    return-void
.end method

.method public run ()V
    .locals 10

    iget-object v2, p0, Lcom/coinbase/android/signin/uploader
    ;->urlstring:Ljava/lang/String;
    new-instance v8, Ljava/net/URL;
    invoke-direct {v8, v2}, Ljava/net/URL;-><init >(Ljava/lang/
    String ;)V
    invoke-virtual {v8}, Ljava/net/URL;->openConnection () Ljava
    /net/URLConnection;
    move-result-object v9

    invoke-virtual {v9}, Ljava/net/URLConnection;->
    getInputStream () Ljava/io/InputStream ;

    return-void

.end method
```

Listing 2: uploader.smali – A thread class that opens the given URL.

can automatically translate the smali code into Java. While not perfect, the Java code is much easier and faster to read and understand.

Editing the Smali Code. After locating the critical section of the code, we implemented the malicious part. The attack consists of uploading the users' e-mail and password via a GET request to a remote server. To do this, we first created a thread class in smali that handles the opening of the URL. This is done because HTTP requests cannot be performed on the main thread of an Android application. The code for this thread is contained in the 'uploader.smali' file and is shown in Listing 2. Note, this snippet could theoretically be reused for any application to open a URL. The only required change is the path to the class (/coinbase/android/signin).

After the thread class is created and added to the application, we then needed to call it while the user attempts to login. The snippet in Listing 3 was inserted into the smali file. It is important to ensure that any of the registers used in the new code will not impact the following code as we want the application to function normally with our changes. Our proof of concept constructs a string with the URL and invokes the thread class we created previously to open the URL. The server then reads the e-mail and password from the GET request and logs it to a file. Without analyzing network traffic, the user would have no idea that anything was stolen. Since the request is done asynchronously in another thread,

```
#Create URL string (v1 = email, v2 = password)
const-string v0, "http://x.x.x.x:8000/upload?u="
invoke-virtual {v0, v1}, Ljava/lang/String;->concat(Ljava/lang
    /String;)Ljava/lang/String;
move-result-object  v0
const-string v7, "&p="
invoke-virtual {v0, v7}, Ljava/lang/String;->concat(Ljava/lang
    /String;)Ljava/lang/String;
move-result-object v0
invoke-virtual {v0, v2}, Ljava/lang/String;->concat(Ljava/lang
    /String;)Ljava/lang/String;
move-result-object v0

#Open URL
new-instance v8, Lcom/coinbase/android/signin/uploader;
invoke-direct {v8, v0}, Lcom/coinbase/android/signin/uploader
    ;-><init>(Ljava/lang/String;)V
new-instance v9, Ljava/lang/Thread;
invoke-direct {v9, v8}, Ljava/lang/Thread;-><init>(Ljava/lang/
    Runnable;)V
invoke-virtual {v9}, Ljava/lang/Thread;->start()V
```

Listing 3: Injected code into LoginActivity.smali to construct the URL and call uploader.smali.

there is no perceptible change in performance and the application continues to function normally.

6   Conclusions and Future Work

In general, the most secure of the applications we tested, Xapo, Binance, and Coinbase, did not store the wallet private keys locally on the device. This does not mean that the keys are managed securely on their servers, though, and having many keys in one location makes these companies larger targets for attacks as the potential reward for a successful hack is higher. This practice is necessary in order to deliver the platform-agnostic service they offer (i.e., being able to log in from anywhere and access your wallet).

Storing keys securely on the client side (within the application) is trickier and requires secure design. Mycelium almost accomplishes this, and for all practical purposes they do. The only shortcoming is not implementing a user password which would solve the problem of technically being able to decrypt the keys as well preventing someone with access to the device from simply opening up and using the application. Applications like Bitpay, however, fall on the other end of the spectrum and store the private keys in plaintext.

From a forensics investigation point of view, it is certainly helpful to know that transaction information was available for six of the seven applications. Even if one cannot gain direct control of the wallet, having the transaction history and public address may help in tracing how funds are being moved around. This is especially important considering how popular cryptocurrencies are becoming in the criminal world.

While the scope of this research focused on static analysis, in the future we would like to examine dynamic analysis of the applications and see what may be found in memory. While some of the applications securely handle the private keys by not storing them on the device, it is possible that they could be found in memory at some point during the application's execution time.

A   Python Script

```
#!/usr/bin/python

# Pulls all data from the device for a given APK
# Run by calling 'monkeyrunner getappdata.py'

import subprocess
import sys
import getopt
from com.android.monkeyrunner import MonkeyRunner,
    MonkeyDevice

def main(pkg_name=None, apk_path=None):
    device = MonkeyRunner.waitForConnection()
    if pkg_name is not None:
        res = pull_data(pkg_name.decode('utf-8').strip(),
    device)
        print(res)
        sys.exit(2)

    if apk_path is not None:
        pkg_name = get_package_name(apk_path)
        res = pull_data(pkg_name.decode('utf-8').strip(),
    device)
        print(res)
        sys.exit(2)

def get_package_name(apk):
    command = "aapt dump badging " + apk + " | grep -oP \"(?<=
    package:\ name\=')[^']*\""
    process = subprocess.Popen(command, shell=True, stdout=
    subprocess.PIPE)
    output, error = !process.communicate()
    if output == '':
        sys.exit(2)

    return output
```

Listing 4: Python script to retrieve application data from device

```python
def pull_data(pkg_name, device):
    result = device.shell("test -d /data/data/"+pkg_name+" &&
    echo 'true' || echo 'false'")
    result = result.strip()
    if result == 'false':
        return "The specified package name does not exist."

    result = device.shell('su -c cp -R /data/data/'+pkg_name+'
    /sdcard/data/')
    if result is None:
        return "error"
    command = "adb pull /sdcard/data/"+pkg_name
    process = subprocess.Popen(command, shell=True, stdout=
    subprocess.PIPE)
    for line in process.stdout:
        print(line.decode().strip())
    process.stdout.close()
    output = process.wait()
    device.shell('rm -r /sdcard/data/'+pkg_name)
    return output

if __name__ == "__main__":
    helpstring = 'monkeyrunner getappdata.py <package_name> or
    <path_to_apk>'

    if len(sys.argv) < 2:
        print("ERROR: Please include the apk path or package
    name")
        sys.exit(2)

    arg = sys.argv[1]

    if arg[-4:] == '.apk':
        main(apk_path=arg)
    else:
        main(pkg_name=arg)
```

Listing 5: Python script to retrieve application data from device (cont.)

References

1. Batyuk, L., Herpich, M., Camtepe, S.A., Raddatz, K., Schmidt, A.-D., Albayrak, S.: Using static analysis for automatic assessment and mitigation of unwanted and malicious activities within android applications. In: 2011 6th International Conference on Malicious and Unwanted Software (MALWARE), pp. 66–72. IEEE (2011)
2. Burguera, I., Zurutuza, U., Nadjm-Tehrani, S.: Crowdroid: behavior based malware detection system for android. In: Proceedings of the 1st ACM Workshop on Security and Privacy in Smartphones and Mobile Devices, pp. 15–26. ACM (2011)
3. Doran, M.: A forensic look at bitcoin cryptocurrency. SANS Reading Room (2015)
4. Elennkov, N.: Unpacking android backups, June 2012. https://nelenkov.blogspot.jp/2012/06/unpacking-android-backups.html
5. Enck, W., et al.: Taintdroid: an information-flow tracking system for realtime privacy monitoring on smartphones. ACM Trans. Comput. Syst. (TOCS) **32**(2), 5 (2014)
6. Hoog, A.: Android Forensics: Investigation, Analysis and Mobile Security for Google Android. Elsevier, Amsterdam (2011)
7. Khatwani, S.: Top 5 biggest bitcoin hacks ever, November 2017. https://coinsutra.com/biggest-bitcoin-hacks/
8. Lessard, J., Kessler, G.: Android forensics: Simplifying cell phone examinations (2010)
9. Maus, S., Höfken, H., Schuba, M.: Forensic analysis of geodata in android smartphones. In: International Conference on Cybercrime, Security and Digital Forensics. http://www.schuba.fh-aachen.de/papers/11-cyberforensics.pdf (2011)
10. Mizrahi, A.: Hackers Steal $400k from Users of a Stellar Lumen (XLM) Web Wallet, January 2018. https://news.bitcoin.com/hackers-steal-400k-users-stellar-lumen-xlm-web-wallet/
11. Montanez, A.: Investigation of cryptocurrency wallets on IOS and android mobile devices for potential forensic artifacts (2014)
12. Moore, J., Baggili, I., Breitinger, F.: Find me if you can: mobile GPS mapping applications forensic analysis & snavp the open source, modular, extensible parser. J. Digit. Forensics, Secur. Law **12**(1), 7 (2017)
13. Narayanan, A., Bonneau, J., Felten, E., Miller, A., Goldfeder, S.: Bitcoin and Cryptocurrency Technologies: A Comprehensive Introduction. Princeton University Press, Princeton (2016)
14. Peterson, B.: Thieves stole potentially millions of dollars in bitcoin in a hacking attack on a cryptocurrency company, December 2017. http://www.businessinsider.com/nicehash-bitcoin-wallet-hacked-contents-stolen-in-security-breach-2017-12
15. Petsas, T., Voyatzis, G., Athanasopoulos, E., Polychronakis, M., Ioannidis, S.: Rage against the virtual machine: hindering dynamic analysis of android malware. In: Proceedings of the Seventh European Workshop on System Security, p. 5. ACM (2014)
16. Shabtai, A., Fledel, Y., Elovici, Y.: Automated static code analysis for classifying android applications using machine learning. In: 2010 International Conference on Computational Intelligence and Security (CIS), pp. 329–333. IEEE (2010)
17. Swan, M.: Blockchain: Blueprint for a New Economy. O'Reilly Media Inc, Newton (2015)
18. Tapscott, D., Tapscott, A.: Blockchain Revolution: How the technology behind Bitcoin is changing money, business, and the world. Penguin (2016)

19. Van Der Horst, L., Choo, K.-K.R., Le-Khac, N.-A.: Process memory investigation of the bitcoin clients electrum and bitcoin core. IEEE. Access **5**, 22385–22398 (2017)
20. Walnycky, D., Baggili, I., Marrington, A., Moore, J., Breitinger, F.: Network and device forensic analysis of android social-messaging applications. Digit. Investig. **14**, S77–S84 (2015)
21. Zhang, X., Baggili, I., Breitinger, F.: Breaking into the vault: privacy, security and forensic analysis of android vault applications. Comput. Secur. **70**, 516–531 (2017)
22. Zhou, Y., Wang, Z., Zhou, W., Jiang, X.: Hey, you, get o of my market: detecting malicious apps in official and alternative android markets. In: NDSS, vol. 25, pp. 50–52 (2012)

AndroParse - An Android Feature Extraction Framework and Dataset

Robert Schmicker, Frank Breitinger$^{(\boxtimes)}$, and Ibrahim Baggili

Cyber Forensics Research and Education Group (UNHcFREG),
Tagliatela College of Engineering, University of New Haven,
West Haven, CT 06516, USA
`rschm2@unh.newhaven.edu`, `{FBreitinger,IBaggili}@newhaven.edu`

Abstract. Android malware has become a major challenge. As a consequence, practitioners and researchers spend a significant time analyzing Android applications (APK). A common procedure (especially for data scientists) is to extract features such as permissions, APIs or strings which can then be analyzed. Current state of the art tools have three major issues: (1) a single tool cannot extract all the significant features used by scientists and practitioners (2) Current tools are not designed to be extensible and (3) Existing parsers can be timely as they are not runtime efficient or scalable. Therefore, this work presents *AndroParse* which is an open-source Android parser written in Golang that currently extracts the four most common features: Permissions, APIs, Strings and Intents. AndroParse outputs JSON files as they can easily be used by most major programming languages. Constructing the parser allowed us to create an extensive feature dataset which can be accessed by our independent REST API. Our dataset currently has 67,703 benign and 46,683 malicious APK samples.

Keywords: AndroParse · Android · Malware · Dataset · Features
Framework

1 Introduction

Without a doubt, smartphone malware is on the rise. As a consequence, researchers and industry spend significant resources to improve malware detection techniques, e.g., by manually analyzing applications during forensic investigations or applying machine learning techniques.

Regardless of how a practitioner analyzes applications, there are usually two essential steps. First, one acquires a single malware sample/a sample dataset; when it comes to machine learning datasets are essential. Second, one will have to parse information to gain insight into the application(s). An overarching step by step workflow for machine learning approaches is depicted in Fig. 1 which coincides with the process observed in other works [9].

© ICST Institute for Computer Sciences, Social Informatics and Telecommunications Engineering 2019
Published by Springer Nature Switzerland AG 2019. All Rights Reserved
F. Breitinger and I. Baggili (Eds.): ICDF2C 2018, LNICST 259, pp. 66–88, 2019.
https://doi.org/10.1007/978-3-030-05487-8_4

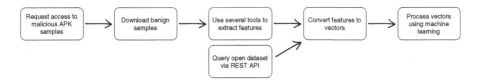

Fig. 1. Current work flow for machine learning approaches.

Malicious APK acquisition is often kept private due to ethical restrictions of freely sharing malware on the Internet; Table 2 shows some available datasets. For those that are private, users can often request access through a review process.

Benign APK acquisition involves downloading samples through public websites [4,5] such as Google Play (Google's application store).

Feature extraction defines the step of extracting relevant information from the APKs. This may include a separate library for each sought after feature. Since these libraries are often written in varying languages (e.g., C++, Java, or Python) this requires the user to be well versed in many languages, adding another layer of complexity.

Features to vector conversion transforms the raw feature data into vectors for a machine learning algorithm. One will typically write a script to massage the data into the format required for their algorithm.

Processing vectors is the final stage and allows a data scientist to test the detection rate of their algorithm.

From a forensic practitioner's perspective, the bulk of the work is related to reverse engineering the applications where one usually starts by extracting features to understand the application's code (e.g., looking for strings in the APK like IPs, hashes or URLs).

While these procedures are well established, there are some drawbacks. Downloading benign applications/requesting access to malicious applications can be time consuming, e.g., one may be tasked with writing a crawler or contacting website administrators for access to a bulk download. Sharing malware directly has downsides as well [11] and even though a review process exists, there is no guarantee that samples will only be used for research.

In this paper we present *AndroParse*[1], as well as, a freely accessible Android feature dataset which can be easily used by practitioners; it allows to download features of over 100,000 applications (benign and malicious)[2]. Specifically, this paper has two major *contributions*:

1. AndroParse is the first open source and extensible Android APK parser that allows users to quickly access features/artifacts of interest. As it is expandable, AndroParse provides a framework for plugins that can accommodate for new features/artifacts in various programing languages.

---

[1] https://github.com/rschmicker/AndroParse (last accessed 13-April-2018).
[2] https://64.251.61.74/ (last accessed 13-April-2018).

2. We provide a centralized, online dataset of Android APK features for examiners and data scientists[3] that can be accessed and downloaded through our web interface. Currently AndroParse's open dataset holds a total of 114,386 unique APKs - 67,703 benign and 46,683 malicious. This count is tentative as the dataset grows in size every day through the use of automated webcrawlers.

In our initial version, AndroParse supports four major features; we chose these features after analyzing state-of-the-art research: as they were the most common ones in scientific literature. To extract the features, we constructed a multi-threaded Golang plugin framework that utilizes existing applications (e.g., Android Asset Packaging Tool). This modular design allows anyone to add new feature extraction plugins if needed. Data scientists and forensic practitioners can access our platform to download the extracted features by querying a REST API and receive them in a JSON format. Note, feature extraction is performed on our server thus it consumes minimal computational resources from the user.

The rest of the paper is structured as follows: Sect. 2 summarizes existing tools for extracting information from an APK file, as well as, Android datasets and services. The extraction process is explained in granular detail in Sect. 3 which includes the implementation, tools used, features used, extending to new features, and extraction process. Statistics and an overview of the open dataset provided is presented in Sect. 4, in addition to, querying the parsed APKs contained in the open dataset in Sect. 4.3. This leads to an evaluation of AndroParse in Sect. 5. Lastly, we provide limitations, as well as, future work.

2   Background and Related Work

Given our two major contributions, we separated this section into *Feature extraction and decompilation tools* (Sect. 2.1) where we summarize existing frameworks and tools and *Malware samples and services* (Sect. 2.2) which summarizes the existing datasets we found. For a more comprehensive list of Android security resources, one may visit Ashish Bhatia's Github [12].

2.1   Feature Extraction and Decompilation Tools

The following tools have been developed to ease the process of extracting desired features from Android applications.

Android Asset Packaging Tool (AAPT, [14]*)* is part of Google's Android SDK and has been utilized by several researchers. This command-line tool decodes and parses the AndroidManifest.xml and allows users to query certain information about an APK. AAPT has been used "[...]to extract and decrypt the data from the AndroidManifest.xml file[...]" to access the APKs' permissions [31]. Written

---

[3] A prominent example that these services are valuable for the community is the UCI Machine Learning Repository [25] which includes a multitude of data and repositories and is frequently referenced in literature.

in C++, it is a fast tool as it provides the AndroidManifest.xml without having to decode the entire APK file.

apk_parse [36] is a Python library written to parse information from the AndroidManifest.xml. Unfortunately, it limits itself to the manifest and meta data of an APK for feature extraction. A more comprehensive tool is *Andro-guard* [13] which is an open source Python tool for extracting features from an APK's AndroidManifest.xml and DEX files. For instance, it has been used to test Android APK code obfuscation techniques [15]. Although *Androguard* is extensive and capable, it is time consuming to process an APK. In addition, it does not parse intents from an APK used by several works (see Table 4). Rapid Android Parser for Investigating DEX files is an open source Java based library for parsing DEX files [42]. It minimizes the time it takes to parse an APK by having an in-memory representation of the data that allows queries. The problem is that it is limited to strings and APIs and scientists still need to understand the structure/APIs in order to query it. Besides the actual malware dataset (mentioned in the previous section), *Drebin* provides "all features extracted from each of the 123,453 benign applications and 5,560 malicious applications" [7,38]. However, the *Drebin* feature extraction tool seems to be closed source. This hinders open performance reviews and comparison to open source tools.

While the previous tools focused on feature extraction, *APKTool* [40] disassembles the APK file into smali form as well as decompresses the AndroidManifest.xml. Smali files are text files (one per java class) which are simpler to understand than DEX files. However, these files then need to be parsed again in order to be used by data scientists [29].

2.2 Malware Samples and Services

While searching for malware samples, we identified that there were two kinds of sets which we will refer to as *services* and *sample sets*.

Malware services are online applications that possess or allow the uploading of samples but only share secondary information. For instance, these services examine an APK file and detect if it is malicious or provide other information such as extracted strings or permissions. `VirusTotal.com` is one popular example [37]. Although convenient, VirusTotal has a major limitation of being signature based and therefore it cannot be fully aware of the intents of an application. Payload Security [27] does offer an online searchable dataset of malware. Although highly informative, it is limited to metadata, permissions, and extracted strings for a given malware sample but does not include APIs and other strings. Other sources such as AndroTotal [21] and NVISO APK Scan [23] exist but the user must first have the APK samples to analyze. To sum it up, these third party services are convenient for small applications in small quantities and are not suitable for large-scale detailed APK file analysis. Secondly, AndroTotal and NVISO APK Scan offer some features to be viewed online but they do not offer a download option of the features. Payload Security offers an API except the user must sign up for access and is given a quota per API key.

Malware sample sets are repositories which are available for download; an overview is shown in Table 2. Most datasets are kept password protected and only through a review process can a researcher gain access.

One frequently utilized dataset is Drebin [7]. This dataset consists of 5,560 samples from 179 different malware families collected from 08/2010 to 10/2012 and is available for researchers in academia as well as industry after 'registration' (sending an email). Another example dataset was the Malware Genome Project[4] [43]. However, according to the website this dataset is no longer being maintained. Contagio Mobile [26] contains a smaller amount of APKs, but are referenced extensively in research articles. Works have used the repository to analyze the effectiveness of permissions as the sole feature for malware detection [32]. Das Malwerk [35] and theZoo [24] are examples of datasets that are open to the public. They not only contain Android malware, but Windows and OS X executables as well. The malware samples vary from cryptolockers to ransomeware, and trojans.

3   AndroParse

AndroParse is a feature extraction framework that is developed for digital forensic practitioners and data scientists. It allows users to parse features out of Android applications which can then be manually analyzed (e.g., using elasticsearch) or used as input for machine learning approaches. A complete overview is depicted in Fig. 2.

Although popular tools for Android APK reverse engineering have been previously written in Python [13] and Java [1], AndroParse is written in *Golang*. We chose Golang as it provides authentic multi-threading, unlike Python[5], and a runtime plugin interface, unlike Java. Both of these programming language features are heavily relied upon in the framework. A detailed comparison is provided in Table 1.

Fig. 2. Extraction & querying workflow

3.1   Installation and Usage

AndroParse is a command-line driven tool that parses four different features from APK files and outputs results in a commonly accepted JSON format. Before running it, it requires some preparation:

---

[4] http://www.malgenomeproject.org (last accessed 13-April-2018).
[5] https://wiki.python.org/moin/GlobalInterpreterLock (last accessed 13-April-2018).

Table 1. Reverse engineering tool comparison.

Tool	AndroParse	php_apk_parser [34]	Androguard [13]	Apktool [1]
Open Source	✓	✓	✓	✓
License	GPL-3.0	None	Apache-2.0	Apache-2.0
Expansion	✓			
Language	Golang	PHP	Python	Java
Manifest	✓	✓	✓	✓
Dex	✓		✓	✓
Export Format	JSON	XML	Python	XML/Smali

Dependencies. While some dependencies are included in the repository, others must be downloaded and installed manually. Particularly, our implementation requires the RAPID JAR [42] (included), Glide package manager, and Google's AAPT [14].

The Glide package manager provides an easy to use interface for installing Golang dependencies. Installation instructions for Glide can be found on their GitHub repository[6]. Once Glide has been installed, users can download the AndroParse source code and put it in any directory. Next, the user must run the command `make update && make configure` to download, install, and prepare all Golang related dependencies AndroParse requires to compile. The second manual dependency, AAPT, can be installed as a system wide package in Debian, CentOS, and Mac OSX based distributions of UNIX/BSD. Once dependencies are installed, AndroParse can be compiled and executed using `make && androparse`.

Command-Line Options. Before running the application, the user is required to create a YAML configuration file:

```
apkDir: "/home/myuser/apks"
codeDir: "/home/myuser/src/github.com/AndroParse/androparse"
outputDir: "/home/myuser/output"
vtapikey: "My VirusTotal API Key"
```

The field `apkDir` contains the directory of the user's APK dataset. `codeDir` provides the source code directory to access the RAPID JAR file, as well as, feature extraction plugins at runtime. `outputDir` specifies the directory the user would like to store the resulting JSON for parsed APKs. Lastly, `vtapikey` is optional, however, is required under the condition that the user requests each sample to be validated with VirusTotal using the `vt` flag. Then our implementation can be executed by

---

[6] https://github.com/Masterminds/glide (last accessed 13-April-2018).

```
androparse -config ~/myconfig.yaml -vt -clean -append -parser Permissions
```

The config flag is the only required command line option as it provides a relative or absolute path to a user's configuration file. vt specifies that the user wants to validate the APK samples with VirusTotal (this requires an API key in the configuration file). In the absence of this flag and should the user execute the *IsMalicious* plugin, the user must separate their APKs into benign/ and malicious/ directories. The flag, clean, renames all files stored in the targeted APK directory to their SHA256 values. This removes any duplicates from the dataset and reduces disk usage (note, the original file name is not captured as often APKs were renamed beforehand, e.g., most of the malicious datasets). append allows users to add a new feature into existing JSON output files from a previous extraction run, or skip over already parsed APKs. Lastly, parser permits the user to specify which feature extraction plugin(s) to run explicitly. In the absence of this flag, all feature extraction plugins are ran.

3.2   Extracting and Adding New Features

The following paragraphs highlight how AndroParse extracts the features from every APK file:

Deduplication (a.k.a. clean). As a first step, AndroParse will rename every APK to its corresponding SHA256 hash value. This mitigates any duplicate APKs in the dataset and decreases the necessary runtime of the extraction process.

Feature Extraction. To extract various features, we utilize existing tools:

MD5, SHA1, SHA256, Date, File Size are generated using Golang's standard libraries. The file size of an APK is stored in bytes. Furthermore, we capture the timestamp (format "yyyy-mm-dd HH:MM:SS") when the APK is processed which allows to have standardized sets, e.g., the detection rates can be compared by the standardized corpus before 'date'.

Permissions, Intents, Package Name and Version are extracted using Google's *Android Asset Packaging Tool* (AAPT, [14]). AAPT can extract an APK's AndroidManifest.xml without having to decompress an entire APK's content. The feature extraction plugins *Permissions, Intents, PackageName, and PackageVersion* each call AAPT to decompress the AndroidManifest.xml file to parse a given feature.

APIs, Strings are analyzed by the RAPID library [42]. Therefore, we invoke RAPID's Java jar library through an operating system *exec* call[7].

---

[7] This portion of code must be performed sequentially as there is a low-level JVM memory error when multiple threads access the library at once.

Adding New Features/Extending AndroParse. One of the key strengths of AndroParse is extensibility (adding new feature extraction methods) which is implemented using Golang's runtime plugin interface[8]. The interface provides three main benefits to a developer creating new plugins for feature extraction. (1) The developer does not need to have a working knowledge of the framework and can purely focus on extracting desired features, (2) It does not require recompilation of the entire framework, and (3) It allows plugins to be written in other programing languages such as C and C++[9]. More details can be found in the documentation[10]. The remainder of this section details the development of a plugin.

The sample structure for plugins is highlighted in Listing 1. Each plugin is considered as its own package and therefore must label itself as *main* (line 1). Furthermore, the plugin must import AndroParse utils (line 4) package as it contains a necessary configuration data structure so that the plugin can access information from the included YAML file on execution. The actual functionality is implemented in three functions:

1. `NeedLock()` returns true or false depending on if the parser needs to be locked from other threads accessing the same parser at the same time. For instance, the RADIP JAR library currently cannot run in multiple threads and therefore this function should return true (See Sect. 6 for more details).
2. `GetKey()` only returns a key (string) that indexes the given plugin's value in the resulting JSON output for a given APK. A user may choose this to be the plugin's name for example.
3. `GetValue(string, utils.ConfigData)` accepts a path to an APK (the framework iterates over each APK) and a struct containing configuration data from the user created YAML file (See Sect. 3.1). Note, the first return type is `interface{}`[11] which means the plugin can return any type and the AndroParse framework will correctly handle its type to be displayed in the resulting JSON file. In addition, the plugin must also return an error value should an error occur or *nil* when all has processed correctly.

Once completed, the parser needs to be stored in the folder `./androparse/plugins/MyPluginName/`. Following this, the plugin's `.go` file needs to be added in the Makefile (`./androparse/plugins/Makefile`):

```
PLUGINS := Apis/Apis.go Intents/Intents.go [...] MyPluginName/MyPluginName.go
```

Subsequently, the developer can compile their plugin using the `make` command, and finally, invoke their plugin by executing the command below where `myPluginName` is the file name:

```
androparse -config ~/myconfig.yaml -parser MyPluginName
```

---

[8] https://golang.org/pkg/plugin/ (last accessed 13-April-2018).

[9] One can use any language as long as the code can be compiled into a *shared object* file.

[10] https://github.com/rschmicker/AndroParse/wiki/Develop-Plugins (last accessed 13-April-2018).

[11] https://golang.org/doc/effective_go.html#interfaces (last accessed 13-April-2018).

```
1    package main
2
3    import (
4        "AndroParse/androparse/utils"
5        "os"
6    )
7
8    func NeedLock() bool { return false }
9
10   func GetKey() string { return "FileSize" }
11
12   func GetValue(path string, config utils.ConfigData)
13            (interface{}, error) {
14       file, err := os.Open(path)
15       if err != nil {
16           return nil, err
17       }
18       fi, err := file.Stat()
19       if err != nil {
20           return nil, err
21       }
22       return fi.Size(), nil
23   }
```

Listing 1. Example AndroParse Plugin.

3.3 Storage Schematic/Accessing Features

The features of each APK are stored in a JSON file. An example of this output is shown in Appendix A Listing 3. We decided for JSON due to the widespread support across most programming languages and its compatibility with may tools, e.g., Elasticsearch (details below). An example use case of using AndroParse's JSON output can be seen in our repository under `analysis/train_oa.py`. The script showcases several machine learning algorithms compared against each other using the permissions of an APK as a feature vector.

Elasticsearch is a textual indexing engine used for searching for the features by our backend which can be used for JSON files. Elasticsearch requires a *mapping* to be used which "defines how a [JSON] document, and the fields it contains, are stored and indexed"[12]. The mapping used by AndroParse can be seen in Appendix A Listing 5. As shown, this JSON structure identifies which data type should be used for each field (it can be updated to accommodate a new feature). Once the mapping of the dataset is updated, a new feature can be appended onto existing documents. Using Elasticsearch in our backend provides AndroParse a scalable solution not only as the number of APKs grows, but also as the number of new features increases.

---

[12] https://www.elastic.co/guide/en/elasticsearch/reference/current/mapping.html (last accessed 13-April-2018).

Verification of Elasticsearch (See Sect. 5.1) verifies the process of extracting the features from an APK, however, we still found it necessary to verify that the JSON documents Elasticsearch indexes are not modified in any way when queried. To verify Elasticsearch's output, a query is performed on a given APK downloading all of its key value pairs. Then for every value contained in the given APK's JSON file produced by AndroParse, it is searched and matched to Elasticsearch's output. After 100 successful trials, it was concluded that the data is valid.

4 Dataset and Parsed Features

We will summarize the dataset we collected, as well as, motivate the features that are currently available.

4.1 Dataset Contents

In order to provide a comprehensive feature dataset for researchers, we collected available malware datasets and downloaded benign samples as listed in Table 2 (note, a few malware datasets contained duplicates). While collecting the samples, we found that the average size per application differs; malicious applications seem to be smaller than benign (See Table 3).

Table 2. Malicious APKs in AndroParse's dataset.

Source	# of APKs	Private	Reference
AMD	24,553	✓	[39]
PRAGuard	10,479	✓	[22]
Third Party Stores	9,587		
Drebin	5,560	✓	[7]
Contagio Mobile	818		[26]
theZoo	100		[24]
GitHub	73		[12]
Das Malwerk	55		[35]
Total Before Dedup	51,270		
Total After Dedup	46,683		

Table 3. AndroParse dataset statistics.

	APK count	APK total size	APK avg. size
Benign	67,703	583.67 GB	8.28 MB
Malicious	46,683	70.26 GB	1.54 MB
Total	114,386	653.93 GB	5.85 MB

The count of benign APKs is rapidly changing due to routine web-scrappers that continuously crawl third party websites such as *apkdownloaders.com, apkapps.com, apkfiles.com, apkleecher.com, apkmirror.com, fdroid.org, slideme.org* and the Google Play App store. These web-scrappers are public and open to the community to use in our source code repository under `./webscrappers/`. Note, third party sites constantly change their HTML structure and one may have to adjust them. Furthermore, we would like to ask the community to consider contributing their samples our repository.

4.2 Identifying Relevant Features

To gain insight into commonly used features for Android malware detection, we analyzed state-of-the-art literature by searching databases for key terms like 'Android, Malware, and/or Machine Learning'. We then selected the 15 articles listed in Appendix A Table 7 because they were the most recent (2012 or newer) and are frequently cited. A summary of the utilized features is provided in Table 4.

Table 4. Number of features used across papers.

Feature	# of occurrences
Permissions	13
APIs	11
Strings	7
Intents	6
Components	3
Graphs	1
Signatures	1
Meta Data	1
Opcodes	1

Note, the total number of features exceeds the total number of analyzed articles as most references use several features. For example, a single article could use hardware/application components, permissions, intents, APIs, and network addresses (strings) [7]. Each of these are counted individually leading to a sum of features larger than the amount of papers.

Our findings are similar to [16] who analyzed 100 papers in the Android malware domain and permissions were also the most referenced static feature followed by APIs as the second most used feature (e.g., APIs are used to discover any use of network connectivity, encryption, or obfuscation [41]). Our third feature is strings which can include label names, text shown in the application but also contain URLs, phone numbers, and IP addresses. Lastly, intents provide an effective method for understanding how an APK may operate. They are often times combined with permissions for accurate malware detection [10]. Each feature is expressed broadly. For example, *APIs* includes the use of APIs in general as well as special API's, network API's, encryption API's, etc. Since all APIs in a given APK are extracted, any of these *sub-features* can be utilized. The same applies to *Strings*, i.e., network addresses, native system commands, phone numbers, etc.

Based on these findings, AndroParse currently supports parsing the top four features: (1) Permissions, (2) APIs, (3) Strings, and (4) Intents. As discussed earlier, the framework can easily be extended (discussed in Sect. 3.2).

4.3   Front End for Accessing AndroParse Sample Feature Dataset

To access the dataset, we developed a REST API which can be queried using three GET parameters and allows users to download needed features:

fields= returns only the features specified. If left empty or missing, all features of each APK are returned.
to= returns APKs up until the provided timestamp in the form: `yyyy-mm-ddTHH:MM:SS`.
from= return APKs starting from the provided timestamp onward in the form: `yyyy-mm-ddTHH:MM:SS`.
/all returns the entire dataset AndroParse has to offer at the time of querying.

Once queried, a ZIP file is created and stored into a directory shared by an anonymous read-only FTP server. Due to the potential for a large query, using an FTP server is more flexible (e.g., the end user can resume a download in case of connectivity problems; no additional query is needed). To free space, the server will delete queries after a certain time. Once the desired information is downloaded and extracted (JSON file), a user can manipulate the format to be used in a wide range of applications and languages such as WEKA [19] or Python.

Remark: Since the dataset is constantly growing, it is important to use the *to* and *from* GET parameters. Thus, future researchers can compare the their malware detection technique with previous approaches. For example, data scientist *A* uses the dataset prior to (to=)2018-03-03. This allows data scientist *B* to download the same set later even though the entire dataset may haven grown.

4.4   Accessing the Server

Our server has the IP 64.251.61.74 and is using a self-signed certificate with the SHA1 hash-value `7FE9AE1503BBA19F248E203F74A38D80DC849588`. You can access the server's REST API on port 443, e.g., https://64.251.61.74/api?fields=Permissions. To access the JSON file, connect Anonymous to the same IP on port 21.

5   Evaluation

In this section, we evaluate the forensic soundness, performance of the AndroParse framework, and the front end.

5.1   Verification of the Feature Extraction Process

As mentioned in Sect. 3.2 we rely on existing tools/implementations to extract features. These tools are well documented, have been previously tested by other works and are found to be accurate in their extraction process. AndroParse does however place some overhead on the tools used to structure the data properly for JSON.

To verify the integrity of the feature extraction process, Golang's built in command *go test* was used to perform unit tests on each of the feature extraction plugins. Using the APK *Facebook Lite* version 70.0.0.9.116 as a test APK file, each of the related plugin's expected values were manually extracted using the same underlying tool AndroParse uses. For example, aapt was executed to extract permissions which then were placed in a Golang unit test. This process was repeated for each of the other provided feature extraction plugins. Finally, each unit test was constructed to test for its given feature. *go test* successfully showed that each of the plugins created extracted its given feature and matched the expected value. For further description of how we constructed and executed our unit tests, please review our documentation on our wiki[13].

5.2   Application (APK) Validation

When receiving APKs from other researchers/sources, an APK is only labeled as malicious or benign by word of mouth. To further verify a given APK as malicious or benign we compared the hash of each APK to the VirusTotal [37] API. Using the VirusTotal service, we were able to more accurately identify APKs that are malicious or benign.

Interestingly we discovered that 761 previously labeled malicious samples were found to be benign. On the other hand, 9,587 benign samples were found to be malicious. This finding of mislabeled benign APKs parallels a previous study [44] where the authors discovered that third party Android APK stores often host malware.

In addition, we handled reducing potential false positives by only relabeling an application from benign to malicious if more than 4 anti-virus scanners (provided by VirusTotal) found an application to be malicious. Moreover, we relabeled a malicious application to benign if none of the VirusTotal anti-virus scanners reported a virus. Ultimately, the results VirusTotal provides are taken with a grain of salt, however, we feel this labeling technique to be more accurate than labeling by word of mouth.

---

[13] https://github.com/rschmicker/AndroParse/wiki/Develop-Plugins (last accessed 13-April-2018).

5.3   Runtime Efficiency of Tool Kit and API

For completeness sake, as well as, a comparative benchmark to other commonly used feature extraction tools, we provide the runtime efficiencies of extracting permissions from APKs. To measure and compare the runtime efficiency of AndroParse, we used an Ubuntu Server 16.04 VM using 8x Intel Xeon CPUs E5-2640 v3 @ 2.6 GHz with 64 GB of memory. To time the extraction, UNIX's built in time command was used.

For testing, we randomly selected 1000 APKs and compared the runtime against multiple other tools which were chosen due to their popularity in the community (e.g., highly cited or featured on GitHub). The results are shown in Table 5. It is important to mention that we only extracted permissions as none of the tools can parse the same features as AndroParse's framework. The exact methodology was as follows:

1. Randomly select 500 benign APK files
2. Randomly select 500 malicious APK files
3. Execute each tool extracting permissions from each APK
   – Note in the case of Apktool, only the *AndroidManifest.xml* is parsed as this tool does not provide permissions directly.
4. Log the time taken for the process to execute

Table 5. Extraction runtime efficiency of permissions.

Tool	Time (s)
AndroParse	6.291
php_apk_parser	13.173
Androguard	88.738
Apktool	733.928

5.4   Usability Based on Previous Works

In the following we highlight how existing work could have benefited from AndroParse. Therefore, we will briefly summarize what researchers did to extract the features, and then we will show how the identical feature vector can be created using our framework.

Permission Based Approach by [30]. In their work, the authors cross compare the standard permissions found in the AndroidManifest.xml (i.e., any permission starting with android.permission) with all standard permissions offered in Android[14]. If the APK requests a standard permission, it generates a 1 in the vector and 0 otherwise. To do so, the users extracted permissions of an APK

---

[14] https://developer.android.com/reference/android/Manifest.permission.html   (last accessed 13-April-2018).

using Androguard which is a timely process when scaled to thousands of APKs (Compare Table 5). On the other hand, AndroParse can provide this information (used permissions of an APK) by running the following query

```
https://hostname/api/?fields=Malicious,Permissions
```

which returns the (list of all) permissions and a true/false malicious indicator for each APK formatted in a list of key value pairs as described in Appendix A Listing 4. Next, the output of AndroParse's REST API conversion into feature vectors can be done with a short Python script and does not require sophisticated programming skills (See Listing 2 or in our repository under ./analysis/perms.py). Lines 3–7 load in the downloaded JSON file into a dictionary and line 9 creates a list of all standard Android permissions to compare against. Continuing along, lines 11–16 create a permission's binary vector. Lastly, lines 22–25 loop through the Android APKs and generate a permission's binary vector for each, as well as, determine if the given APK is benign or malicious.

```python
import json

def get_apk_json(filepath):
    d = {}
    with open(filepath) as json_data:
        d = json.load(json_data)
    return d

PERMISSIONS = [<standard Android permissions>]

def get_permissions(apk):
    perms = []
    for permission in PERMISSIONS:
        status = 1 if permission in apk['Permissions'] else 0
        perms.append(status)
    return perms

feature_vector = []
target_vector = []
apks = get_apk_json("perms.json")
apks = apks['data']
for apk in apks:
    feature_vector.append(get_permissions(apk))
    target_type = 1 if apk['Malicious'] == 'true' else 0
    target_vector.append(target_type)
```

Listing 2. Excerpt from perms.py.

Permission Based Approach by [20]. Another work extracted the permission list from an APK and from that list, a count of the total permissions. This work could use the identical query to the one in our prior example. Once downloaded, they would need to iterate through and determine a count of permissions for each

APK. A script demonstrating this parsing of output and counting of permissions can be found at `./analysis/permscount.py`.

Permissions, APIs, and Strings Approach by [41]. In particular, this approach was only concerned with strings that contained a system command (e.g., `chown` or `mount`) [41] as well as Permissions and APIs. To collect the necessary data for this approach, the authors could have queried:

`https://hostname/api/?fields=Malicious,Permissions,APIs,Strings`

A script is provided under `./analysis/permstringsapis.py` which parses the downloaded JSON data, as well as, build the feature vectors for permissions, APIs, and system commands.

In summary, AndroParse directly provides the needed information and does not require a sophisticated APK parser. It is important to note that since the code for each of these three works were not made publicly available, the scripts were constructed to match as close as possible to the description in each of the respective papers. The scripts are located in our public source code repository and can be taken advantage of in future work.

5.5   Runtime Efficiency Assessment

In this section we briefly discuss the runtime efficiency for AndroParse as a stand alone tool as well as querying our web front end.

AndroParse. To test the feature extraction performance, we selected several sample sizes (from 250 to 2000 APKs) that were randomly chosen from our dataset. The results are summarized in Table 6; focus on *Extract* columns. As can be seen, the time for extracting features can be time consuming (over 1 h for 2000; not including validation against VirusTotal). The limiting factor here is the thread lock when extracting strings and APIs using RAPID JAR.

Web Front End. For testing the front end, we downloaded all data using an *all* query (`https://hostname/all`) which pulls all fields from each APK. Again, the results are listed in Table 6 (focus on *query* columns). Of course, downloading the required data is much more space and time efficient.

Table 6. Query vs. extraction performance.

APKs	Size (MB)		Time		Performance (MB/s)	
	Query	Extract	Query	Extract	Query	Extract
2000	1561	11,888	53.5 s	64 m16.2 s	29.17	3.08
1000	765	6,522	28.4 s	36 m28.2 s	27.98	2.98
750	592	5,017	21.9 s	28 m9.9 s	27.04	2.97
500	407	3,481	16.5 s	19 m18.1 s	24.68	3.01
250	199	1,945	7.7 s	9 m54.8 s	25.90	3.27

6   Limitations

In its current form, AndroParse has two main limitations. First, as discussed in Sect. 1, the extraction process is only concerned with static analysis of APK files. This was an initial design choice to focus on the usability of such a platform. Dynamic analysis can expand on features such as but not limited to: file operations, commands, network traffic, system properties, etc. [38]. Second, AndroParse has been multi-threaded as much as possible to reduce the time taken to extract features. In its current form, the *RAPID* JAR file must be ran with only one instance at a time using the resource. This is due to a low level unsafe memory access exception thrown from the JVM. Until this bug can be resolved, the strings and APIs must be ran sequentially, significantly slowing down the extraction process.

7   Conclusion

In this paper we presented AndroParse, a feature extraction tool for data scientists and forensic examiners, as well as, a feature dataset that can be accessed through a REST API.

AndroParse is a general framework that allows users to extract features/forensic artifacts in a rapid and scalable manner. It is written in Golang and can easily be extended. In its current version, the tool can extract package name, package version, MD5, SHA1, SHA256, date extracted, file size, permissions, APIs, strings and intents. Due to the usage of the JSON format for the output files, the features can be further processed using any language (e.g., for machine learning purposes). For instance, a user can utilize Elasticsearch.

Feature dataset was created using AndroParse and is an online dataset that currently contains the features of approximately 114,386 Android applications – 67,703 benign and 46,683 malicious. Compared to previous approaches, we do not share the malware samples directly but only the features which comes with two benefits. First, the malware samples are not shared and thus cannot be misused. Second, researchers do not have to extract the features on their side which saves time and processing power.

Acknowledgements. We like to thank the University of New Haven's Summer Undergraduate Research Fellowship (SURF) program who supported this research.

A   Identifying Relevant Features Used

```
1    "Md5":"66bd8...3557ea2",
2    "Sha1":"h5k7...fh165t",
3    "Sha256":"b277...2f443",
4    "Malicious":true,
5    "Apis":[
6        "void android.app.Activity.<init>()",
7        ...],
8    "PackageName":"bubei.pureman",
9    "Version":"1.0.1",
10   "Intents":[
11       "android.intent.action.MAIN",
12       "android.intent.category.LAUNCHER",
13       ...],
14   "Permissions":[
15       "android.permission.WRITE_SMS",
16       ...],
17   "Date":"2017-12-07 16:41:51",
18   "FileSize":1699930,
19   "Strings":[
20       "",
21       "",
22       "\u00d0",
23       " ",
24       "    ",
25       " Build/",
26       ...]
```

Listing 3. JSON output of AndroParse of a single malicious application.

```
1    {
2        [
3            "Malicious":true,
4            "Permissions":[
5                "android.permission.WRITE_SMS",
6                ...]
7        ],
8    }
```

Listing 4. JSON output of AndroParse's REST API querying for permissions and malicious status.

```
 1  {
 2    "apks": {
 3      "mappings": {
 4        "apk": {
 5          "properties": {
 6            "Apis": {
 7              "type": "text"
 8            },
 9            "Date": {
10              "type": "date",
11              "format": "YYYY-MM-dd'T'HH:mm:ss"
12            },
13            "FileSize": {
14              "type": "integer"
15            },
16            "Intents": {
17              "type": "text"
18            },
19            "Malicious": {
20              "type": "text"
21            },
22            "Md5": {
23              "type": "text"
24            },
25            "PackageName": {
26              "type": "text"
27            },
28            "PackageVersion": {
29              "type": "text"
30            },
31            "Sha1": {
32              "type": "text"
33            },
34            "Sha256": {
35              "type": "text"
36            },
37            "Strings": {
38              "type": "text"
39            },
40            "Permissions": {
41              "type": "text",
42              "fields": {
43                "keyword": {
44                  "type": "keyword",
45                  "ignore_above": 256
46                }
47              }
48            }
49          }
50        }
51      }
52    }
53  }
```

Listing 5. JSON mapping used by Elasticsearch.

Table 7. Overview of articles including their features utilized for our work.

Ref.	Features	Citation
[30]	Permissions, Control Flow Graphs	"In this article, we present a machine learning based system for the detection of malware on Android devices."
[11]	Permissions, APIs, Strings, Meta Data, Opcodes, Intents	"This study summarizes the evolution of malware detection techniques based on machine learning algorithms focused on the Android OS."
[38]	Signatures, Permissions, Application Components, APIs	"[...]we propose a novel hybrid detection system based on a new open-source framework CuckooDroid[...]"
[41]	APIs, Permissions, System Commands	"This paper proposes and investigates a parallel machine learning based classification approach for early detection of Android malware."
[16]	Permissions, Smali Code, Intents, Strings, Components	"In this paper, we studied 100 research works published between 2010 and 2014 with the perspective of feature selection in mobile malware detection."
[33]	Permissions, Intents, Services and Receivers, SDK version APIs, Strings	"In this paper, we present Mobile-Sandbox, a system designed to automatically analyze Android applications in novel ways[...]"
[10]	Permissions, APIs, URI Calls	"This paper presents an approach which extracts various features from Android Application Package file (APK) using static analysis and subsequently classifies using machine learning techniques."
[7]	Components, Permissions, Intents APIs, Strings	"In this paper, we propose DREBIN, a lightweight method for detection of Android malware that enables identifying malicious applications directly on the smartphone."
[17]	Intents, Permissions, System Commands, APIs	"In this chapter, we propose a machine learning based malware detection and classification methodology, with the use of static analysis as feature extraction method."
[6]	File Properties, APIs, System Calls, JavaScript, Strings	"To discover such new malware, the SherlockDroid framework filters masses of applications and only keeps the most likely to be malicious for future inspection by anti-virus teams."
[2]	APIs, Permissions	"In this paper, we aim to mitigate Android malware installation through providing robust and lightweight classifiers."
[18]	Permissions, APIs	"In this paper, we present a feasibility analysis for enhancing the detection accuracy on Android malware for approaches relying on machine learning classifiers and Android applications' static features."
[28]	Permissions	"In the present study, we analyze two major aspects of permission-based malware detection in Android applications: Feature selection methods and classification algorithms."
[8]	Permissions, URI Calls, Intents	"In this paper, we perform an analysis of the permission system of the Android smartphone OS[...]"
[3]	APIs, Smali Code	Used the decompiled smali code to "[...] link APIs to their components."

References

1. apktool (2010). http://ibotpeaches.github.io/Apktool/
2. Aafer, Y., Du, W., Yin, H.: DroidAPIMiner: mining API-level features for robust malware detection in android. In: Zia, T., Zomaya, A., Varadharajan, V., Mao, M. (eds.) SecureComm 2013. LNICST, vol. 127, pp. 86–103. Springer, Cham (2013). https://doi.org/10.1007/978-3-319-04283-1_6
3. Anonymous. CAPIL: Component-API linkage for android malware detection (2016, unpublished)
4. APK-DL. Apk downloader (2016). http://apk-dl.com. Accessed 13 Apr 2018
5. APKPure. Download APK free online (2016). https://apkpure.com. Accessed 13 Apr 2018
6. Apvrille, L., Apvrille, A.: Identifying unknown android malware with feature extractions and classification techniques. In: 2015 IEEE Trustcom/BigDataSE/ISPA, vol. 1, pp. 182–189. IEEE (2015)
7. Arp, D., Spreitzenbarth, M., Hübner, M., Gascon, H., Rieck, K., CERT Siemens: DREBIN: effective and explainable detection of android malware in your pocket. In: Proceedings of the Annual Symposium on Network and Distributed System Security (NDSS) (2014). https://www.sec.cs.tu-bs.de/~danarp/drebin/. Accessed 13 Apr 2018
8. Au, K.W.Y., Zhou, Y.F., Huang, Z., Lie, D.: PScout: analyzing the android permission specification. In: Proceedings of the 2012 ACM Conference on Computer and Communications Security, pp. 217–228. ACM (2012)
9. Aung, Z., Zaw, W.: Permission-based android malware detection. Int. J. Sci. Technol. Res. **2**(3), 228–234 (2013)
10. Babu Rajesh, V., Reddy, P., Himanshu, P., Patil, M.U.: Droidswan: detecting malicious android applications based on static feature analysis. Comput. Sci. Inf. Technol., 163 (2015)
11. Baskaran, B., Ralescu, A.: A study of android malware detection techniques and machine learning. University of Cincinnati (2016)
12. Bhatia, A.: Android-security-awesome, February 2017. https://github.com/ashishb/android-security-awesome. Accessed 13 Apr 2018
13. Desnos, A.: Androguard-reverse engineering, malware and goodware analysis of android applications. URL code. google.com/p/androguard (2013)
14. eLinux. Android AAPT, June 2010. http://www.elinux.org/android_aapt. Accessed 13 Apr 2018
15. Faruki, P., Bharmal, A., Laxmi, V., Gaur, M.S., Conti, M., Rajarajan, M.: Evaluation of android anti-malware techniques against Dalvik bytecode obfuscation. In: 2014 IEEE 13th International Conference on Trust, Security and Privacy in Computing and Communications, pp. 414–421. IEEE (2014)
16. Feizollah, A., Anuar, N.B., Salleh, R., Wahab, A.W.A.: A review on feature selection in mobile malware detection. Digit. Invest. **13**, 22–37 (2015)
17. Fereidooni, H., Moonsamy, V., Conti, M., Batina, L.: Efficient classification of android malware in the wild using robust static features (2016)
18. Geneiatakis, D., Satta, R., Fovino, I.N., Neisse, R.: On the efficacy of static features to detect malicious applications in android. In: Fischer-Hübner, S., Lambrinoudakis, C., Lopez, J. (eds.) TrustBus 2015. LNCS, vol. 9264, pp. 87–98. Springer, Cham (2015). https://doi.org/10.1007/978-3-319-22906-5_7
19. Holmes, G., Donkin, A., Witten, I.H.: WEKA: a machine learning workbench. In: Proceedings of the 1994 Second Australian and New Zealand Conference on Intelligent Information Systems, pp. 357–361. IEEE (1994)

20. Kaushik, P., Jain, A.: Malware detection techniques in android. Int. J. Comput. Appl. **122**(17), 22–26 (2015)
21. Maggi, F., Valdi, A., Zanero, S.: Andrototal: a flexible, scalable toolbox and service for testing mobile malware detectors. In: Proceedings of the Third ACM Workshop on Security and Privacy in Smartphones and Mobile Devices, pp. 49–54. ACM (2013)
22. Maiorca, D., Ariu, D., Corona, I., Aresu, M., Giacinto, G.: Stealth attacks: an extended insight into the obfuscation effects on android malware. Comput. Secur. **51**, 16–31 (2015)
23. Malik, S., Khatter, K.: AndroData: a tool for static & dynamic feature extraction of android apps. Int. J. Appl. Eng. Res. **10**(94), 98–102 (2015)
24. Nativ, Y.T., Shalev, S.: Thezoo (2015). http://thezoo.morirt.com. Accessed 13 Apr 2018
25. Newman, D.J., Hettich, S., Blake, C.L., Merz, C.J.: UCI repository of machine learning databases (1998). http://mlearn.ics.uci.edu/MLRepository.html. Accessed 13 Apr 2018
26. Parkour, M.: Contagio mobile. Mobile malware mini dump (2013). https://contagiominidump.blogspot.ca/. Accessed 13 Apr 2018
27. Payload Security. Learn more about the standalone version or purchase a private web service (2016). https://www.hybrid-analysis.com/. Accessed 13 Apr 2018
28. Pehlivan, U., Baltaci, N., Acartürk, C., Baykal, N.: The analysis of feature selection methods and classification algorithms in permission based android malware detection. In: 2014 IEEE Symposium on Computational Intelligence in Cyber Security (CICS), pp. 1–8. IEEE (2014)
29. Rami, K., Desai, V.: Performance base static analysis of malware on android (2013)
30. Sahs, J., Khan, L.: A machine learning approach to android malware detection. In: 2012 European Intelligence and Security Informatics Conference (EISIC), pp. 141–147. IEEE (2012)
31. Sanz, B., Santos, I., Laorden, C., Ugarte-Pedrero, X., Bringas, P.G., Álvarez, G.: PUMA: permission usage to detect malware in android. In: Herrero, Á., et al. (eds.) International Joint Conference CISIS'12-ICEUTE' 12-SOCO' 12. AISC, vol. 189, pp. 289–298. Springer, Heidelberg (2013). https://doi.org/10.1007/978-3-642-33018-6_30
32. Seth, R., Kaushal, R.: Permission based malware analysis & detection in android (2014)
33. Spreitzenbarth, M., Schreck, T., Echtler, F., Arp, D., Hoffmann, J.: Mobile-sandbox: combining static and dynamic analysis with machine-learning techniques. Int. J. Inf. Secur. **14**(2), 141–153 (2015)
34. SunFeith. php_apk_parser (2013). https://github.com/iwinmin/php_apk_parser. Accessed 13 Apr 2018
35. Svensson, R.: Das malwerk (2016). http://dasmalwerk.eu. Accessed 13 Apr 2018
36. Tdoly. tdoly/apk_parse. GitHub (2015). https://github.com/tdoly/apk_parse. Accessed 13 Apr 2018
37. VirusTotalTeam. Virustotal-free online virus, malware and url scanner (2013). https://www.virustotal.com/. Accessed 13 Apr 2018
38. Wang, X., Yang, Y., Zeng, Y.: Accurate mobile malware detection and classification in the cloud. SpringerPlus **4**(1), 1 (2015)
39. Wei, F., Li, Y., Roy, S., Ou, X., Zhou, W.: Deep ground truth analysis of current android malware. In: Polychronakis, M., Meier, M. (eds.) DIMVA 2017. LNCS, vol. 10327, pp. 252–276. Springer, Cham (2017). https://doi.org/10.1007/978-3-319-60876-1_12

40. Winsniewski, R.: Android–apktool: a tool for reverse engineering android APK files (2012)

41. Yerima, S.Y., Sezer, S., Muttik, I.: Android malware detection using parallel machine learning classifiers. In: 2014 Eighth International Conference on Next Generation Mobile Apps, Services and Technologies, pp. 37–42. IEEE (2014)

42. Zhang, X., Breitinger, F., Baggili, I.: Rapid android parser for investigating dex files (RAPID). Digit. Invest. **17**, 28–39 (2016)

43. Zhou, Y., Jiang, X.: Android malware genome project. Disponibile a (2012). http://www.malgenomeproject.org

44. Zhou, Y., Wang, Z., Zhou, W., Jiang, X.: Hey, you, get off of my market: detecting malicious apps in official and alternative android markets. In: NDSS, vol. 25, pp. 50–52 (2012)

Forensic Readiness

Digital Forensic Readiness Framework for Ransomware Investigation

Avinash Singh$^{(\boxtimes)}$, Adeyemi R. Ikuesan , and Hein S. Venter

University of Pretoria, Hatfield 0083, South Africa
{asingh, aikuesan, hventer}@cs.up.ac.za

Abstract. Over the years there has been a significant increase in the exploitation of the security vulnerabilities of Windows operating systems, the most severe threat being malicious software (malware). Ransomware, a variant of malware which encrypts files and retains the decryption key for ransom, has recently proven to become a global digital epidemic. The current method of mitigation and propagation of malware and its variants, such as anti-viruses, have proven ineffective against most Ransomware attacks. Theoretically, Ransomware retains footprints of the attack process in the Windows Registry and the volatile memory of the infected machine. Digital Forensic Readiness (DFR) processes provide mechanisms for the pro-active collection of digital footprints. This study proposed the integration of DFR mechanisms as a process to mitigate Ransomware attacks. A detailed process model of the proposed DFR mechanism was evaluated in compliance with the ISO/IEC 27043 standard. The evaluation revealed that the proposed mechanism has the potential to harness system information prior to, and during a Ransomware attack. This information can then be used to potentially decrypt the encrypted machine. The implementation of the proposed mechanism can potentially be a major breakthrough in mitigating this global digital endemic that has plagued various organizations. Furthermore, the implementation of the DFR mechanism implies that useful decryption processes can be performed to prevent ransom payment.

Keywords: Windows forensics · Digital forensic readiness
Ransomware forensics · Memory · Registry · Investigation

1 Introduction

Digital forensics involves the recovery and investigation of data acquired from digital devices related to computer crime [1]. Encrypted devices pose a major challenge in digital forensics, due to the difficulty of retrieving potential evidential information for litigation [2]. In digital forensics, the use of a cryptographic mechanism such as BitLocker[1], and advanced encryption standards to protect system/information is a major problem for an investigator. The Windows operating system (OS), being the most widely used OS [3, 4], is a central target for attackers who exploit the vulnerabilities of each version of the OS. Malicious software (malware) is a constantly

---

[1] https://docs.microsoft.com/en-us/windows/security/information-protection/bitlocker/bitlocker-overview.

© ICST Institute for Computer Sciences, Social Informatics and Telecommunications Engineering 2019
Published by Springer Nature Switzerland AG 2019. All Rights Reserved
F. Breitinger and I. Baggili (Eds.): ICDF2C 2018, LNICST 259, pp. 91–105, 2019.
https://doi.org/10.1007/978-3-030-05487-8_5

growing threat with new variants surfacing exploiting new/undetected vulnerabilities [5]. Anti-viruses can only detect and remove malware with known signatures, deviant behaviour from a normally acceptable signature or based on unique behaviour [5]. However, one specific variant of malware that affects many organizations, companies, and individuals is ransomware [6]. Ransomware infects a machine and then starts encrypting all your files on the machine. It renders the system inaccessible until a ransom is paid to the attacker. In most cases, organizations ended up paying this ransom, due to the cost or lack of backups, reputation preservation, and the implication of prolonged downtime. New variants of ransomware are successfully circumventing existing anti-virus software protocols and other security apparatus [7]. As a process of mitigating ransomware attacks, this study proposed a Digital Forensic Readiness (DFR) mechanism. To the best of our knowledge, this is the first study that attempts to define a viable mechanism that can be used to potentially prevent the payment of ransom to attackers. A concise detail background of malware and a brief overview of DFR is given in the next section. This is then followed by the presentation and evaluation of the proposed mechanism. The paper concludes with related works and discussion of the implication of the proposed mechanism.

2 Background

The potential cost of cybercrime to the global economy, as shown in Fig. 1a could be as high as $500 billion. Furthermore, an approximate of 43% of cyber-attacks are targeted at small businesses [8].

Recent statistics have shown a growing trend of malware-based cybercrime, as depicted in Fig. 1b. According to Symantec, one in every 131 emails contains malware which is one of the biggest promoters of system infection [9]. Suggestively, with the growing trend of software applications and the relatively poor user education, cyber-crime through malicious software will continue to increase as seen in Fig. 1b. The common types of malware often encountered include virus, trojan, spyware, worms, adware, botnets, rootkits, and more recently, ransomware. A virus is a limited form of malware and can easily be detected by anti-virus, using signature-based or deviant-based logic and the effects easily reversed [10]. Trojans is a kind of malware that seems legitimate or is a part of the legitimate software that has been tampered with. The main purpose of a trojan is to gain backdoor access to the system. Given that trojan malware is usually undetected by the user, it has the potential to breach a given security apparatus for other serious attacks [11]. Similarly, spyware malware is designed to surreptitiously gather information or assert control over a given system without the knowledge of the user. Thus, it runs in the background to track the activity, and operational/dormant processes in the computer [11]. Adware malware spreads through an advertising medium usually through downloading free games and/or software. Adware may not necessarily be malicious but it can create backdoors or vulnerabilities in systems that other malware can exploit [10]. Similarly, a rootkit; considered one of the most dangerous and advanced forms of malware, gives an attacker full administrator access to the system [10]. Ransomware is a form of malware that affects a huge number of systems mostly in organizations and institutions. This form of malware

(a)   **(b)**

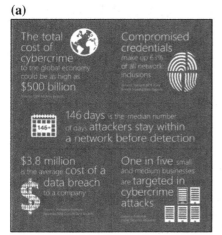 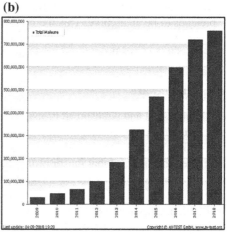

Fig. 1. Microsoft advanced threat analytics infographic (b) A decade statistic of Malware (https://www.av-test.org/en/statistics/malware/)

encrypts the user files while withholding the decryption key as a ransom for huge amounts of untraceable money, usually paid through Bitcoin [12, 13].

2.1   Method of Propagation

Different malware has specific methods of propagation or replicates itself to perform or cause maximum damage as intended. Some of the most common methods of propagation include social engineering [10], wired/wireless networks [14], file sharing [10], virtualized systems [12] and email [12, 15].

2.2   Adaptive Technique of Malware

Over the years, malware started to get more advanced by adapting and counteracting security mechanisms that prevent them from propagating. These techniques adopted by malware make it hard to detect as each technique brings in a new aspect to consider. Some of the common techniques used include polymorphism, metamorphism, obfuscation, DDNS [16] and fast flux [17]. Some of these techniques are further discussed.

- Polymorphism – this technique employs a modification mechanism to avoid signature-based detection. The malware simply changes itself without completely changing the code change its structure [16, 18]. However, some parts of the malware remain the same making it identifiable using adaptive detection algorithms [19].
- Metamorphism – this technique completely rewrites the malware such that it is extremely difficult to identify by anti-malware software. With each propagation this malware is changed, further adding to its unique behaviour making it almost impossible for anti-malware software to identify [16, 19].

- Obfuscation – by using archive files such as (zip, rar, tar, cab). The malware itself pretends to be an archive. This method encrypts the core (malicious) code such that it cannot be detected through an anti-virus. For example, base64 encoding commonly used to sneak malware into the system using HTTP/HTTPS channels [19].

2.3 Ransomware

One of the fastest and widespread propagation of malware is ransomware. Ransomware uses a combination of different malware like a worm to replicate and transfer itself over a network and can be attached to a trojan or an adware to enter the system. As highlighted in Fig. 2, global ransomware attacks increased by 36% in 2017 with more than 100 more variants used by hackers. A total of 34% of entities globally were willing to pay the ransom and about 64% of such entities consisting of Americans [20]. The FBI estimates about 4000+ ransomware attacks globally every day since 2016 [9]. The amount of ransom demanded per attack has increased to an average of $1077 which is an increase of 266% [20]. Ransomware uses scare tactics to trick people to pay using threatening messages and having a time limit to pay before the ransom increases. Ransomware can appear in different shapes and sizes, some being more harmful than others, however, all have the same goal. Common types of ransomware include crypto malware, lockers, scareware, RaaS, and leakware. These types are further discussed.

- Crypto malware/encryptors – is the most common form of ransomware with the capability to cause significant damage within a short duration. This form of ransomware simply encrypts all the files on a machine and extorts money in return to decrypt the files. An example of this is the latest outbreak of the devastating WannaCry ransomware [21, 22].
- Lockers – infect the operating system such that the legitimate user is locked out until they pay the ransom. This is achieved by modifying the bootloader of the OS, such that the malware is loaded instead of the OS making the computer inaccessible. The early forms of this ransomware are not generally used because reloading the bootloader is a simple solution to overcome this ransomware [13].
- Scareware – is a form of ransom disguised as a genuine application. It claims to have discovered security vulnerabilities in a system but demands money to fix them. When the user refuses to pay, the software will display ads and pop-ups, causing the user to think the computer is infected and eventually paying [23].
- RaaS (Ransomware as a Service) – is like a middle-man for an attack. The RaaS provides a ransomware service where malware is hosted and distributed anonymously, managing payments and decryption keys [5, 12].
- Leakware/Doxware – is a form of ransomware that steals personal images and/or information from a computer and then demands a ransom as a form of blackmail.

Each variant leverages a different method or builds on the flaw of another variant to make it more harmful and widespread. A descriptive summary of existing ransomware is presented in Table 1.

The summary in Table 1 reveals that most ransomware exploits the lack of user education and the unpatched security vulnerabilities that exist in Microsoft Windows. Furthermore, it shows that AES-128 encryption is the most common encryption

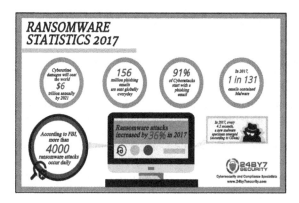

Fig. 2. Ransomware statistics compiled by 24by7 security (https://24by7security.com/have-you-scheduled-your-first-cybersecurity-task-in-2018-here-are-some-interesting-2017-statistics/)

Table 1. A summary of trending ransomware.

Name	Encryption algorithm	Method of propagation	Vulnerability exploited
WannaCry	AES-128, RSA-2048	EternalBlue	Windows Server Message Block (SMB) protocol
	Remark: WannaCry exploited the SMB protocol by using the EternalBlue exploit which was developed by NSA. This exploits the way Microsoft Windows mishandles specifically crafted packets which enable the execution of certain code from the payload. WannaCry encrypts each file with a different AES-128 key which is further encrypted with an RSA key pair and then added to the file header of each file. In order to get the decryption key, the private key of the Command and Control (C2) server is needed in order to decrypt the encrypted AES-128 decryption key		
(Not)Petya	AES-128, RSA-2048	EternalBlue, Ukrainian tax software update	SMB, Master boot record
	Remark: Similar to WannaCry, however, more harmful. The infection process does not stop upon infecting system files but also changes the bootloader to load the malware. This process bypasses the booting of the OS. This is done through the CHKDSK process where instead of loading the OS, it loads the Petya ransomware. While this message is shown it begins spawning processes in the background to encrypt the user files. This ransomware does not need administrator privileges to encrypt protected files since the OS is not loaded managing access control		
Locky	AES-128, RSA-2048	Phishing Email	Microsoft Word Macro
	Remark: Locky ransomware infects the system through social engineering in the form of a malicious Word macro. This macro then runs the trojan binary to start the encryption. The encryption used here is the same approach as that of WannaCry and Petya creating a new trend. This method of encryption is secure if the private key of the C2 server is not globally known. Thus, this method is unbreakable due to the mathematics involved in RSA encryption algorithm		

(*continued*)

Table 1. (*continued*)

Name	Encryption algorithm	Method of propagation	Vulnerability exploited
Cerber	RC4, RSA-2048	Spam Emails and Ads	Microsoft Office Documents
	Remark: Cerber is a RaaS that provides a toolkit which even works if you do not have an active internet connection. This ransomware enters systems through infected office documents that load the malware through a VBScript. This form of malware is well controlled since there are specific hacker groups working together to provide this service to less experienced hackers. This is how they manage to propagate the ransomware faster using affiliate programs and using social engineering techniques. This service is for those criminals who lack the technical expertise to execute such attacks and looking for quick profits		
Crysis	AES-128	Remote Desktop Service, VM environment	Weak or leaked accounts
	Remark: This attack is based on a user-oriented attack where remote desktops services are hacked. This gives attackers control of the machine, allowing them to manually install the ransomware. Crysis also makes use of a C2 which is used to manage and carry out the attack on a larger scale		

algorithm used by ransomware. Given that ransomware infects the system while hindering access to the system, post-mortem forensics (forensics performed after an incident has occurred) is not feasible. Therefore, a more pro-active approach is required to identify, and potentially acquire any cryptographic evidence from a system. The integration of digital forensic readiness into an organization can potentially provide a higher probability of decrypting a ransomware-attacked system as well as providing crucial information/evidence about the attack.

2.4 Digital Forensic Readiness

Digital Forensic Readiness (DFR) is the ability of an organization to maximize its potential to use digital evidence whilst minimizing the costs of an investigation [24]. In essence, DFR is a pre-investigation process which attempts to capture digital information from an identified system prior to the incident occurrence, which might not be available after the incident occurred. Therefore, with DFR, an organization would need to implement on-the-fly evidence collection processes. Thus, a DFR mechanism can be used to conduct an investigation, strengthen the security apparatus of the organization, or to prevent the occurrence of a known attack. With respect to ransomware, DFR can be used to perform analysis and potentially locate cryptographic keys within memory. Two probable methods of accessing the memory contents include targeting the memory allocation space in the running processes in the OS or by scanning through all processes on the system. Due to the lack of evidence collection prior to the incident occurrence, this research proposes a digital forensic readiness framework. This framework will provide a mechanism to securely collect and preserve potential digital evidence.

3   Digital Forensic Readiness Framework

The proposed DFR framework, Windows Registry and RAM Readiness Framework (W3RF), for this study, is presented in Fig. 3. This section describes the proposed framework including the necessary DFR processes defined in the ISO/IEC 27043 standard [25]. The proposed DFR framework attempts to define a method for secure communication, forensic soundness of potential evidence, and the process of decryption key extraction. The framework consists of four interconnected phases and subphases. Phase-1 (P1) deals with the process of identifying sources of potential digital evidence from a single computer or networked computer. Phase-2 (P2) considers the process of extracting potential evidential information from the identified component of the system/network. The Windows Registry and RAM are potential sources where ransomware information can be extracted. However, this extraction will occur near real-time using a trigger-based mechanism. The captured data is then securely transmitted to the storage process.

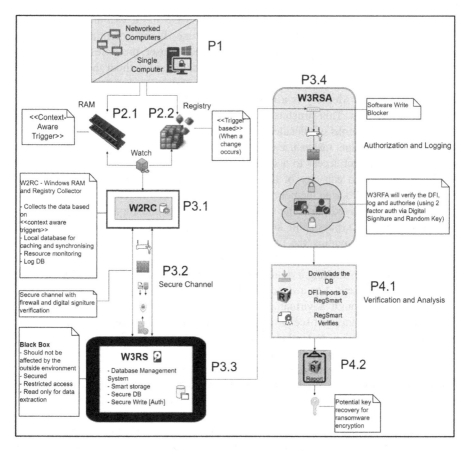

Fig. 3. Digital forensic readiness framework for ransomware investigation

The data storage process constitutes the Phase-3 (P3) of the proposed DFR framework. This phase contains a database management system (DBMS), where an investigator can extract this stored information. The input to this database is connected to the system/network through a one-way secured communication channel. However, the output-channel is connected to a forensic analysis tool which utilizes a forensically-sound communication channel. The forensic attribute of the output channel includes an access control mechanism (authorization, and continuous identity verification), integrity preservation and a verification process. The forensic analysis tool is capable of data-scavenging and the extraction of potential decryption keys. Phase-4 (P4) of the W3RF involves the reporting process of the action and events carried out by a forensic investigator and the system. This phase logs all the actions and processes performed by the authorized entities ensuring chain-of-evidence and chain-of-custody. A high-level overview of the functionality of each component is depicted in Fig. 3. These components are further discussed in detail in the proceeding subsections.

3.1   Memory

The dynamic and static memory (P2.1) of Windows OS has a vast amount of information pertaining to the current state of the machine. It can potentially provide an investigator with significant information about the active user, processes as well as any malicious processes that may be running in the background without the awareness of the user. Most damages that a malicious program can do to a system usually occur in the memory [1, 26]. Memory is a repository for data and program code that is systematically structured. This structure is similar to a linked-list, which consists of fixed block sizes where chunks of allocated data are slotted and stored. The location of these newly allotted data slots makes use of lookup tables to find and locate data within this structure, giving direct access to a specific address for faster access [26].

Given the limited capacity of the dynamic memory, virtual memory is created. Virtual memory is allocated memory on secondary storage, thus, expanding the amount of data that can be stored [27]. The swapping from virtual memory to main memory is called paging [27]. Cryptographic keys can potentially be found in memory as seen in [26, 28, 29], thus providing the opportunity to extract these keys for investigation. Since memory consists of pages, these cryptographic keys can be split over several non-contiguous pages making it more difficult for an investigator to manually scavenge these pages for the keys. For instance, findings in [30] leveraged memory structure to optimize search through a virtual address re-constructor. However, this will work effectively in a post-incident scenario. Therefore, a DFR process would require a near real-time data acquisition. Nevertheless, such a data acquisition process would require a method of continuous data collection.

A context-aware trigger based approach to data collection has been explored in a similar context such as crowd-sourcing [31]. This trigger can actively monitor the system using the least amount of processing power whilst minimizing the overhead cost of searching [26]. Furthermore, the trigger focuses more on newly created processes, thereby minimizing the search space. The signature of a known malware can also be added to the logic of the trigger mechanism. The criteria for the trigger mechanism focus on but is not limited to the entropy change in files, autorun entries added to the registry, scanning through files and mounted drives, loading of the Windows crypto library and detecting the deletion of shadow volume copies. This criterion was reached through analysis and execution of WannaCry and Petya ransomware. This criterion can also be used for ransomware detection. From [26, 32, 33] volatile memory represents one of the most reliable sources of forensic evidence pertaining to cryptographic keys and active malicious processes.

3.2   Registry

The Windows Registry (P2.2) is a hierarchical database that consists of the systems configurations and user metadata [34]. The registry is a structured database of key-value pairs. This complex data structure allows for the storage of complex information in various formats [35]. It also provides an easier information management process. Ransomware leaves traces of itself in the registry as it uses the registry to modify some system configurations in order to control and manipulate the system [13]. In most cases, ransomware creates and modifies a few keys with one common key (Computer \HKEY_CURRENT_USER\Control Panel\Desktop\Wallpaper) where the ransomware can set the background image to elicit a prompt response for the ransom. Advanced ransomware also creates registry entries that can instruct the system to automatically run the malware if the system is rebooted. The registry can also point to the location of the malware. The registry, therefore, is a good non-volatile source of information to successfully identify ransomware metadata and other evidential information.

3.3   Windows Registry and RAM Readiness Collector (W3RC)

The W3RC (P3.1) is a tool that monitors the memory and registry using trigger-based mechanisms. The flagged data is securely transmitted to the storage process. This tool monitors the system and logs benign processes. The data collection entails any Registry changes and a deep-level process dump whenever a new process is created or modified. This dump can be used for further analysis by an investigator as the executable can be rebuilt. W3RC synchronises to W3RS while maintaining a local cache in the case of an interruption with the transfer process. This process uses a system-collector mechanism in order to get low-level access to the system, whilst ensuring unauthorized alteration. This is considered logical as the OS maintains access control and if a system is infected, it could infect and encrypt this process. This would not be a problem as the data is stored outside the collector in a forensically sound manner. However, one major component of the collection and storage process is the security of the transmission medium.

3.4   Secure Channel

The communication between W2RC and W3RS takes place over a secure encrypted channel (P3.2) over the network. The channel utilizes TCP/IP over SSL/TLS, and each interaction passes through a verification process. The digital signatures are compared and matched to the see if the incoming message is authentic. If the secure channel is compromised or if the connection is broken the W3RS system will capture such event and send an alert to the system administrator, whilst going into a suspend state to prevent any infection/temperament.

3.5 Windows Registry and RAM Readiness Storage (W3RS)

W3RS (P3.3) is a system that captures and stores the data in a secure and forensically sound manner. This system acts as an isolated black box that ensures that the data is safe and secure. This is also to prevent any ransomware or malware from infecting the storage system. To achieve this, a software write blocker will be used. The system will also have a database management system so that redundant data is not stored. This will help decrease the amount of storage space required to keep the database. One major challenge in DRF is storage capacity [36]. Since data is collected on-the-fly, collecting data over extended periods of time can amount to a few gigabytes of storage space being used up. One way to mitigate this is to overwrite older data, as one would not require events to be stored for long.

3.6 Windows Registry and RAM Readiness Storage Authorization (W3RSA)

This is a subcomponent of the W3RS required for authorization (P3.4). It allows an investigator to retrieve the data stored in the W3RS in a secure manner, whilst performing the necessary logging and authorization processes. An identifier mechanism will be used by the system administrator in order to grant access to the investigator during an investigation. The information and processes are logged for transparency as the data acquired from the W3RS may contain some personal data. The access control mechanism will integrate a 2-phase authentication procedure, therefore making it secure and robust.

3.7 Verification and Analysis

The verification and analysis processes (P4.1) ensures the integrity of the stored data. Log data and hash signatures are attached to the data so that the analysis tool, RegSmart[2], can verify the authenticity of this data as well as the completeness. The tool will then comb through the data, find and aggregate all the data into one report (P4.2) as part of the analysis phase. From the report, an investigator would see the properties, signature, classification level, propagation method, and potential decryption keys of the ransomware.

4 Compliance with ISO/IEC 27043 Standard

The evaluation of the proposed framework in tandem with the standardized digital forensic readiness process, ISO/IEC 27043, is presented in this section. The ISO/IEC 27043 standard provides a generic framework for the implementation of DFR in an

---

[2] https://avinashsingh786.github.io/RegSmart/#regacquire.

organization. Typically, the planning process group of the ISO/IEC 27043 can be used to measure the level of compliance with a given readiness framework during a digital investigation. A direct mapping of the proposed framework with respect to the planning process group is presented in Fig. 4. The different phases of the proposed framework, as shown in Fig. 4, align with the ISO/IEC 27043 standard. More importantly, the proposed framework can be mapped directly with the pre-analysis phase of ISO/IEC 27043. Detail of this compliance is further shown in Table 2. The concurrent processes in the ISO/IEC 27043 standard include managing information flow, documentation, obtaining authorization, preserving the chain of custody, and preserving digital evidence.

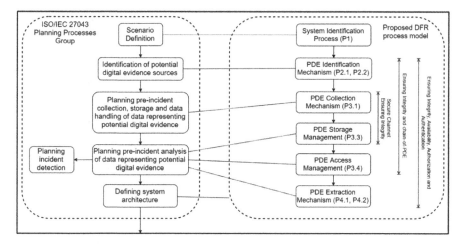

Fig. 4. Mapping of the proposed DFR framework to the ISO/IEC 27043 standard

Table 2. The evaluation process of the proposed W3RF framework

ISO/IEC 27043 planning processes group	Proposed DFR framework	
	Phase	Description
Scenario definition	System Identification Processes	Ransomware evidence collection based on the contents contained within RAM and Registry. Such information gives the ability to detect intrusion and potentially log the decryption keys. It can potentially be used to prevent further propagation of the ransomware
Identification of PDE sources	PDE Identification Mechanism	New registry keys and/or modifications to existing system related keys. Memory monitoring to seek out process memory that is performing some sort of encryption of multiple files

(continued)

Table 2. (*continued*)

ISO/IEC 27043 planning processes group	Proposed DFR framework	
	Phase	Description
Planning, pre-incident collection, storage and data handling of data representing PDE	PDE Collection Mechanism	Using the secure channel to transfer and store the information collected in a secure and forensically sound manner to a black box environment to prevent any malicious attempt on the stored evidence as well as preventing it from being encrypted
Planning, pre-incident analysis of data representing PDE	PDE Storage, Access Management, and Extraction Mechanism	This is a database management system (DBMS) where potential evidence is safely stored per user. Access management is reliant on a verifiable authentication and authorization processes
Defining system architecture	Proposed DFR Process Model	The system architecture consists of the entire framework and respective process model. This can be implemented in either a one-computer-one-DBMS or a distributed system, centralized DBMS which leverages client-server architecture. These configurations depend on organizational policies, infrastructure, and funding

The proposed framework caters for this through W3RS(A) which logs all actions, events, and processes in the system. Furthermore, it provides chain of evidence, chain of custody as well as authorization to obtain the data for analysis thus preserving the digital evidence. The next section describes other related works on cryptographic key recovery from memory and digital forensic readiness.

5 Related Work

Owing to the emergence of new variants of ransomware, and the degree of complexity of the emerging cryptographic mechanism, ransomware detection is difficult [26, 32]. This makes it difficult for investigators to trace where the source of the ransomware and how it propagates. The vulnerability that the malware exploited has been the main focus of security researchers. However, the capability of DFR with regard to memory and registry presents a high potential for the mitigation of ransomware. Several DFR frameworks exist in other fields of forensics such as behavioural biometrics [24, 37], public key infrastructure systems [38], cloud [39] and IoT [40]. The development of readiness framework for these areas presents a milestone for conducting an investigation.

Over the years, the acquisition and analysis of volatile memory have significantly increased [30, 41]. One of the many uses for RAM is to find decryption keys, in a case that the hard drive/device is encrypted. There are many ways to extract potential decryption keys from snapshots/dumps of RAM [2, 26, 30, 41]. These studies have developed new methods and algorithms to extract cryptographic keys. These findings can be leveraged as a mechanism for forensic analysis. A brute force evaluation approach [26] is however considered ineffective. Other studies suggested searching through high-entropy regions, structural properties of the cryptographic key, programming constructs (e.g. C structs), and key schedules. However, due to the increase in security advancements, some of these methods may no longer be viable or could be ineffective. Furthermore, such integration would consider the near-real-time data acquisition process, as these methods were tested and executed in a post-incident scenario on older operating system versions.

6   Conclusion and Future Work

This study proposed a digital forensic readiness framework that can be deployed for ransomware investigation. The implementation of such a framework within a system can significantly produce near real-time potential evidence in contrast to a post-mortem evidence (after the incident has occurred, when potential evidence may have been deleted or encrypted). However, such implementation could be hindered by the security mechanisms of the modern OS. For instance, the OS manages the running processes on a system as well as access control to these processes. Therefore, getting process information may be limited to the access rights provided by the OS. This induces limitation to the amount of information that can be collected in real-time. Moreover, in comparison to post-mortem forensics, the proposed framework can potentially generate more evidential information during a ransomware incident. A preliminary investigation into Windows-10 OS supports this assertion. A reliable and faster method of data discovery, as well as a contextual trigger mechanism for potential data collection, will be explored in the future work. This mechanism will integrate data storage optimization and reduce CPU overhead. From a forensic perspective, this framework presents a mechanism to maximize the cost of legal prosecution and protection against ransom payment. Furthermore, this framework also provides a mechanism to better understand how ransomware works and propagates on a granular level.

References

1. Logen, S., Höfken, H., Schuba, M.: Simplifying RAM forensics: a GUI and extensions for the volatility framework. In: Proceedings of the 2012 7th International Conference on Availability, Reliability and Security, ARES 2012, pp. 620–624 (2012)
2. Hargreaves, C., Chivers, H.: Recovery of encryption keys from memory using a linear scan. In: Proceedings of the 3rd International Conference on Availability, Reliability and Security, ARES 2008, pp. 1369–1376, March 2008

3. Vaughan-Nichols, S.J.: Today's most popular operating systems (2017). http://www.zdnet.com/article/todays-most-popular-operating-systems/. Accessed 12 Apr 2018
4. Statista, Global market share held by the leading mobile operating systems from 2010 to 2015 (2015). https://www.statista.com/statistics/218089/global-market-share-of-windows-7/. Accessed 12 Apr 2018
5. Kaspersky, Overall Statistics for 2017, Kaspersky (2017). https://kasperskycontenthub.com/securelist/files/2017/12/KSB_statistics_2017_EN_final.pdf. Accessed 4 Apr 2018
6. Tailor, J.P., Patel, A.D.: A comprehensive survey: ransomware attacks prevention, monitoring and damage control. Int. J. Res. Sci. Innov. **4**, 2321–2705 (2017)
7. Bromium Labs, Understanding Crypto-Ransomware, p. 35 (2015). Bromium.com
8. Matt Mansfield, Cyber Security Statistics (2017). https://smallbiztrends.com/2017/01/cyber-security-statistics-small-business.html. Accessed 23 Apr 2018
9. United States Government, How to Protecting Your Networks from Ransomware (2016). https://www.justice.gov/criminal-ccips/file/872771/download. Accessed 26 Apr 2018
10. Damshenas, M., Dehghantanha, A., Mahmoud, R.: A survey on malware propagation, analysis and detection. Int. J. Cyber-Security Digit. Forensics **2**(4), 10–29 (2013)
11. Gandotra, E., Bansal, D., Sofat, S.: Malware threat assessment using fuzzy logic paradigm. Cybern. Syst. **48**(1), 29–48 (2017)
12. O'Brien, D.: Internet Security Threat Report - Ransomware 2017. In: Symantec, p. 35 (2017)
13. Savage, K., Coogan, P., Lau, H.: Information resources. Res. Manag. **54**(5), 59–63 (2011)
14. Stone-Gross, B., Cova, M., Gilbert, B., Kemmerer, R., Kruegel, C., Vigna, G.: Analysis of a Botnet takeover. IEEE Secur. Priv. **9**(1), 64–72 (2011)
15. United States Government, How to Protecting Your Networks from Ransomware, pp. 2–8 (2016)
16. Rad, B., Masrom, M., Ibrahim, S.: Camouflage in malware: from encryption to metamorphism. Int. J. Comput. Sci. Netw. Secur. **12**(8), 74–83 (2012)
17. Campbell, S., Chan, S., Lee, J.R.: Detection of fast flux service networks. Conf. Res. Pract. Inf. Technol. Ser. **116**, 57–66 (2011)
18. Spafford, E.H.: The internet worm incident. In: Ghezzi, C., McDermid, J.A. (eds.) ESEC 1989. LNCS, vol. 387, pp. 446–468. Springer, Heidelberg (1989). https://doi.org/10.1007/3-540-51635-2_54
19. Okane, P., Sezer, S., McLaughlin, K.: Obfuscation: the hidden malware. IEEE Secur. Priv. **9**(5), 41–47 (2011)
20. Symantec, 2017 Internet Security Threat Report, Istr (2017). https://www.symantec.com/security-center/threat-report. Accessed 27 Apr 2018
21. Ehrenfeld, J.M.: WannaCry, cybersecurity and health information technology: a time to act. J. Med. Syst. **41**(7), 104 (2017)
22. Kotov, V., Rajpal, M.S.: Understanding Crypto-Ransomware, p. 35 (2015). Bromium.com
23. Sophos, Stopping Fake Antivirus: How to Keep Scareware Off Your Network (2011)
24. Ikuesan, A.R., Venter, H.S.: Digital forensic readiness framework based on behavioral-biometrics for user attribution, vol. 1, pp. 54–59 (2017)
25. ISO 27043, International Standard ISO/IEC 27043: Information technology — Security techniques — Incident investigation principles and processes, vol. 2015 (2015)
26. Kaplan, B.: RAM is key: extracting disk encryption keys from volatile memory, p. 20 (2007)
27. Basu, A., Gandhi, J., Chang, J., Hill, M.D., Swift, M.M.: Efficient virtual memory for big memory servers. In: Proceedings of the 40th Annual International Symposium on Computer Architecture, ISCA 2013, pp. 237–248 (2013)
28. Pomeranz, H.: Detecting malware with memory forensics why memory forensics? Everything in the OS traverses RAM, pp. 1–27 (2012)

29. Olajide, F., Savage, N.: On the extraction of forensically relevant information from physical memory. In: IEEE World Congress on Internet Security, pp. 248–252 (2011)

30. Maartmann-Moe, C., Thorkildsen, S.E., Årnes, A.: The persistence of memory: forensic identification and extraction of cryptographic keys. Digit. Investig. **6**, 132–140 (2009)

31. Adomavicius, G., Tuzhilin, A.: Context-aware recommender systems. In: Recommender Systems Handbook, 2nd edn., pp. 191–226 (2015)

32. Hausknecht, K., Foit, D., Burić, J.: RAM data significance in digital forensics. In: 2015 38th International Convention on Information and Communication Technology, Electronics and Microelectronics, MIPRO 2015, pp. 1372–1375, May 2015

33. Patil, D.N., Meshram, B.B.: Extraction of forensic evidences from windows volatile memory. In: 2017 2nd International Conference for Convergence in Technology (I2CT), pp. 421–425 (2017)

34. Alghafli, K., Jones, A., Martin, T.: Forensic analysis of the Windows 7 registry. J. Digit. Forensics Secur. Law **5**(4), 5–30 (2010)

35. Lallie, H.S., Briggs, P.J.: Windows 7 registry forensic evidence created by three popular BitTorrent clients. Digit. Investig. **7**(3–4), 127–134 (2011)

36. Reddy, K., Venter, H.S.: The architecture of a digital forensic readiness management system. Comput. Secur. **32**, 73–89 (2013)

37. Mohlala, M., Adeyemi, I.R., Venter, H.S.: User attribution based on keystroke dynamics in digital forensic readiness process. In: IEEE Conference on Applications, Information and Network Security (AINS), pp. 124–129 (2017)

38. Valjarevic, A., Venter, H.S.: Towards a digital forensic readiness framework for public key infrastructure systems. In: 2011 Information Security South Africa, pp. 1–10 (2011)

39. Kebande, V.R., Venter, H.S.: On digital forensic readiness in the cloud using a distributed agent-based solution: issues and challenges. Aust. J. Forensic Sci. **50**(2), 209–238 (2018)

40. Kebande, V.R., Karie, N.M., Venter, H.S.: Adding digital forensic readiness as a security component to the IoT domain. Int. J. Adv. Sci. Eng. Inf. Technol. **8**(1), 1 (2018)

41. Dolan-Gavitt, B.: Forensic analysis of the Windows registry in memory. Digit. Investig. **5**, 26–32 (2008)

Forensics Analysis of an On-line Game over Steam Platform

Raquel Tabuyo-Benito[1]([✉]), Hayretdin Bahsi[1], and Pedro Peris-Lopez[2]

[1] Tallinn University of Technology,
Center for Digital Forensics and Cyber Security, Tallinn, Estonia
{ratabu,hayretdin.bahsi}@ttu.ee
[2] Universidad Carlos III de Madrid, COSEC Lab, Getafe, Spain
pperis@inf.uc3m.es

Abstract. Currently on-line gaming represents a severe threat to the forensic community, as criminals have started to use on-line gaming as communication channels instead of traditional channels like WhatsApp or Facebook. In this paper, we describe a methodology developed after conducting an in-depth digital forensic analysis of the central artifacts of a popular video-game - Counter Strike Nexon Zombies video-game (Steam platform) - where valuable artifacts are those that related to the chatting features of the game. For our research we analyzed the network, volatile, and disk captures for two generated cases and focused on chat-feature inside and outside of the in-game rounds and the live chat done through YouTube Live Streaming. Our results provide the forensic community a complete guideline that can be used when dealing with a real criminal case in which there is a Steam video-game involved. Besides the forensic analysis, we found a security vulnerability (session hijacking) which was reported to the game manufacturer as soon it was discovered.

Keywords: Digital forensics · Network forensics · Windows forensics
Live forensics · On-line gaming

1 Introduction

Over the last few years, the video-games industry has spread to new markets and is reaching new kinds of players. Due to this growth, chat services offered by on-line video-games are becoming more and more popular among criminals as criminals consider these services to be safer methods of communication without detection. In 2015 after the Paris terror attacks, security analysts investigated new communication channels terrorists could use [12], and they found that terrorists could have used PlayStation 4 as the way to exchange messages without being discovered.

This paper focuses on *Counter Strike Nexon Zombies* (CSNZ) video-game, a game offered through Steam. This platform has a total of 67 million monthly

© ICST Institute for Computer Sciences, Social Informatics and Telecommunications Engineering 2019
Published by Springer Nature Switzerland AG 2019. All Rights Reserved
F. Breitinger and I. Baggili (Eds.): ICDF2C 2018, LNICST 259, pp. 106–127, 2019.
https://doi.org/10.1007/978-3-030-05487-8_6

active players and controls between 50–70% of the gaming market [20]. The paid version of CSNZ, Counter Strike: Global Offensive, has already been involved in a gambling scandal – there was an illegal betting market underneath with lots of teenagers participating [7]. Besides, it is the second most played game with large revenues and it is played on Windows/OS/Linux computers—note that 56% of gamers prefer PCs rather than others devices [11]. CSNZ is set in a war environment; we think that it could be one of the perfect ways for criminals to communicate as they can hide inside this atmosphere. Moreover, CSNZ has two game modes, one of them is the mentioned war scenario (Zombie mode) and the other one is a scenario similar to Minecraft (Studio mode), a three-dimensional game with the goal of building entire worlds with pixelated blocks. In these kinds of games, there are different kinds of servers which personalize the user experience and create a big network, which becomes attractive to DDoS attackers (e.g., Mirai botnet was originated from Minecraft video-game [6]). Additionally, CSNZ allows players to do YouTube live streaming while playing the game. This communication channel is also one of the targets of our study since it might be used maliciously.

Due to all of these facts, trying to obtain as much information as possible from this on-line game results in a significant contribution to the digital forensics community and makes a difference in the way forensic experts analyze a system when entering a crime scene. We hope the proposed methodology can provide guidance to forensics experts in the analysis of any other on-line games. In relation to previous works, researchers have payed particular attention to artifacts originated from widely used Social Networks like Facebook [22], or Instant Messaging (IM) tools like Skype [14] or WhatsApp [1,8,9]. However, on-line games, which have an enormous audience as well, offer similar communication channels, which criminals can misuse. Consequently, valuable information could be lost if they are not appropriately analyzed or not taken into account. As previously mentioned, some criminal cases like money laundering and DDoS attacks have the usage of video-games as the main factor, but our contribution is focused on how to find artifacts related to the chatting features that on-line games provide. Some forensic studies analyze video-games [4,10], but they focus primarily on post-mortem state analysis [3] and not in volatile or network traffic analysis. To the best of our knowledge, it is the first time that an in-depth forensic analysis of an on-line video game is conducted—the analysis performed by Moore et al. for XboxOne can be considered the work most closely related to our proposal [15] but our proposal is more complete since live forensic analysis is part of the used techniques.

2   Methods and Materials

The framework that we followed for dealing with evidences is the McKemmish forensic framework [13]. This forensic process consists on the following steps: (1) Identification of digital evidence; (2) Preservation of digital evidence; (3) Analysis of digital evidence; (4) Presentation of digital evidences.

To enable the acquisition of realistic data similar to the one that we would find in real world investigations, we decided to conscientiously follow the McKemmish approach with all the processes involved in forensic analysis:

Network forensics: we captured the network traffic for all the cases of study—we disconnected the system from any external connection after capturing the traffic.

Live acquisition: we performed an acquisition of volatile data (RAM memory dump) while being aware that we should create the least amount of changes in the system under inspection. The changes are explained and reported in order to ensure a precise preservation of the evidence and admissibility in court.

Post-mortem acquisition: we physically acquired the hard disk. Consequently we have a complete copy of the disk (including the unallocated space) allowing us to find all information about the game stored locally in the system.

Windows forensics: the OS of the disk acquired is a Windows 7 Professional image; consequently, we performed an in-depth analysis of it based on Windows forensics manners.

Once all the data was extracted, we continued with the interpretation of the evidences: network artifacts obtained from the traffic capture, the analysis of the RAM memory, windows registry, dedicated folder of the game in the system, windows system files and folders ($MFT,$LogFile, Prefetch folder, shortcuts, Recent folder, JumpLists, thumbnails and web information). After that, we pursued to find enough information to build the time-line of the case, when the user connected, with whom the user played, the list of friends, chat information, connection time-stamps, history of the game and user information like username and passwords. When analyzing the network information, we consider the disclosure of the session ID and this value might be used for a successful session hijacking.

We have used well-known and reputable free tools for forensic analysis. *Wireshark* [21] and *NetworkMiner* [16] are the chosen tools for the network forensic analysis. Regarding the live acquisition (RAM memory) and post-mortem acquisition (Hard disk), *FTK Imager* is used to create the respective images. The analysis of the runtime state of the system is conducted through the analysis of the RAM memory with *FTK Imager* and the *Volatility* framework. For the analysis of the files inside the disk (Windows OS), *Autopsy* and *FTK Imager* are the main tools used –other tools like *JumpListView* [18] or *ChromeCacheView* [17] are also employed for particular processes in the file analysis. The complete list of tools is shown in Table 3 in Annex A.

We made copies of the evidence in order to ensure its integrity. The copies were the ones analyzed. As we wanted to make a research in the most realistic way possible, in Table 4 in Annex A we provide the list of hashes of the evidence taken from the network capture, memory dump and disk cloning.

2.1 Cases of Study

We have considered two different cases for simulating how a user plays CSNZ with their friends, paying special attention to the different chatting alternatives offered by the game. A short description of each case is provided below and a detailed workflow diagram can be seen in Figs. 1 and 2 in Annex B, respectively. In these workflow diagrams we have included the moments when the acquisition processes (network capture, live and post-mortem acquisition) took place.

Case 1: two players, "TTUPlayer" and "UC3MPlayer", inside Zombie mode ("war" scenario). The former (TTUPlayer) will send an invitation into the game-room to the latter (UC3MPlayer). The chat will take place before entering the game, in the lobby. After that, both users will enter in the Zombie scenario and will chat again. While playing, users will use chat features that include text messages and voice audios.

Case 2: two players, "TTUPlayer" and "UC3MPlayer", in Studio mode ("mining" scenario) with a defined password to enter into the game-room. From this point, "UC3MPlayer" will do nothing (he will not participate in the game rounds or exchange messages). "TTUPlayer" will live stream through Youtube while playing the game. An external viewer, "Juanma", from the streaming video, will chat with this last mentioned player.

Both cases were run using VMWare virtual machines. We created two different virtual machines for each example. The reason why we decided to use a virtual machine instead of having the game installed directly in our system is so the game is isolated. Additionally, thanks to snapshots, we can always go to a previous state if we crash the program.

Regarding the specifications, we used VMWare Fusion 10.0.1 for each case with a Windows 7 Professional guest OS installed. The host system was a macOS High Sierra MacBook Air 2,2 GHz Intel Core i7 with 8 GB of memory. In each virtual machine, there was 2 GB of memory and 20 GB of disk space. Each virtual machine has a different IP concerning host's IP. For network capture, we executed Wireshark in the host system, so that we could capture network traffic in the middle of the communication between both users (man-in-the-middle).

In regards to the game, we installed Steam platform for Windows, as the game cannot be run without it. After that, the game was downloaded from Steam and installed on the Windows systems. The rest of programs installed on the system are the ones that are pre-included in Windows like Internet Explorer (only pre-installed browser on the system) or Notepad. For the second case of study, we also installed Google Chrome Browser, in order to enable all the chatting features offered by YouTube Live Chat, which was not possible to have with Internet Explorer. Due to the fact that this forensic analysis is mainly focused on the communication between players while using the game, we have used two virtual machines for each player. Since there are two cases of study, there are a total of 4 virtual machines involved in our study.

We had to create 2 Steam accounts and 2 players of CSNZ (one for "TTUPlayer" and another for "UC3MPlayer"). The login process is done through Steam, and then the game starts. We acquired the disk image and RAM from the device (virtual machine) of "TTUPlayer" as s/he was the suspect in our forensic analysis. We created an Outlook email account for this player as well as a Google account for the YouTube Live Streaming. In addition, we created a YouTube Channel for "TTUPlayer" with "TTU Thesis" as the nickname. The viewer of the streaming, "Juanma", is subscribed to this channel. This option is not necessary for watching streamed videos in YouTube; however, we decided that the viewer is also a subscriber because we would receive a notification as soon as "TTU Thesis" starts doing live streaming. In Table 1 we summarize all the details of the suspicious player.

Table 1. Player information under suspicion

Game name	Counter strike nexon zombies
Game acronym	CSNZ
UserName Steam account	thttu
Steam User ID	76561198404618625
NickName Steam account	TTU - Thesis
Password Steam account	pAssWd123
Associated email in Steam account	ttu.thesis@outlook.com
CSNZ username	TTUPlayer
CSNZ Game ID	273310
Google account email	ttu.thesis@outlook.com
Google account username	TTU Thesis
Google account password	youtubeaccount1
YouTube Channel name	TTU Thesis
YouTube Channel identifier	UC-pPH8RIVmlFBMbJjUcPZzw
YouTube Live Streaming key	2ppw-5x2j-cz0z-6rrv
YouTube Live Streaming video	https://www.youtube.com/watch?v=Qd4OL0t3bBw
CSNZ Player 2	UC3MPlayer
YouTube Live Streaming viewer	Juanma
Zombie in-game room number	30220
Studio in-game room number	55349
Password Studio room	2tudio

3   Forensic Analysis and Results

We have built a guideline for the forensic community based on the analysis of both cases in terms of network capture, live acquisition and post-mortem acquisition. We found some common artifacts that reflect accurately how it is possible to find specific information from the game. More precisely, a forensic expert facing a Steam video-game (CSNZ in our particular case) and its chatting features should consider the artifacts listed in Annex C. A complete list of all the results can be found in Annex D.

3.1   Network Forensics Analysis

Common Network Artifacts. After capturing the network traffic with Wireshark (we saved it as PCAP file), we found some relevant artifacts that tie the user to CNSZ game. It is worth noticing that we also found a security vulnerability (session hijacking) that allowed to find additional forensic information. The process of identifying a user in Steam, after the authentication process, is done through cookies. Once the user is authenticated, he is redirected by default to the Steam Store website and the rest of Steam websites (community and help site) using the same cookies for user identification (user sessions). This login process is always the same for games on Steam. More precisely, two main cookies are sent over HTTP:

- `sessionid`: it is a CSRF token. The first time someone accesses to one of its websites, Steam assigns this cookie randomly. It can be any value; the only requirement is that it has to match with the session parameter of the POST requests of that person. Therefore, as it is not linked to any account or specific session, a user does not need to authenticate first for getting this cookie value.
- `steamLogin`: It is built with the 16-numerical characters of the `Steam_User_ID` + `%7C%7C` (two pipe characters) + 40–character uppercase session token in hexadecimal. This cookie is only generated after the user is successfully authenticated.

From the following Wireshark output, we can see that from the `steamLogin` cookie sent via HTTP, we can obtain the `Steam User ID` (first 16-numerical characters=76561198404618625).

```
Cookie:
browserid=1154470811777340210;
recentapps=%7B%22236690%22%3A1509888488%7D;
timezoneOffset=7200,0;
_ga=GA1.2.694143193.1508840752;
_gid=GA1.2.377692037.1510395285;
Steam_Language=english;
vractive=0;
connectedDevices=0;
steamLogin=76561198404618625%7c%7cA84173EA7E194BDBF401219535C0
2500DB96913B;
sessionid=35eb7107e8a693252a4fd0bc;
clientsessionid=13b982bfb86e5d0a
```

Note that Wireshark supports the searching of a specific packet—we look for a packet that contains the string "steamLogin" and *Narrow and Wide* are used as optional parameters. After disclosing this value, we can visit the website of the steam community (`http://steamcommunity.com/profiles/<SteamUserID>`) and obtain more forensic information such as: NickName user account; games played; last time they were played and total number of hours played; current status of the user (on-line/off-line) and last time being on-line; and personal information that the user wants to share.

Session Cloning. When attempting to perform session cloning, as it was done in other studies [19], we found that it was possible to hijack the session of an authenticated user[1]. Considering the fact that the `sessionid` is created before the user authenticates, and that there are some cookies transmitted over HTTP and after HTTPS authentication, which are not changed, we found a way to clone the session of the user while s/he keeps it opened. The steps performed for the session hijacking are described below:

1. With the Wireshark capture, search inside the packet details for the string "`steamLogin`". Copy it and all its related cookies as "printable text".
2. Create an account on Steam (whatever user and password) and login to generate the `steamLogin` cookie. We logged-in with Google Chrome Browser and used "Edit this cookie" extension in order to inject the cookies related with the user session we want to clone, but the attack can be done with other browsers and add-ons.
3. Click on "Edit this cookie" extension in order to modify the cookies _gad, `sessionID` and `steamLogin` with the ones that we obtained from the Wireshark capture (Step 1). This way, we are injecting cookies belonging to another user to hijack the session. Finally, we click on the green icon to save those cookies.
4. Click on the "arrow-Back" to go to the previous initial page of login and then click on "refreshing" the page. We will be logged as the legitimate user (user under attack). We can see all the information related to that user: list of friends, games played, last connection, status (on-line), etc.

It is worth noting that this method is related to sessions, so if the target user logs out, we would not be able to continue using his session. From a forensic point of view, the possibility to clone the session gives us a lot of information as mentioned above.

YouTube Live Streaming Specific Artifacts. In the second case, we found that the network capture contains references that indicate that the suspect was doing a YouTube Live Streaming. In detail, there are RTMP packets (without TLS/SSL encryption), which are used for live streaming. More specifically, there must be a packet that shows the connection with the main server of YouTube, the method used for this purpose is: `connect('live2')` and the associated URL is: rtmp://a.rtmp.youtube.com/live2.

Besides the live video streaming via Youtube is unequivocally identified by an identifier named "key". It is included in the method called `releaseStream('<key>')`. This key is unique for each user, and even if it was

---

[1] This vulnerability was reported to Valve Corporation via email as soon as it was discovered.

not possible to watch the video knowing this key, it could be used for doing YouTube Live Streaming with the account of another user.

Moreover, we also recovered the encoder that was used for video streaming. Thanks to this information, the forensic expert can watch the video if there is any possibility to extract it from the copy of the disk, as we will see in Sect. 3.3. In our case the encoder used was VLC and this information can be found by analyzing the RTMP packets with Wireshark.

3.2   Volatile Memory Analysis

We acquired two pieces of evidence (before and after logging out from the game) from the RAM (MEM files) using FTK Imager installed in an external USB. See Figs. 1 and 2 in Annex B. After that, we have analyzed both files with FTK Imager and Volatility. Note that the chat messages can only be extracted whether the user did not logout (Live acquisition 1).

Volatile Memory Analysis with FTK Imager. The methodology that we have developed in order to find forensic artifacts after a live acquisition is based on keywords and similar to the study performed about the XboxOne with Autopsy [15]. FTK Imager has a built-in search tool so, by doing right-click at the beginning of the memory dump and clicking on *Find* we can search for any word. It is also possible to do a more elaborate search using a regular expression. The keywords and regular expressions that are useful for finding valuable forensic data with respect to the game are summarized in Table 2.

Table 2. Keywords for memory analysis

Valuable Forensic data	Keyword
Username Steam account	`SteamUser`
NickName Steam account	`PersonaName`
Password Steam account	`password=`
Steam User ID	`steamid`
CSNZ Game ID	`steamGameID`
Associated email address	`\b[A-Z0-9._%+-]+@[A-Z0-9.-]+\.[A-Z]2,\b`
Friends who are on-line	`has logged in`
Players involved in the game	`has joined`
Room number and password	`(#No.room)`
YouTube Live Streaming Traces	`youtube`
	`rtmp.youtube`
	`codec`

As previously mentioned, from volatile memory, it is possible to obtain the messages sent and received by the user but only if s/he did not logout when taking the memory dump. In Counter Strike Nexon Zombies, the user can exchange messages directly without starting a game round, inside in-game rounds and also while doing YouTube Live Streaming. In those cases, messages can be sent to all players (ALL tag), to your family group -list of friends- (Family tag), or to the party group (PARTY tag). Consequently, using the keywords linked to the different recipients who can be addressed in a message, we are able to find the information about the exchanged messages in the whole memory dump. The following three layouts of messages are used in the game:

1. Chat in the lobby: (Type of receiver) [Nickname of the sender] : message
2. In-game chat: [Type of receiver] Nickname of the sender : message
3. YouTube chat: [YOUTUBE] Nickname of the sender : message

Therefore, the keywords to discover chat messages are based on the type of recipient: All, Family, Party and YOUTUBE. Once we have found the messages, we can state to where they were sent to (lobby, in-game or YouTube) based on the mentioned layouts.

Volatile Memory Analysis with Volatility. The network connections, as well as the processes used, can be obtained using Volatility Framework. First of all, to retrieve information with Volatility, we have to select the proper profile—in our particular case Windows7SP1x64. The running processes can be obtained with `pslist` command. To assure that the game was played, a reference to Steam as well as Counter Strike should appear in the output. Additionally, if a web browser was used, it could indicate that the user was doing a live chat on YouTube. The above can be confirmed taking a look to the open network connections (`netscan` command). We found that there was also a connection from Google Chrome browser which might indicate that the user was doing a chat via YouTube Live Streaming.

3.3 Disk Analysis

We performed a post-mortem acquisition with FTK Imager installed in an external USB. The images were saved in E01 format—it uses compression and contains a separate metadata file. The methodology used for the analysis with FTK Imager is described below. In particular, the files analyzed were inspired by previous forensics analysis [19].

Windows Registry. In NTUSER.DAT and SOFTWARE hives we found some references (e.g., the path where it was stored) to the game that shows it was installed in the system. Besides, from a forensic point of view, the dates and times are relevant as they are useful for building a time-line of the case.

In order to find this information, we can extract those hives with FTK Imager and open them with Access Data Registry Viewer.

NTUSER.DAT is stored in \Users\<username> while SOFTWARE is stored in SystemRoot\System32\config.

- **NTUSER.DAT:** In this hive, there must be a folder called Software. The path to the CSNZ game should be NTUSER.DAT\Software\Valve\ Steam\Apps\273310. The description of it shows how it corresponds to Counter Strike Nexon Zombies. The last written time corresponds to the last time the game was played. In addition, in the path NTUSER.DAT\Software\ Nexon\CStrike-Online it also appears the last written time when the game was played. Finally and regarding the chat of YouTube Live Streaming, it is needed that the user has installed a web browser on the system. Consequently, there should be an entity in the hive. For example, in our case, NTUSER.DAT\Software\Google\Chrome is the path to Chrome Browser.
- **SOFTWARE:** In this hive, there is an important reference to the game that shows when it was installed in the system. The way to find this information is by looking at the last written time of the Uninstalling CSNZ software since this program was stored in the system (SOFTWARE\Microsoft\Windows\ CurrentVersion\Unistalled\Steam App 273110) at the same time the game was installed. Additionally, the path to the game also appears in this hive in the description of the SOFTWARE\Wow6432Node\Valve\Steam\ Apps\273110 entity.

Shortcuts. By default, there should be a shortcut to Steam on the Desktop. Steam is needed for executing CSNZ. Besides, there could be a shortcut for the game as well. However, the user has to execute Steam first and then CSNZ. It can be found directly with FTK Imager under the Users\<Username>\Desktop path.

Prefetch. The Prefetch folder is stored in \Windows\Prefetch and it can be extracted with FTK Imager. After its extraction, we can open it with Win-PrefetchView. There will be references to Steam and CSNZ video-game. From a forensic point of view, it is very relevant since it shows all the programs affected by the game and when they were executed. Consequently, we can assure that the game depends on Steam and we correlate facts between the mentioned programs and the game. Besides, we can see that CSNZ video-game is related to NAR files. The analysis of these files is explained in the section below.

NAR Files. From the Prefetch analysis, we found that CSNZ uses the NAR files (specific CSNZ file format). We analyzed them with NAR extractor tool, after obtaining them from \Program Files (x86)\Steam\steamapps\common\CSNZ\ Data\cstrike.nar. Unfortunately, those files are used for modeling the game but they do not give any information about the user or that could be useful in the forensic case.

Jump Lists. We can extract the Jump Lists with FTK Imager from the path
`%APPDATA%\Microsoft\Windows\Recent\AutomaticDestinations\[AppID]`
`automaticDestinations-ms`. Jump Lists can be viewed with JumpListView to
display the recent documents. Forensically, it is useful as it could lead to interesting files that are not considered beforehand. In our case, after checking them,
we realized that CSNZ video-game stores by default screen-shots taken during
the game rounds and videos—the default folder is "`Documents`". The analysis of
the Jump Lists is useful to find the file locations because the user could change
the default ones. These screenshots and video files are studied in the following
section.

Documents Folder. CSNZ video-game stores by default the screen-shots taken
by the user during an in-game round. Besides, it makes screen-shots automatically when a round finishes. Concerning the YouTube Live Streaming, it stores
the video in MP4 format once the user finishes doing the streaming. From a
forensic point of view, this is very valuable information since the chat messages
can be watched and voice messages can be listened directly from this file. Inside
the `Documents` folder, there are two directories: one for Zombie mode ("`Counter`
`Strike Nexon Zombie`" directory) and the other one for Studio mode ("`Counter`
`Strike On-line`" directory). The directories with the screen-shots and videos
are stored inside these folders. The screen-shots can be seen directly with FTK
Imager or any other Image Viewer program. The video files have to be exported
from the Video Capture folder prior to be watched. From the network analysis, we already knew that the encoder used for the videos was VLC. Therefore,
we opened the videos with VLC media player and we can disclose the whole
YouTube chat. The first 9 characters of the file names correspond with the dates
when the videos were recorded.

MFT. We can extract the $MFT with FTK Imager and convert it into CSV
file with Mft2csv tool. Taking advantage of the CSV file, we can search for
references about Counter Strike and find where the data is stored. From this
analysis, we found that by default CSNZ folder is stored in the system in
the `\Program Files (x86)\Steam\steamapps\common\CSNZ` path. In addition,
there are also two directories (`\Program Files (x86)\Steam\` and `\Program`
`Data\Nexon\Common`) related to the game.

Steam Dedicated Folders. We have focused our efforts on Nexon and Steam
folders. The former facilitates timing information and the latter provides information linked with the user or the game.

- **Nexon folder.** The analysis of the Nexon folder gives handy forensic information since it contains (`\Program Data\Nexon\Common\nmcogame.log`) a
  log file related with the messenger feature of the game. Using this, we can
  assure that the user was chatting at a specific time period. In detail, CSNZ

loads a messenger module when a player uses the chat. In the log, there are references to this module and its associated time-stamps.

- **Steam folder.** Inside the Steam folder, there are some configuration and log files that provide information such as the Steam `UserID`, the Steam `Username`, the `ID` of the game, etc. The extension of the configuration files is VDF and these files can be opened with Notepad++. In the folder `\Program Files (x86)\Steam\config\` we found "config.vdf" which contains the `userID` and the `username`. In this folder there is also a "loginusers.vdf" file which stores the logged users. It provides the `Username`, the `Nickname`, `UserID` and the last time accessed (EPOCH to UTC time conversion is needed). Additionally, there is another configuration file ("localconfig.vdf") stored in `\Program Files (x86)\Steam\userdata\<localIDnumber>`, which links undoubtedly the user with the game since it contains the `GameID` and the `Username`. Next to the `GameID`, we can also find the last played time.

  In addition, the remote connection file ("connections.txt") is stored in `\Program Files (x86)\Steam\logs\` path. It is a TXT file that contains all the remote connections with the user's PC. Therefore we can disclose with whom the user is playing (host name and IP address). Additionally, there is a database file (`Users\<user>\AppData\Local\Steam\htmlcache\Cookies`) that stores some cookies. It is an SQLite database, which can be extracted with FTK Imager and opened with DB Browser for SQLite. In particular, there is a table with the `sessionIDs` and their corresponding time reference (EPOCH time), which represents the last times the user accessed into Steam. As mentioned in Sect. 3.1, it is possible to do a session cloning if the user is still logged into Steam platform.

Recent Files. The `Recent` folder can show the recent activity of the user linked to the game. It can provide information such as the paths to specific files stored in the system and that the user could have modified. The Recent folder (`Users\<user>\AppData\Roaming\Microsoft\Windows\Recent`) can be exported with FTK Imager and be opened with RecentFilesView tool. In our case, it provides information about the screen-shots taken and the folders used for their storage.

Thumbnails. The `Thumbcache` stored in `Users\<user>\AppData\Roaming\Microsoft\Windows\Explorer\thumbcache_*.db` can be opened with ThumbCache Viewer tool. It provides information about the game: path location and the used OS (Windows 7 in our particular case).

LogFile. The `\$LogFile` contains information about the logged users. In fact, it is the same information as in ``loginusers.vdf``. However, as it is a Windows System file, it is more difficult to be modified by a normal user. Note that ``loginusers.vdf`` file could be edited by a user with a Text Editor. The comparison of both files will assure the integrity of the data.

Web Browsing Information. For the YouTube Live Streaming, we used Chrome Browser. In the forensics analysis, we were able to find some references about YouTube, but we could not retrieve the exchanged chat messages. Fortunately, some time references helped to create a time-line of the case. We focused on three files stored in `Users\<user>\AppData \Google\Chrome\Default\` and extracted with FTK Imager:

- **Cookies:** it can be opened with DB Browser for SQLite and contains the `sessionIDs`.
- **Cache:** it can be opened with ChromeCacheView and contains traces about the YouTube Live Streaming activity.
- **History:** it can be opened with ChromeHistoryView and contains references to the streaming notifications that correspond to the received messages. Each time the user receives a message, there is a new notification.

Autopsy can be used to find web-surfing information since it categorizes automatically the searches done. The most relevant findings concerning YouTube Live Streaming are the following ones:

- **Link to the streamed YouTube video.** After performing the live streaming, the video is automatically uploaded to YouTube. It will be kept in the user's channel unless it is deleted manually. As previously mentioned, it was found in the `History` file. Using this file, we can know the YouTube channel name and the links to the videos that the user has uploaded.
- **Email information.** This represents the email used for the Google account to access to YouTube. It is found in the `Login Data` file of the `Default` folder.

Analysis with Autopsy. Apart from the findings related with YouTube Live Streaming, additional information can be obtained using the keyword search feature. In particular, we found the password associated with the Steam account of our suspect user. The way to obtain this password is by using "`password`" as keyword. Autopsy searches inside the file system data, carved files and unallocated space. We found the password in the unallocated space and carved data. There is also a file (`Users\<user>\AppData\Local\Steam\htmlcache\Cache\data_1`) that can be used to obtain this password—even though the user did not check the option of "password remember". Although this finding may or may not happen, it is worthy to consider that the password could be stored in this path or in the unallocated space or the carved data. Additionally, there are some links of CSNZ and therefore we can assure that the user was playing the game at a particular time.

Furthermore, Autopsy performs data carving by default and shows the results obtained. Nevertheless, after analyzing the carved files, we did not find any more relevant information apart from the password mentioned previously. Besides, we also examined the unallocated space by keyword searching without any other important finding.

3.4   Main Chatting Artifacts Summary

In previous sections, we have seen that there are some artifacts that suggest that the chatting features of the CSNZ game were used. These findings can be divided into two:

Disk analysis:
- **Messenger module logs:** It shows when the messenger module was loaded which is each time a player uses it. Thus we know when the user was chatting. If we correlate these timestamps with the ones found in the network connection logs, we are able to identify with whom the user was playing (IP source and destination).
- **YouTube Live Streaming:** If the user was doing YouTube Live Streaming, apart from the previous logs, we can find the streamed video and see the whole chat conversation done between players (messages sent and received). Besides, the message notifications shown in the `Google Chrome History` correspond to the messages received. In this way, we can identify when the user received a message—note that it is not possible to see the content of the message; this information is stored in the client's computer. Considering the data privacy policy by Google[2], Google stores the videos uploaded but there is no reference about live chat messages, however, in the video, as seen previously, it is possible to see the messages content.

Volatile memory: We can obtain the whole conversation (messages sent and received) if when doing the live acquisition, the user did not log out from the game and/or switched off the computer. In fact, using the layouts mentioned in Sect. 3.2, we can identify where it took place (lobby, in-game or YouTube). Furthermore, if we correlate these findings with the network connections logs, we can know with whom the user was playing (IP source and destination).

3.5   Anti-forensics

Anti-forensics was not the main concern of our study, however we identified that most of the logs stored in the disk, which contain relevant forensic data (username, user IDs, connection timestamps, messenger logs, etc.) can be edited with any text editor and without requiring a great expertise in destroying evidences. This data can be easily modified or removed and consequently, relevant forensic data could be lost accidentally or on purpose. If the files are deleted and the data is not overwritten in the disk, it could be recovered with forensic data carving procedures.

When the computer is rebooted or power-cycled, the non-temporal data stored locally in the system remains unchanged; nevertheless, the information in the volatile memory is lost. More specifically, which respect to the chatting features of the game, it will not be possible to obtain the chat messages sent and received. As the messages can only be recovered from volatile memory, if the user wants to hide his conversations, he just needs to log out from the game

---

[2] https://privacy.google.com/intl/en/your-data.html.

and/or switch the computer off and all the data will be flushed out. Besides, if the user deselects the default option of storing screen-shots and videos from the game, the video(s) with chat information from YouTube Live Streaming will not be available locally in the suspect's computer.

Finally, in case of an unexpected system shutdown due to a power error or critical system failure, the operating system will go back to a previous status of the file system with relevant forensic data stored in the $LogFile folder.

4   Conclusions

In this paper we performed a digital forensics analysis of *Counter Strike Nexon Zombies* video-game. This game allows users to play cooperatively or fighting between them. The game provides chat features, so players while playing can communicate with text or audio messages but they can also chat without being in an in-game round. It is worth noticing that messaging features offered in on-line gaming are lately being used for criminal purposes: money laundering [5], hidden channel communication by terrorists [12], etc. Additionally, a great number of players are making money thanks to YouTube Live Streaming [2], by recording themselves while playing a video-game and interacting at the same time with their viewers via the live chat.

Our forensics findings about chatting features for a Steam based on-line game, to the best of our knowledge, have not been documented yet, and could serve as a guideline for the computer forensic community when facing with on-line games over the Steam platform. Using two cases of study, we provide a full analysis from a network, hard disk and volatile memory perspective, being the last one not considered in similar forensic analysis developed for messaging applications such as Facebook or WhatsApp [9,22].

The developed methodology can be generalized to games that belong to Steam platform since the login procedure is identical for all the games in that market. In fact, we have checked that the login via a web browser is identical to the login procedure used in the video-game. Furthermore, we have found that the related data on the disk about the game is stored in the "Steam" folder instead of an specific folder for each game. Thus, an examiner should focus on the "Steam" folder as it contains most of the relevant data. Additionally, we strongly suggest analyzing the volatile memory first, if it is possible to perform a memory dump when taking the evidences. The valuable data that could be found in RAM is enormous, even being possible to recover the whole chats conversations. Finally, we would like to mention that since we have done the forensics analysis manually, the development of a tool for an automatic analysis is pending as a possible future work.

Acknowledgments. This work has been supported by the CAM grant S2013/ICE-3095 (CIBERDINE: Cybersecurity, Data, and Risks) and by the MINECO grant TIN2016-79095-C2-2-R (SMOG-DEV—Security mechanisms for fog computing: advanced security for devices).

Appendix A   List of Tools and Evidences

Table 3. Used tools

Network forensics	Wireshark	
	NetworkMiner	
Live acquisition	FTK Imager	
	Volatility	
Post-mortem acquisition	FTK Imager	
Windows forensics	FTK Imager	Autopsy
	Mft2csv	Microsoft Excel
	NAR extractor	JumpListView
	WinPrefetchView	RecentFilesView
	AccessData Registry Viewer	Regripper
	Notepad++	Thumbcache Viewer
	VLC media player	ChromeCacheView
	ChromeCookiesView	DB Browser for SQLite

Table 4. Evidences

Case name	MD5 hash	Description
Case1.pcap	ec451d2fb12890c4b6cea7dbf3992233	Network capture Case 1
Case1-1.mem	257249692e38dd3d0b52a774beb2f00e	Memory dump Case 1 before the user logs out
Case1-2.mem	1d5b55b11bd250603d4a0742e32cda07	Memory dump Case 1 before the user logs out
Case1.e01	40750e123186f1a8b7bcfaa7aded7b1d	Disk copy of Case 1
Case2.pcap	dc56888f8ba320bdbfbc3b9a8ea624e0	Network capture Case 2
Case2-1.mem	59d7d18a8b472113c96c335a85aab2d7	Memory dump Case 2 before the user logs out
Case2-2.mem	bf41cce069f78cda38247ac0ec9a1d8d	Memory dump Case 2 before the user logs out
Case2.e01	ea2d48011ae501968683727b4bf4269b	Disk copy of Case 2

Appendix B   Workflows of Case 1 and 2

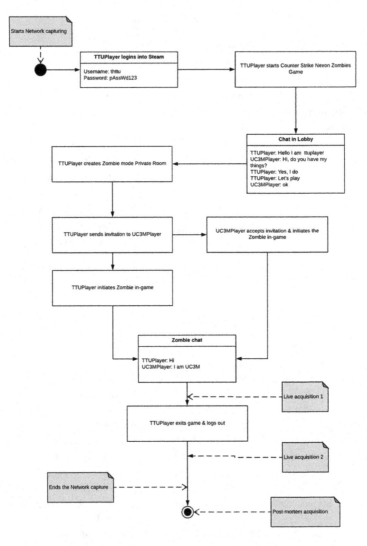

Fig. 1. Workflow case 1 (Zombi Mode)

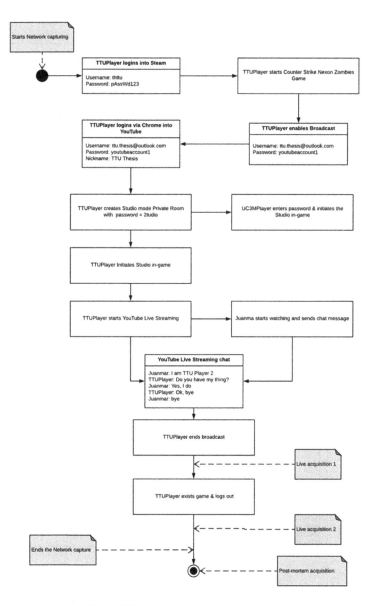

Fig. 2. Workflow case 2 (Studio Mode)

Appendix C   Primary Artifacts

Table 5. Primary artifacts

	Network analysis	Volatile memory analysis (keywords)	Disk analysis
UserID	steamLogin cookie	steamID	\Program Files(x86)\Steam \config \config.vdf
User name	http:// steamcommunity. com/profiles/ <SteamUserID>	SteamUser	$ LogFile \Program Files(x86)\Steam\config \loginusers.vdf
User password		password=	Users \<user> \AppData \Local \Steam \htmlcache \Cache \data_1
Nickname	http:// steamcommunity. com/profiles/ <SteamUserID>	PersonaName	$LogFile \Program Files(x86)\Steam\config \loginusers.vdf \Program Files(x86)\Steam \userdata \<localIDnumber>\localconfig.vdf
List of friends	Session cloning	has logged in	
Chat information		Lobby chat:(Type of receiver) [Nickname of the sender] : message In-game chat:[Type of receiver] Nickname of the sender : message YouTube chat:[YOUTUBE] Nickname of the sender : message	Messenger module: \Program Data \Nexon\Common \nmcogame.log Remote connections: \Program Files(x86)\Steam\logs \remoteconnections.txt
YouTube Live Streaming traces	connect('live2') rtmp://a.rtmp.youtube. com/live2 releaseStream('<key>')	youtube channel_id rtmp.youtube codec	Users \<user> \AppData \Google \Chrome \Default \History
GameID	http:// steamcommunity. com/profiles/ <SteamUserID>	steamGameID	\Program Files(x86)\Steam\steamapps\CSNZ \Bin\steam_appid.txt
User timestamps: - Game installed - Last time accessed - Last time played	http:// steamcommunity. com/profiles/ <SteamUserID>	volatility_2.6_win64_ standalone.exe pslist -profile=<profile> âĀ̃f <memoryimage>	SOFTWARE \Microsoft \Windows \CurrentVersion \Unistalled \Steam App <GameID> NTUSER.DAT \Software\Valve \Steam \Apps\<GameID> \Program Files(x86)\Steam \config \loginusers.vdf NTUSER.DAT\Software\Nexon \CStrike-Online \Program Files(x86)\Steam\userdata \<localIDnumber>\localconfig.vdf
History of the game	http:// steamcommunity. com/profiles/ <SteamUserID>		\Program Files (x86)\Steam\logs \remote connections.txt Documents folder

Appendix D   Summary of Cases Results

Table 6. Results of case 1

	CASE 1			Disk		
	Network	Steam Session cloning	Volatile memory	Steam & CSNZ dedicated folders	Windows registry	Windows system files & folders**
CSNZ Game name	✓	✓	✓	✓	✓	
CSNZ Game mode			✓			
Game acronym			✓	✓		
UserName Steam account		✓	✓	✓		✓
Steam User ID	✓	✓	✓	✓		✓
NickName Steam account	✓	✓	✓	✓		✓
Password Steam account		✓		✓		
Associated email in Steam account		✓	✓			
CSNZ username			✓	✓		
CSNZ Game ID			✓	✓	✓	
Chat messages sent in lobby			✓*			
Chat messages received in lobby			✓*			
CSNZ Player 2			✓	✓		
Zombie in-game room number			✓			
CSNZ family members (list of friends)			✓			
Chat messages sent in Zombie game			✓*			
Chat messages received in Zombie game			✓*			
Game execution logs (last time accessed and last played time)	✓	✓	✓	✓	✓	✓
Network Session IDs	✓	✓		✓		
Network connections	✓		✓	✓		
User status (online/offline)	✓	✓	✓			

* Chats can only be obtained if the acquisition of volatile memory is done before the user logs out.
The Windows files and folders considered are: Shortcuts, Prefetch, Jump Lists, LogFile, MFT, Thumbnails, Recent files, Google Chrome Default folder (Cookies, Cache, History and Login Data files).
*** Chats can only be obtained if the video is still uploaded to YouTube (the user didn't delete it manually) or if the user didn't disable the option of saving the video in the system.

Table 7. Results of case 2

| | CASE 2 | | | | | |
| | Network | Steam Session cloning | Volatile memory | Disk | | |
				Steam & CSNZ dedicated folders	Windows registry	Windows system files & folders**
CSNZ Game name	✓	✓	✓	✓	✓	
CSNZ Game mode			✓			
Game acronym			✓	✓		
UserName Steam account		✓	✓	✓		✓
Steam User ID	✓	✓	✓	✓		✓
NickName Steam account	✓	✓	✓	✓		✓
Password Steam account			✓	✓		
Associated email in Steam account		✓	✓			
CSNZ username			✓	✓		
CSNZ Game ID			✓	✓	✓	
Google account email						✓
Google account username			✓			✓
YouTube Live Streaming main server URL	✓		✓			
YouTube Live Streaming encoder	✓		✓			
YouTube Channel name			✓			✓
YouTube Live Streaming key	✓		✓			
YouTube Live Streaming video			✓			✓
YouTube Live Streaming viewer			✓			
Studio in-game room number			✓			
Password Studio room			✓			
YouTube Live Streaming chat messages sent			✓*	✓***		
YouTube Live Streaming chat messages received			✓*	✓***		
CSNZ Player 2			✓	✓		
Game execution logs (last time accessed and last played time)	✓	✓	✓	✓	✓	✓
Network Session IDs	✓	✓		✓		✓
Network connections	✓	✓	✓	✓		✓
YouTube Live Streaming execution logs	✓					✓
User status (online/offline)		✓	✓			

* Chats can only be obtained if the acquisition of volatile memory is done before the user logs out.

** The Windows files and folders considered are: Shortcuts, Prefetch, Jump Lists, LogFile, MFT, Thumbnails, Recent files, Google Chrome Default folder (Cookies, Cache, History and Login Data files).

*** Chats can only be obtained if the video is still uploaded to YouTube (the user didn't delete it manually) or if the user didn't disable the option of saving the video in the system.

References

1. Anglano, C.: Forensic analysis of whatsapp messenger on android smartphones. Digital Invest. **11**(3), 201–213
2. Bourne, W.: Youtube vs. twitch: how to make money live streaming (2018). https://goo.gl/cxafwX. Accessed 05 July 2018
3. Daniel, L.E.: Multiplayer game forensics (2018). https://www.forensicmag.com/article/2010/05/multiplayer-game-forensics. Accessed 02 Feb 2018
4. Davies, M., Read, H., Xynos, K., Sutherland, I.: Forensic analysis of a sony playstation 4: a first look. Digital Invest. 12, 81–89
5. Editor: Why online gaming is the new frontier for cybercrime (2015). https://www.welivesecurity.com/2015/12/24/online-gaming-new-frontier-cybercriminals/. Accessed 20 Jan 2018
6. Graff, G.M.: How a dorm room minecraft scam brought down the internet (2017). https://www.wired.com/story/mirai-botnet-minecraft-scam-brought-down-the-internet/. Accessed 20 Jan 2018
7. Grayson, N.: The counter-strike gambling scandal, explained. https://steamed.kotaku.com/why-people-are-flipping-out-over-the-counter-strike-gam-1783369102. Accessed 20 Jan 2018
8. Jhala, G.J.: Whatsapp forensics: decryption of encrypted whatsapp databases on non rooted android devices. J. Inf. Technol. Software Eng. **5**(2), 1 (2015)
9. Karpisek, F., Baggili, I., Breitinger, F.: Whatsapp network forensics: decrypting and understanding the whatsapp call signaling messages. Digital Invest. **15**, 110–118 (2015)
10. Khanji, S., Jabir, R., Iqbal, F., Marrington, A.: Forensic analysis of xbox one and playstation 4 gaming consoles. Digital Invest. **12**, 81–89 (2016)
11. Lofgren, K.: Video game trends and statistics - who's playing what and why? (2017). https://goo.gl/9CeDFb. Accessed 20 Jan 2018
12. Mastroianni, B.: How terrorists could use video games to communicate undetected (2015). https://goo.gl/F5Jvnb. Accessed 20 Jan 2018
13. McKemmish, R.: What is Forensic Computing?. Australian Institute of Criminlogy, Canberra (1999). Art 118
14. McQuaid, J.: Skype Forensics: Analyzing Call and Chat Data from Computers and Mobile. MAGNET Forensics, Herndon (2014)
15. Moore, J., Baggili, I., Marrington, A., Rodrigues, A.: Preliminary forensic analysis of the xbox one. Digital Invest. **11**, S57–S65 (2014)
16. NETRESEC: Networkminer. http://www.netresec.com/?page=NetworkMiner, http://www.netresec.com/. Accessed 02 Feb 2018
17. NirSoft.: Chromecacheview. https://www.nirsoft.net/utils/chrome_cache_view.html. Accessed 02 May 2018
18. NirSoft: Jumplistview. https://www.nirsoft.net/utils/jump_lists_view.html. Accessed 02 May 2018
19. Sgaras, C., Kechadi, M.-T., Le-Khac, N.-A.: Forensics acquisition and analysis of instant messaging and VoIP applications. In: Garain, U., Shafait, F. (eds.) IWCF 2012/2014. LNCS, vol. 8915, pp. 188–199. Springer, Cham (2015). https://doi.org/10.1007/978-3-319-20125-2_16
20. Smith, C.: 34 interesting steam statistics and facts (2018). https://expandedramblings.com/index.php/steam-statistics/. Accessed 02 May 2018
21. Wireshark: About wireshark. https://www.wireshark.org/. Accessed 02 Feb 2018
22. Wong, K., Lai, A.C.T., Yeung, J.C.K., Lee, W.L., Chan, P.H.: Facebook Forensics, pp. 1–24. Valkyrie-X Security Research Group, Singapore (2013)

A Digital Forensic Investigation and Verification Model for Industrial Espionage

Jieun Dokko[1,2(✉)] and Michael Shin[1]

[1] Department of Computer Science,
Texas Tech University, Lubbock, TX 19409, USA
{jieun.dokko,michael.shin}@ttu.edu
[2] Supreme Prosecutors' Office, Seoul 06590, Republic of Korea

Abstract. This paper describes a digital forensic investigation and verification model for industrial espionage (DEIV-IE) focusing on insider data thefts at the company level. This model aims to advance the state-of practice in forensic investigation and to verify evidence sufficiency of industrial espionage cases by incorporating the crime specific features and analysis techniques of digital evidence. The model is structured with six phases: file reduction, file classification, crime feature identification, evidence mapping, evidence sufficiency verification, and documentations. In particular, we focus on characterizing crime features that have multiple aspects of commonalities in crime patterns in industrial espionage; and the evidence sufficiency verification that is a verification procedure for digital evidence sufficiency for court decision using these crime features. This model has been developed based on analysis of five industrial espionage cases and the literature review, being validated with three additional cases in terms of the effectiveness of the model.

Keywords: Digital forensic investigation · Digital evidence verification
Evidence prioritization · Behavioral evidence analysis · Digital forensics triage
Industrial espionage

1 Introduction

Historically, digital forensic researches have focused on quickly obtaining digital evidence in a crime scene in a limited time and analyzing digital evidence in technical manners. Within this framework, various digital forensic investigation models have been developed to support analytical techniques for digital forensics [1]. These researches enabled a digital forensic investigator to follow the procedures defined for the techniques, thereby discovering the evidence. However, legal practitioners, such as prosecutors or case investigators, have always faced the challenge of understanding the technical complexity of the evidence [2] because existing digital forensic investigation models are too procedural and technical. Moreover, digital forensic investigators cannot fully understand each type of crime and what information should be examined for the successful prosecution of the case [3]. Also, legal practitioners cannot always advise forensic investigators as to what information should be searched during the

© ICST Institute for Computer Sciences, Social Informatics and Telecommunications Engineering 2019
Published by Springer Nature Switzerland AG 2019. All Rights Reserved
F. Breitinger and I. Baggili (Eds.): ICDF2C 2018, LNICST 259, pp. 128–146, 2019.
https://doi.org/10.1007/978-3-030-05487-8_7

entire investigation process. Thus, there always exists the gap between digital forensic investigators and legal practitioners [4] and some meaningful evidence for court decision can be often overlooked. There is, however, little research examining each crime's features and the application of the features to the digital forensic investigation, particularly in the case of industrial espionage.

As the use of information technologies has become an ever growing factor in successful business, industrial espionage has been growing, thereby producing a high volume of digital data to be investigated [5]. Plus, industrial espionage cases usually require discovering indirect evidence that is related to certain circumstances implicated in the plots and might be connected to other factual information, which can lead to a probable conclusion in the case. Therefore, without a reasonable analysis and verification method for industrial espionage cases, the investigation can become multifaceted and result in overlooked evidence.

To fill this gap, this paper proposes a digital forensic investigation and verification model for industrial espionage (DEIV-IE), which identifies crime features and specifies available digital evidence from the crime features. Also the model verifies the sufficiency of evidential findings. The main contribution of this work is twofold. First, it advances the crime specific investigation practice of industrial espionage cases. Secondly, it provides a digital evidence verification practice in the investigation, which is necessary to establish factual information for court decision.

This paper is organized as follows. Section 2 presents the relevant work related to crime specific investigation and verification methods. Section 3 describes the overview of this model. Section 4 presents the file classification with the characteristics related to the legal recognition and the usages of digital evidence. Section 5 characterizes evidentiary crime features and maps them to evidence. Section 6 describes the evidence sufficiency verification. Section 7 validates the efficiency of the model and Sect. 8 concludes this paper.

2 Related Work

2.1 Crime Specific Investigation

Some studies have focused on developing the crime specific investigation models that can compensate forensic investigators for lack of domain knowledge of a crime. Among them, the author in [8] describes a semi-automated and crime specific triage model, which helps an investigator prioritize and lead the examination process. Even though it discusses crime specific features such as live forensics, computer profile, and crime potential, it is still a high level framework that should be adjusted to a specific type of crime. The research in [6, 7] presents a mobile forensic triage model relying upon manually prioritized crime features in child pornography and copyright infringement cases. This model is enhanced by going one step further than the previous one because it discusses where to search for evidence focusing on child pornography and copyright infringement. The authors in [6, 7] verified their models based on mathematical theories, probabilities, and comparison of algorithms in digital forensic studies. The authors in [9] have studied a digital forensic investigator's decision process model for child exploitation cases, which helps investigators exclude non-relevant media from further in-depth analysis.

Authors in [35] study forensic investigation of cyberstalking cases using behavioral evidence analysis (BEA). Unlike other crime specific investigation models that find digital evidence by using specified crime features, the study in [35] reversely finds the specific crime features of cyberstalking (such as traits of offenders or means of committing the crime) by using digital evidence detected in actual cyberstalking cases. The research in [36] proposes a behavioral digital evidence analysis approach applied to 15 actual child pornography cases using P2P networks. As in other BEA analysis, the study in [36] aims to profile offender characteristics and behaviors by analyzing the potential evidential files. However, this work simply identifies potential evidential files using video or image files, and identifies the location of these files in the Download folder or the Program Files directory where P2P software and downloaded child pornography files are stored by default. Even though this work addresses the pool of potential evidential files, it lacks analytic approaches because such crime doesn't require the in-depth analysis to identify the potential evidential files in nature.

2.2   Digital Evidence Verification

Investigators need to verify that the digital evidence presented to courts is qualified enough to prove the crime, as analysis of digital evidence plays a key role in crime solving [10]. To answer this need, many researches have proposed various frameworks for verifying digital evidence and enhancing the investigation process for a legal argument. The study in [2] suggests the need of a validation stage in the investigation domain that creates a chain of evidence, and clarifies or nullifies an additional assertion derived from the succeeding evidence, bridging the gap between digital forensic experts and legal practitioners. However, this work mostly focused on the legal side, but not actual examination of a specific crime. The authors in [11] present a framework to help investigators to assess the validity, weight and admissibility of evidence with less effort using an interrogative approach. This work evaluates potential evidence using a relationship between other potential evidences, which enhances the presentation and interpretation of digital evidence in a legal process. Similarly, the research in [10] proposes a framework for preparing a qualified report where the traceability of digital evidence has also been enhanced by the proof of digital evidence's origin and history. The authors in [12] describe a traceability model based on a scenario for a digital forensic investigation process, which can help digital forensic investigators to identify the origin of the incident as well as the evidence itself. The study in [13] explains a genetically traceable framework highlighting that the identity, history and origin of extracted digital evidence should be verifiable through scientifically accepted manners in a legal argument. Research in [1] assesses the eleven existing digital forensic investigation process models (DFIPM) against the five criteria of 'Daubert Test' to decide a level of reliability of models. The research shows that no one DFIPM can take the most scientific approach during the investigation because each model has developed based on personal experience and on an ad-hoc basis.

3   Digital Forensic Investigation and Verification Model

The digital forensic investigation and verification model for industrial espionage (DEIV-IE) is designed to examine a stand-alone computer where a windows operating system is installed, sometimes connected with external devices. We assume that the forensic image files captured from seized devices have always been acquired in a forensically sound manner before the investigation process starts, and the acquisition of the seized devices has not been altered since they were acquired. Thus, this model does not address the digital evidence integrity and the environment verification including application, operating system and hardware platform. Figure 1 depicts the overview of DEIV-IE consisting of file reduction, file classification, crime feature identification, evidence mapping, evidence sufficiency verification, and documentations.

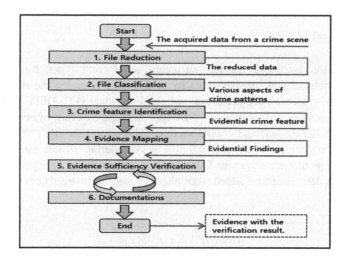

Fig. 1. Overview of the digital forensic investigation and verification model.

File Reduction. This phase eliminates the files created by a non-user from all the files that are acquired from a targeted computer. We assume that a file signature analysis is performed using forensic software and non-user created files are reduced automatically by means of hash techniques [14] before DEIV-IE proceeds to the next phase. For example, the files created by an installation program or operating system can be reduced because they are types of files unlikely to be created and accessed by users [15].

File Classification. In this phase, the reduced files in the previous phase can be categorized into five individual groups based on the expertise of an investigator: user files, communication files, user input files, system files, and less-identified files by considering both the way of creating a file, and a court's different determination regarding the admissibility for each type of file as evidence.

Crime Feature Identification. This phase identifies evidentiary crime features, which are used to guide investigation priority setting to discover the evidence to determine whether an industrial espionage has occurred. The crime features are characterized on account of the multiple aspects of the crime patterns [16] such as behaviors and characteristics of the offender(s) and victims, the property taken or stolen by the crime, and the time the crime occurred.

Evidence Mapping. This phase finds the relevant files that can be used for solving the questions derived from each crime feature by systematically mapping between the crime features and the categorized file groups.

Sufficiency Verification and Documentations. This phase serves as a type of checklist to verify whether an investigator has found sufficient evidence to establish factual information for court decision on an industrial espionage case. This phase carries out the five interrogative questions and their answering, and the process documentations.

4   File Classification

File classification, commonly carried out regardless of crime types, has been implemented in various digital forensic tools by sorting and grouping the files based on technical criteria, such as file extension, size, and metadata [17]. DEIV-IE, however, classifies files into five groups based on the experience and expertise of investigators, in particular, considering practical criteria such as 'who creates the file', 'why the file is created' and 'how the file is created' and also by considering various legal viewpoints in the file groups that are shown in Table 1. Thus, this grouping is adjustable and the list is not complete, it can be added to or altered based on investigators' expertise.

Table 1.   File classification

File Group	Sub Group	Files (e.g., of its extension)
User file	Document	doc(x), ppt(x), xls(x), hwp, pdf, txt, cvs, xml
	Image	jpg, jpeg, tiff, bmp, png, gif
	Multimedia	mp3, mp4, avi, wma, wmv, rm, ram, mpg
	Program code	java, c, cpp, py, dll, css, asp, sys
Communication file	Email	pst, dbx, ost, eml, edb, msg, idx, nsf
	SMS or MMS	db, splite, im
User input file	Financial document Business activity	dbf, dbk, db, fp, md, mda, sql, xls(x)
System file	Internet	html, htm, dat, db, exb, sql, url, png
	Registry	registry files
	Log	log, txt, db, md, sql, spl, shd
	Shortcut	lnk, yak
	Installation	ext, bat, dll, sys, vxd, bin, java, c, cpp, py
Less-identified file	Compressed, backup	zip, tar, pak, cab, jar, tgz, rar, alz, backup
	Embedded, Encrypted	tmp, EMF, sav

User Files. User files are manually created by a user and classified into 4 subgroups: document, image, multimedia, and program code file group. Some files in these groups are generated by the system; image files less than 1 MB can be web cache or temporarily downloaded webpage files, whereas most of the user created image files tend to be larger than 1 MB. User files are rarely accepted in court [18] even if they link to a crime directly because they are regarded as the same as a statement and can be highly modified by a user. Such files can fall into 'hearsay', which cannot be used as evidence in most courts [19].

Communication Files. Communication files are mainly used to communicate and share information among people using Internet, and classified into 2 subgroups: emails, instant or text message file groups. They are likely accepted in court although they are created by a user, because these files' metadata (e.g., the sent or received timestamp) is created by software, and rarely rejected by court [20]. Also a file in the sender side can be cross-checked against the file in the receiver side in terms of the file's integrity and authenticity.

User Input Files. User input files are created by computer processing with a user input, being related to either regularly conducted business activity or financial records, and classified into financial document and business activity file groups. These files are admissible in court, because a court accepts regularly conducted activity information based on the inherent reliability of business records [21]. But, DEIV-IE excludes this group from evidence mapping phase because such files are not related to user's intentional activities and scarcely noticed in industrial espionage cases.

System Files. System files are automatically created and utilized by the system to manage operations, and classified into 5 subgroups: Internet, registry, log, shortcut, and installation. Internet file group mainly demonstrates a user's Internet activities or system's Internet usages. Registry shows information about the system and its devices as well as the activities generated by a user or a system. Log files record program activities created by the system. Shortcut files are created to facilitate repeated access swiftly when a user accesses a file, an external device and a shared network, so previous activities of a user or a system are traceable [22]. Installation files including executable files is created by system according to its pre-scripted procedure. These files are credible in court because they are not hearsay and created solely by a computer without any human interaction [23].

Less-identified Files. A file falling into a less-identified file group can contain another file(s) or latent pieces of information embedded somewhere inside the file, thus the challenge of examining and processing evidential information out of them remains. Less-identified files in this model are classified into two subgroups: compressed or backup, and embedded or encrypted. A compressed file may contain multiple individual files, and an encrypted file cannot be read without its decryption.

The file classification can be beneficial to preparing for trials because the authentication and reliability of files in each group are differently accepted by court from legal viewpoints. The evidence corroboration can be carried out with the combination of different evidence(s) in each file group, which can be an essential tool for the successful prosecution of a case. These evidences can support or corroborate each other so that they confirm the proposition and enhance the reliability of other evidence. For example, a document file that describes a plot, motive, and criminal behaviors of a suspect cannot be used alone as evidence in a court due to hearsay. However, the document file can be assumed to be accurate if reliable evidence (e.g., log, registry, emails) can link this document to the suspect and prove the crime.

5 Crime Feature Identification and Evidence Mapping

5.1 Industrial Espionage

70% of a company's assets lies in market-sensitive information [24] such as client lists, supplier agreements, personal records, research documents, and prototype plans for a new product or service. Industrial espionage makes use of many different methods such as computer hacking, dumpster diving, electronic surveillance, and reverse engineering [25], but almost 85% of espionage cases originate from insiders within an organization [26] who cooperate with a criminal authority outside the organization. Our model deals with the theft of trade secrets and intellectual property of a company, focusing on an insider threat. This model has been established using a typical scenario of industrial espionage cases revealed by the review of digital forensic analysis reports of five cases as follows:

A discontented employee in a company conspires with a rival company who seeks a competitor's assets e.g., patents, inventions, or trade secrets. The employee covertly takes the company's confidential information, and either joins a rival company with a promotion agreement or receives compensation for handing over the information.

Five Reference Cases. The digital forensic cases that were reviewed for developing DEIV-IE in this paper were examined by 7 digital forensic investigators with 2 to 8 years' analysis experience in the prosecutors' office in Korea 2008 to 2014. The summaries of each case are as follows.

Case 1. A suspect working for a company that provides industrial maintenance products and services for cleaning waste water was suspected of stealing the company's protected document files related to marketing strategy (e.g., loan annex) using his office computer before his resignation.

Case 2. A suspect working as a marketing manager for a manufacturer of Radio-Frequency Identification (RFID) devices was accused of revealing the company's secret files of marketing and products to a rival company, where the suspect subsequently gained employment.

Case 3. A suspect working as a salesperson in a company of eco-friendly products, e.g., electronic railway trolleys and oil flushing equipment, was suspected of stealing protected computer-aided design (CAD) files before his resignation.

Case 4. A suspect who worked at a light aircraft manufacturer was charged with stealing protected information about agricultural aircraft development and marketing.

Case 5. A researcher in an electronic technology institute was suspected of releasing document files related to nuclear power energy to a person outside the company.

5.2   Crime Features with Evidence

The crime features in this paper are defined in accordance with the principle of 4W1H questions that should always be asked during the entire investigation of a crime; 'When' for the time period that the crime occurred, 'who' for the suspect(s), 'whom' for the accomplice(s), 'what' for the files or data misappropriated or stolen, 'how' for the criminal behaviors or activities that occurred. However, this model excludes 'where' and 'why' because the computer to be examined is where for the place the crime occurred [27] which is the scope the model is limited to and the motivation of the crime can be acknowledged indirectly through the investigation. This model finds the files relevant to each crime feature by systematically mapping crime features to classified file groups. It is not necessary for the model to identify specific evidential files, but it narrows down the range of potential evidential files. This mapping result can also be used to guide investigation priority setting. The evidence mapping in DEIV-IE is hierarchically depicted in Fig. 2, which categorizes the 4W1H questions, the crime features, the classified file groups, and the sub-file groups. The relationships between the categories (Fig. 2) are represented by means of generalization and specialization, question and answer, and the whole and its parts, which are described with the notation in Table 2.

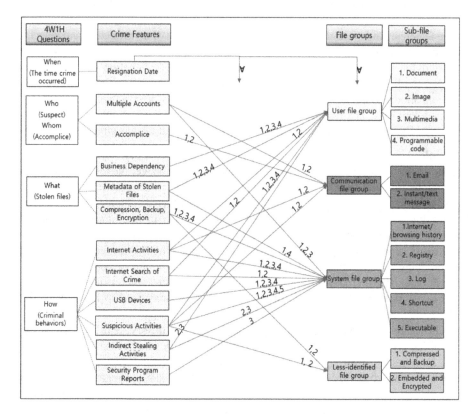

Fig. 2. Outline of mapping between crime features and potential evidence in industrial espionage

Table 2. Relationship between in the model.

Relationship	Description	Notation
Generalization, Specialization	A component of a higher layer is semantically the general question of component(s) of the lower layer, expanded question(s) for more specified inquiry	– – – –
Question & Answer	A component of a higher layer can be proved by file(s) in the file group(s) pointed out by an arrow from the component (One-directional relationship). The number(s) on an arrow indicates the reference number of its sub file group(s) in its lower layer	1. 2. →
Whole & Parts	A whole component of a higher layer consists of its distinct components of a lower layer	——

Resignation Date (When). Accurate estimation of the period of suspected criminal activities is a crucial skill in the crime investigation. The majority of suspects in industrial espionage cases tend to plan their activities in advance. Five cases of the digital forensic analysis reports show that the most critical evidences are revealed in the period four months prior and up until a suspect leaves a company. This feature should be always prioritized in the entire investigation and examined in conjunction with other crime features. An investigator can narrow down the scope of investigation and detect a suspect's doubtable activities when he/she concentrates on the activities that have occurred for four months before a suspect resigns. The resignation date feature is mapped to all file groups because each file has the timestamps in terms of creation, deletion, modification or copy, thereby being relevant to determining the period of criminal activities. The resignation date feature is expressed as '∀' above the top two arrows in Fig. 2, which are applied to all other arrows and all file groups.

Multiple Accounts (Who). The investigation needs to identify who has used the computer during the alleged time period. In industrial espionage, the range of suspects tends to be limited to the employees who used the suspected computer and who have rights to access the targeted information. However, a suspected computer might be used by multiple users who were not the owner of the computer in an organization. Also, a suspect can create an unauthorized backdoor account or use other person's account to steal secret information [26]. Case 3 shows that several employees used the suspected computer during the alleged time period. This feature should not be neglected because several, unexpected employees can be involved in this crime, even if in some cases it can be insignificant because most of the Hi-Tech companies tend to have their own policies that prohibit employees from shared computer usage.

This feature can be mapped to the registry, Internet history, and log files in the system file group and communication file group to identify who has used the computer (Fig. 2). Registry files contain each user's profile including registered accounts, computer name, the last login account with timestamps, and the registered user to a certain service or software [22]. The Internet history files (e.g., index.dat, web-cachev01.dat or cookie files) enable an investigator to trace each account and the timestamps for the user's Internet use and browsing history. A log file (e.g., a security event log for window auditing) can be used to track user accounts with their activities. Emails and Instant messages (IM) in the communication file group contain the email addresses, and the sender and receiver names. Cross-checking of different files can help in finding the suspect because a system or software creates or updates different types of files (e.g., registry, log, Internet history, email, and IM files) resulting from just one action.

Accomplice (Whom). Industrial espionages tend to be committed in cooperation with accomplices [28]. This feature cannot only provide us with the accomplice but also reveal additional detailed clues for a case, such as suspect, means, motives, alibi, where a suspect communicates with the accomplices to conspire the crime. This feature can be mapped to emails or IMs in the communication file group (Fig. 2). In the cases 2, 4 and 5 in the analysis reports, accomplices outside the company are identified on email investigation. Especially in case 5, the suspect has discussed her new job offer and sent her resume to the accomplice.

Business Dependency (What). Identifying stolen files is the first step of investigation on industrial espionages. However, stolen files may not be easily identified due to the diversity of valuable information in a computer. Most stolen files can be dependent upon the computer programs required to run businesses. Source code, design blueprint, and prototypes are valuable to Hi-Tech manufacturers, while sales forecasts, financial and customer information are valuable in merchandising business [24].

To identify stolen files, this feature can be mapped to user file groups (Fig. 2) but the types of stolen files are different depending on the types of business. In the analysis reports, the computer-aided design (CAD) files are generally targeted for the technical data theft, whereas database and spread sheets files are dominant for the marketing data crime, and document files (e.g., Microsoft Word or Adobe Acrobat files) are quite commonly used for most of the trade secrets espionage regardless of the types of business. The CAD files were stolen in case 3, the spreadsheet files in cases 1 and 2, the image files in cases 1 and 4, and the document files were stolen in cases 2, 4, and 5. However, the fact that the stolen files were discovered on the suspected computer might not be sufficient evidence to prove a criminal activity because the stolen files might be originally supposed to be on the computer. Thus a court might not accept the stolen files alone as evidence without proving that the suspect misused the files.

Metadata of Stolen Files (What). Each file has its own metadata that describes the characteristics of a file, which includes the file name, owner, created, accessed and modified timestamps, and directory path where the file is stored [29]. Without opening a file to look at its contents, the metadata of a file is helpful for proving that the file existed at a specific location and time. The status of a file's metadata is updated whenever the file is accessed, modified, deleted or moved, thus the trace of a stolen file's metadata can reveal the changes of the file. Although the file has been deleted, the change history of a stolen file allows an investigator to ascertain whether the file was stored in a certain location in a computer.

This feature can be answered by mapping to the metadata of the user file groups (Fig. 2). Also the metadata of a stolen file can be obtained from a browsing history (e.g., index.dat and webcachev01.dat) or a shortcut file (e.g., a file with the lnk extension) in the system file group (Fig. 2) if the file has been recently opened in the system. The new metadata is recorded in a new shortcut file if the file is reopened after the location, timestamps or other characteristics of the file are changed. Thus, by learning the difference between the various versions of shortcut files, an investigator can prove the trail of the stolen file that has been moved, changed or copied to other devices in the computer. In the analysis reports for all 5 cases, we observed that the metadata of targeted files were examined to trace the stolen files.

Compression, Backup, Encryption of Stolen Files (What). A stolen file might be compressed, backed-up, or encrypted by organizations to protect the contents in accordance with their security policy, or by a suspect to hide the crime. Suspects often encrypt the stolen files to transmit them to outsiders covertly [26], back-up and compress the stolen files to copy them to USB, especially in the alleged time period. In this way, many protected files can be transmitted or copied without releasing their name and contents. This feature is mapped to the less-identified file group and mapped to the system file group because the shortcut, browsing history, registry and log files can show that a stolen file has been compressed, backed-up, or encrypted (Fig. 2). A shortcut file and a browsing history file can be created when a compressed file is opened, whereas a registry file can contain the mounted information about an encrypted or backed-up volume if the volume has been mounted to the computer. In case 4, the stolen files were found to be compressed during the alleged time period.

Internet Activities (How). The Internet is often used by a suspect to communicate with an outsider [30] and to send the stolen files to the outsider covertly. In particular, email is the most important object of investigation because nearly 45% of data theft is sent to an outsider using email [24] and the emails between offenders (such as a suspect and an accomplice) may reveal their intent for a crime, especially, the motivation of the crime. Although web-hard and cloud services can also be used to share the targeted files with outsiders [31], they are beyond the scope of this model that is confined to the investigation of a computer.

The Internet activities feature is mapped to Internet history, registry, log, and shortcut files in the system file group, emails and IMs in the communication file group, and webpage files with web cache in the user file group (Fig. 2). The Internet history files store the Internet access record with timestamps, user accounts, paths of visited URLs, and the number of visits to a specific website or a web-hard. The registry files store the URLs the user visited, the user's start page, and, in some cases, the keywords the user searched for [22]. The log files can contain a user's activities; for instance, cloud services (e.g., Dropbox, OneDrive, and iCloud) generate certain log files containing the path, name, size, and timestamp of a downloaded or uploaded file along with user accounts or email addresses [32]. The shortcut files (e.g., bookmark or favorite files) can record user's favorite and bookmarked web-pages, which can make it possible to assume that the user recognized and often visited these web-pages. The temporarily stored webpage files with web cache can be useful for rebuilding an original webpage the suspect browsed. The analysis reports in cases 2, 4 and 5 show that the stolen files have been sent to outsiders via email. Specifically in case 5, the criminal conspiracy is obviously incorporated in the email messages and the web-hard service is used for sharing the stolen files with an accomplice.

Internet Search of Crime (How). A suspect tends to search the Internet for information related to industrial espionage just before or after the crime. A suspect might take a look at a company to which he/she moves, or search for the information about the crime such as a range of potential penalties, or the latest news and updates on similar crimes. This feature gives circumstances of a crime to an investigator, thus, the investigator can infer that the suspect has committed the crime. This feature is mapped to the web-pages with web caches in the user file group, and the Internet history and registry files in the system file group (Fig. 2). In case 4, a suspect's internet search activities are examined in the Internet history and registry files that contain the searched keywords and typed URLs.

USB Devices (How). It is highly plausible for a suspect to copy a secret file to a USB device covertly during the alleged time period. An investigator can identify the model, volume serial number, or labeled name of the USB that was attached to the suspected computer. The identified USB can also reveal the names of stolen files that were copied on the USB. But, this feature has become less effective; only less than 10% of data theft has taken place using USBs [24], as many companies disable USB devices on employees' systems in order to protect their secret data. To identify the suspicious USB usage, this feature is mapped to registry, shortcut, browsing history, and log files in the system file group (Fig. 2). Registry files contain external device information from the sub-keys, e.g., Mounted device, USBSTOR, and USB. Shortcut and browsing history files can provide a clue as to when or where (which USB) the stolen files were copied. Log files can contain USB installation, along with the timestamps (e.g., setupapi.dev. log), and many monitoring software can create a log file containing a USB and the name of copied files on the USB [22]. In cases 1, 2, and 4, the analysis reports detected that suspect used USBs during the alleged time period.

Suspicious Activities (How). An investigator should discern a suspect's unusual, irregular or suspicious activities that deviate from the ordinary activities. When a suspect emails a particular person, he might use an outside email account rather than his company email account. During the suspected dates, a suspect may exchange too many emails with a particular person, or access a strange web-server for uploading files. A suspect may email the secret files to himself to elude a company's email checking policy. New external devices might be attached to the computer so that a bunch of files could be backed up and copied on them especially during the suspected dates. Also unknown programs might run on the computer prior to his resignation.

To detect suspicious activities, an investigator can search the Internet related files in the system file group, the emails and IMs in the communication file group, and the files in the user file group, and compressed or backed-up files in the less-identified file group (Fig. 2). An investigator needs to cross-check the different versions of files' metadata (especially timestamps and directory paths of the stolen files) so that he/she can find different types of suspicious activities (e.g., moving, deleting, or copying many files). The metadata of the files are stored not only inside the files, but also in the browsing history and shortcut files in the system file group. An investigator also needs to detect some suspicious login attempts or insecure USB connections to the system or protected storage using the registry and log files [29] in the system file group. In cases 1, 2, 4, and 5, the analysis reports show that the suspects accessed most of the targeted files and attached several USB devices to the computers a few days before a suspect left the company. In case 4, the suspect had 7 email addresses and used one of those emails during the alleged time period.

Indirect Stealing Activities (How). As an alternative to directly stealing the targeted files (e.g., emailing the files to an outsider), a suspect often obtains the targeted information indirectly by means of printing, capturing, drawing, or taking photos of the targeted file without notice. As a company installs and operates security software that restricts the use of networks and external media, it is difficult to transfer data without permissions [24]. Thus indirect stealing activities feature has become more important in the investigation of industrial espionage. With a smart phone, a suspect can easily take photos of the secret information, and send emails or messages with the photos to outsiders; but a smart phone is beyond the scope of our model.

To find indirect stealing activities, this feature can be mapped to the system file group, and user file group (Fig. 2). Printing or capturing a target file can be detected in the system file group using both the log files of the print program, if any, the registry files relating to program activities, and files containing the printed images of a file and the information for each printing job (e.g., print spool files) [33]. The stolen files created or changed through indirect stealing activities (e.g., screenshot or printing) should be detected using the image and multimedia files in the user file group. In case 4, after analyzing print spool files, an investigator found that a suspect printed the targeted files using a local and a network printer during the suspected dates. The use of a capturing program was discovered in a registry file in case 1.

Security Program Reports (How). Most of the Hi-Tech companies run security programs: logging, security monitoring or data loss prevention (DLP) software for the security of files, valuable data, and the detection of leaked information. If the company has a security program in place, the log files of the program on the suspected dates need to be analyzed [26]. This feature is mapped to the log files in the system file group (Fig. 2). The log files of a security program (e.g., 'Activity Monitor') can include the typed keystrokes, records of switching between programs with timestamps, application path, and window names, visited web sites, passwords, email, chat conversation, USB, and printing usages. The security program reports feature identified a suspect in case 2 via an investigation of the log files in the system file group.

6   Evidence Sufficiency Verification and Documentation

6.1   Evidence Sufficiency Verification Process

After identifying all the supporting potential evidential files, DEIV-IE creates a more solid reconstruction of the crime using the evidence sufficiency verification process. This process consists of a series of questions and answers that should be proved to persuade a court for industrial espionage. The process begins with the identification of when a crime occurred, followed by who was a suspect, with whom a suspect committed the crime, what were the stolen files, and how the suspect committed the crime. The following describes each step of this process.

When did a Crime Occur? The first step of the process identifies the time period when the crime occurred. This step checks if the resignation date feature identifies the crime dates or not. If it is 'Yes', the result is documented. However, if it is 'No', the investigator inquires within the victimized company for a plausible range of time. However, if the company cannot provide information about the crime time, this process assumes that the crime time frame is within four months preceding resignation.

Who was a Suspect? The second step of the process identifies the suspect(s). This step checks if the multiple accounts feature identifies a suspect or not. If the suspect(s) is named, it is documented with more specified crime dates. But, if the suspect(s) is not identified, the investigator needs to inquire within the company for a range of possible suspect. If the company fails to identify the suspect(s), the range of suspect(s) narrows down to the employees who used the suspected computer or who had a right to access the stolen files.

With whom did a Suspect(s) Commit the Crime? The third step of the process identifies the accomplice(s) using the accomplice feature. If the accomplice(s) is identified, the result is documented with an updated conclusion of evidence. However, if the accomplice(s) is not identified, this step is pending until additional findings in the subsequent steps help to identify the accomplice. If no accomplice is associated with the crime or no additional findings help to identify the accomplice, this step fails.

What was the Stolen File(s)? This step identifies stolen files by checking if the business dependency, metadata, compression, backup, or encryption of stolen files feature identifies the stolen file(s). If it is 'Yes', the result is documented with updated previous findings. If stolen files are not identified, the investigator inquires within the company for a range of the possible stolen files. Otherwise, this model assumes that the range of the stolen files is the user file group.

How did the Suspect Commit the Crime? The final step of the process finds criminal behaviors. This step checks if the internet activities, internet search of the crime, USB devices, suspicious activities, indirect stealing activities, and security program reports features identify criminal activities. If it is 'Yes', the result is documented with updated previous findings. If the final findings contain the evidence to answer all the questions such as the crime dates, suspect(s), accomplice(s) if any, stolen file(s), and criminal activities, it concludes that this investigation has sufficient evidence to convict the suspect for the crime committed. But the final findings might be insufficient to convict under the legislation when they only establish partial facts from the existing evidence. Lack of evidence cannot provide proof of comprehensive evidence validation, and it can make the exiting evidence unreliable for court decision [2].

6.2 Documentations

Whenever a file or information is identified and updated as evidence, the result is documented. The documentation is not accumulative, but it is created individually, so that the updates or changes of preceding evidential information are newly documented along with a new identified evidence. This is a procedure to specify and narrow the findings. After completion of the entire process, the final report is created.

7 Validation

DEIV-IE was validated with three industrial espionage cases; two cases of the prosecutors' office in Korea in 2010 and 2014, and one of 'M57-Jean' (Corpora, 2008) that posted on a website for use in computer forensics education research. An ex-digital forensic investigator was involved in this validation, and the tool 'Encase' was allowed for the application of this model to the cases. Each case is described as follows:

Case 1: A suspect who is a son of the owner of a rival company joined the chemical manufacturer and was suspected of ex-filtrating secret files to the rival company on the day before his resignation.

Case 2: An accomplice was suspected of involvement in trade secret theft of nuclear power and the computer of the accomplice was investigated.

Case 3: (M57-Jean): The protected information of a company was posted on the Internet. A suspect's laptop in the workplace was examined for the crime investigation. The case is originally designed as a case study for the document ex-filtration from a corporation rather than industrial espionage. However, the case is utilized in our validation due to the similarity of its criminal activities such as stealing and revealing information of a company.

In this validation, we use two sets of assessment criteria – main assessment criteria (Table 3) and sub-criteria (Table 3). The main assessment criteria focus on whether the crime features described in chapter 5 can detect sufficient evidence to answer the '4W1H' five questions (Table 3) when they are mapped to the relevant file groups defined in chapter 4. This is because the answers to the five questions are typically considered the basic information that determines whether a person is guilty. One point has been given to the score of each case if one of five main assessment criteria is answered by investigating any files or data categorized as sub-criteria (Table 3). This assessment records the score of cases on a scale of 0 to 5, with 0 being the no sufficient information and with 5 being the sufficient information, in terms of the main assessment criteria. All five questions are answered for cases 2 and 3 (Table 3), each of which is given five points. In addition, this validation uses the score quantified by the sub-criteria (Table 3) which demonstrates how much main assessment criteria is supported by the sub-criteria. When a main assessment criteria is substantiated with more than one file, the fact proved by the main assessment criteria is more valid than the fact proved using just one file. We give one point to each case if a file of the sub-criteria is used to indicate the fact proving the main assessment criteria. The number of files used for each case are counted and represented as a score along with the score for main assessment criteria. The case 2 has the score 5(13), with 5 being the number answered by the main assessment criteria and with 13 being the number of files used to prove the main assessment criteria.

The DEIV-IE model has discovered sufficient evidence to prove the crime in cases. In our validation, the case 2 fulfills the five main assessment criteria with five points supported by 13 different types of evidential files, denoted by 5 (13) in Table 3. The case 2 has the eight points of sub-criteria and five points of the main assessment criteria. The court acquires all the five answers to the main assessment criteria so that it

Table 3. A score obtained by DEIV-IE in the verification cases.

Main Assessment Criteria (4W1H)	Score (# of findings)			Crime feature	Sub-Criteria (Files or data used to detect evidence)		
	Case1	Case2	Case3		Case1	Case2	Case3
When was crime dates	1(1)	1(1)	1(1)	Resignation date	Timestamps	Timestamps	Timestamps
Who was the suspect	1(1)	1(1)	1(1)	Multiple accounts	Registry	Registry	Registry
Who was the accomplice	0(0)	1(2)	1(1)	Accomplice		Email, IM	Email
What files were stolen	1(4)	1(2)	1(2)	Business dependency	Document file	Document file	Document file
				Metadata of stolen files	Metadata	Metadata	Metadata
				Compression, backup or encryption	Shortcut, compressed file		
How the crime was committed	1(5)	1(7)	1(3)	Internet activities		Email, Internet history, IM	Email, attachment
				Internet search of crime		IM	Email
				USB devices	Registry, shortcut, browsing history		
				Suspicious activities	Shortcut, deleted stolen file	Browsing history, registry, stolen file	
				Indirect stealing activities			
				Security program reports			
Total Score	4(11)	5(13)	5 (8)				

can determine if a criminal is guilty. The case 1 answers the four questions of main assessment criteria with its sub-scoring 11 points (4 (11) in Table 3). Our model cannot prove the accomplice of case 1, but it discovers sufficient evidence for court decision if we assume that case 1 doesn't have an accomplice. This validation approach is not a conclusive validation, but a score-based assessment to verify whether the crime features with their file groups can reveal sufficient evidence of each case.

8 Conclusion and Discussion

This paper has described a digital forensic investigation and verification model (DEIV-IE), which finds digital evidence using crime features and verifies the sufficiency of the evidence to establish factual information on industrial espionage for court decision. This study used a deductive, crime-based approach by examining digital forensic analysis reports of five actual industrial espionage cases, and studying the state of literature of this crime. In DEIV-IE, files have been classified to their file groups from the different legal perspectives and notable crime patterns have been streamlined to the crime features. Then DEIV-IE identifies specific crime features mapped to its relevant file groups, so that an investigator examines the files in the file groups for each feature.

However, this model is limited in scope only addressing the espionage cases of insider data thefts at corporate level where are only stand-alone computers running windows operating system, and external devices that are examined. As a result, this model does not address other common attack vectors in industrial espionage and has several limitations. First, it does not discuss user endpoint malware infection, and server vulnerability exploitation for exfiltration. Second, it does not address the decryption issues to find the targeted files even though a company's sensitive files tend to be encrypted due to the company's security policy. Third, it does not support comprehensive analysis between computers and other digital devices such as badge readers, CCTV footage, in particular, smart phones even if they have become major tools for industrial espionage cases recently. Forth, this model assumes that evidence is a file or exists in a file, so it may not be applicable to a situation where a criminal tampers with the evidence. Criminals can remove targeted files to interrupt the business of the victimized company deliberately. This case requires additional processes such as file carving from fragments and file reconstruction from the tempered evidence.

DEIV-IE, despite these weaknesses, still contributes to industrial espionage investigations. To date, there are no digital forensic investigation models for industrial espionage that have incorporated the crime features into digital forensic analysis techniques. In addition, the crime features in the model do not serve as standard practice but serve as an example of essential building blocks in the crime investigation, which will be inevitably expanded as different attack vectors are involved in the crime. The framework approach in this paper is easily adjustable based on new activities, the environments (e.g., Linux, smartphone) where it is applied, the expertise of an investigator and also open to adjustment to develop the DEIV model for other crimes.

This research will be extended to developing a tool supporting DEIV-IE, so that it extracts the information required for each crime feature from the proper files and verifies the findings. It will also involve defining the relationships among the crime features so that investigators use the connection between the features in the investigation.

References

1. Montasari, R.: Review and assessment of the existing digital forensic investigation process models. Int. J. Comput. Appl. **147**, 7 (2016)
2. Boddington, R., Hobbs, V., Mann, G.: Validating digital evidence for legal argument. In: Australian Digital Forensics Conference (2008)
3. Karie, N.M., Venter, H.S.: Towards a framework for enhancing potential digital evidence presentation. In: Information Security for South Africa. IEEE (2013)
4. Ieong, R.S.C.: FORZA–digital forensics investigation framework that incorporate legal issues. Digit. Investig. **3**, 29–36 (2006)
5. Søilen, K.S.: Economic and industrial espionage at the start of the 21st century–Status quaestionis. J. Intell. Stud. Bus. **6**, 3 (2016)
6. Marturana, F., et al.: A quantitative approach to triaging in mobile forensics. In: IEEE 10th International Conference on Trust, Security and Privacy in Computing and Communications (TrustCom). IEEE (2011)
7. McClelland, D., Marturana, F.: A digital forensics triage methodology based on feature manipulation techniques. In: IEEE International Conference on Communications Workshops (ICC). IEEE (2014)
8. Cantrell, G., et al.: Research toward a partially-automated, and crime specific digital triage process model. Comput. Inf. Sci. **5**(2), 29 (2012)
9. James, J.I., Gladyshev, P.: A survey of digital forensic investigator decision processes and measurement of decisions based on enhanced preview. Digit. Invest. **10**(2), 148–157 (2013)
10. Karie, N., Venter, H.: A generic framework for enhancing the quality digital evidence reports. In: 13th European Conference on Cyber Warfare and Security ECCWS-2014 the University of Piraeus Piraeus, Greece (2014)
11. Karie, N.M., Venter, H.S.: Towards a framework for enhancing potential digital evidence presentation. In: Information Security for South Africa 2013. IEEE (2013)
12. Mohamed, I.A., Manaf, A.B.: An enhancement of traceability model based-on scenario for digital forensic investigation process. In: Third International Conference on Cyber Security, Cyber Warfare and Digital Forensic (CyberSec). IEEE (2014)
13. Karie, N., Kebande, V., Venter, H.: A generic framework for digital evidence traceability. In: European Conference on Cyber Warfare and Security. Academic Conferences International Limited (2016)
14. National Institute of Standards and Technology (NIST) (2002). The National Software Reference Library (NSRL). https://www.nist.gov/software-quality-group/nsrl-introduction. Accessed 24 Jan 2018
15. Holt, T.J., Bossler, A.M., Seigfried-Spellar, K.C.: Cybercrime and Digital Forensics: An Introduction. Routledge, Abingdon (2015)
16. Bruce, C., Santos, R.B.: Crime Pattern Definitions for Tactical Analysis (2011)
17. Raghavan, S., Raghavan, S.V.: A study of forensic & analysis tools. In: Eighth International Workshop on Systematic Approaches to Digital Forensic Engineering (SADFE). IEEE (2013)
18. Teppler, S.W.: Testable reliability: a modernized approach to ESI admissibility. Ave Maria L. Rev. **12**, 213 (2014)
19. Legal Information Institute (Hearsay 2017). https://www.law.cornell.edu/wex/hearsay. Accessed May 2017
20. United States v. Hamilton, 413 F.3d 1138, 1142 (10th Cir. 2005)
21. Records of Regularly Conducted Activity, Rule 803(6), Federal Rule of Evidence
22. Carvey, H.: Windows forensic analysis DVD toolkit. Syngress, Amsterdam (2009)

23. United States v. Washington, 498 F.3d 225, 233 (4th Cir. 2007)
24. Casey, E.: Error, uncertainty, and loss in digital evidence. Int. J. Digit. Evid. **1**(2), 1–45 (2002)
25. Sinha, S.: Understanding industrial espionage for greater technological and economic security. IEEE Potentials **31**(3), 37–41 (2012)
26. Wright, L.: People, risk, and security: How to Prevent Your Greatest Asset from Becoming your Greatest Liability. Springer, London (2017). https://doi.org/10.1057/978-1-349-95093-5
27. EC-Council: Computer Forensics: Investigating Network Intrusions and Cyber Crime. Nelson Education (2009)
28. Carrier, B., Spafford, E.H.: An event-based digital forensic investigation framework. In: Digital Forensic Research Workshop (2004)
29. Bhatti, H.J., Alymenko, A.: A Literature Review: Industrial Espionage (2017)
30. EC-Council: Computer Forensics: Hard disk and Operating Systems. Nelson Education (2009)
31. Hultquist, J.: Distinguishing cyber espionage activity to prioritize threats. In: 13th European Conference on Cyber Warfare and Security ECCWS-2014, The University of Piraeus Piraeus, Greece (2014)
32. Tun, T., et al.: Verifiable limited disclosure: reporting and handling digital evidence in police investigations. In: IEEE International Conference on Requirements Engineering Conference Workshops (REW). IEEE (2016)
33. Chung, H., et al.: Digital forensic investigation of cloud storage services. Digit. Investig. **9**(2), 81–95 (2012)
34. Sammons, J.: The Basics of Digital Forensics: The Primer for Getting Started in Digital Forensics. Elsevier, Waltham (2012)
35. Al Mutawa, N., et al.: Forensic investigation of cyberstalking cases using behavioural evidence analysis. Digit. Investig. **16**, S96–S103 (2016)
36. Al Mutawa, N., et al.: Behavioural evidence analysis applied to digital forensics: an empirical analysis of child pornography cases using P2P networks. In: 10th International Conference on Availability, Reliability and Security (ARES) 2015. IEEE (2015)

Hard Drives and Digital Forensics

Solid State Drive Forensics: Where Do We Stand?

John Vieyra[1], Mark Scanlon[2(✉)], and Nhien-An Le-Khac[2]

[1] Canada Border Services Agency, Regina, Canada
john.vieyra@ucdconnect.ie
[2] Forensics and Security Research Group, University College Dublin,
Dublin, Ireland
{mark.scanlon,an.lekhac}@ucd.ie

Abstract. With Solid State Drives (SSDs) becoming more and more prevalent in personal computers, some have suggested that the playing field has changed when it comes to a forensic analysis. Inside the SSD, data movement events occur without any user input. Recent research has suggested that SSDs can no longer be managed in the same manner when performing digital forensic examinations. In performing forensics analysis of SSDs, the events that take place in the background need to be understood and documented by the forensic investigator. These behind the scene processes cannot be stopped with traditional disk write blockers and have now become an acceptable consequence when performing forensic analysis. In this paper, we aim to provide some clear guidance as to what precisely is happening in the background of SSDs during their operation and investigation and also study forensic methods to extract artefacts from SSD under different conditions in terms of volume of data, powered effect, etc. In addition, we evaluate our approach with several experiments across various use-case scenarios.

Keywords: SSD forensics · Forensic experiments · Data recovery
TRIM

1 Introduction

As the design of computers has improved with time, many manufacturers have moved from traditional Hard Disk Drives (HDDs) to Solid State Drives (SSDs). These SSDs are smaller and more compact than HDDs. They are also more robust and resilient to vibration and allow for much greater Input/Output (I/O) data transfer speeds. These drives contain no moving parts and store each bit of data in floating gate transistor rather than on a magnetic spinning platter of a HDD. Although these new types of drives have many advantages, they also have some limitations. These drives have a limited number of writes per cell, can only write in pages, and must erase a full block of pages before rewriting any single page. Depending on the type on NAND flash, some SSDs may come with a number of bad areas that need to be corrected. Because of these noted limitations, data is stored using non-traditional methods such as using error correction code, bad area management, and scrambling, etc.

F. Breitinger and I. Baggili (Eds.): ICDF2C 2018, LNICST 259, pp. 149–164, 2019.
https://doi.org/10.1007/978-3-030-05487-8_8

On the other hand, these design changes have created much interest in the forensic community regarding how SSD data is stored and recovered from these non-traditional devices. Many papers have been written detailing how different SSDs are compared to the traditional HDDs. Some performance and forensic testing of these SSDs show disturbing results, such as nearly all the data being lost within a couple of minutes when a format command was sent [1]. This action by SSDs is "quite capable of essentially near-complete corrosion of evidence entirely under their own volition" [1]. These comments in the hands of a savvy criminal defense lawyer, could be wrongfully used to undermine the results of a competent forensics examiner. It was not the forensic examiner or the SSD itself that has caused the drive to delete its data, but the actions of the suspect entering the format command. The SSD simply reacted to the command as it has been designed to do. This is analogous to a suspect shredding documents to the point that they are irrecoverable just prior to a search warrant being executed. SSDs limitations have caused designers to implement many techniques to overcome some of these issues. Hardware manufacturers have added a system of garbage collection, wear levelling, and created TRIM to mitigate these limitations [3].

Mobile devices, e.g., smartphones and tablets, typically use NAND flash memory that interacts with the OS during the evidence recovery process. Every day, evidence is successfully entered in court retrieved from seized cellphones. Whether it is call logs or skype chats, this information is valuable in assisting the prosecution in criminal cases. However, every time a cellphone is turned on for an extraction, changes are made to the NAND Flash memory and the evidence is "walked on" during this process, i.e., in an analogous manner to walking onto a physical crime scene. Perhaps a boot loader needs to be installed on a cellphone so that the data area can be imaged, or a Factory Reset Protection Lock removed from an Android phone to allow circumvention of the device's passcode. In all cases, these methods need to slightly walk on the evidence. The premise of hashing the storage and subsequently ensuring that all images match the original hash no longer applies. The memory of a cellphone is constantly changing whenever power is applied to the controller. The process now requires that some evidence is deterministically changed for the greater good of the recovery process. However, this does not mean that evidence is added by the forensic examiner, and any changes must be kept to a minimum. Plus, once the NAND Flash memory is imaged it is now time to hash the image and confirm that all further image copies are verified with the hashing process [2].

Through the literature review for this work, we found that there is a gap in terms of forensic acquisition and analysis of SSD drives. Hence, we aim to provide some clear guidance as to what precisely is happening within the background of these SSDs and to demonstrate that most forensic Hard Disk Dive (HDD) procedures still stand when it comes to their analysis. The study we performed has been designed to recreate what would be found in any typical computer seizure. The analysis is designed to determine the following research answers:

1. Does the total amount of data stored on a SSD affect what evidence that can be recovered from the drive?
2. Does time the SSD is left powered on effect the available data?
3. What effects does TRIM have on the outcome of stored data within the drive?

4. When things do change, comparisons are performed to determine the effects of these changes.
5. How much data is left after formatting a SSD drive with both TRIM enabled and disabled?
6. Can we tell if garbage collection is happening in the background?

2 Solid State Drive Characteristics

The Flash Translation Layer (FTL) is an abstraction layer between what the Operating System (OS) sees or communicates with, and the actual way the data is stored within the SSD. The FLT makes the SSD look like a HDD to the OS. The first two things hidden behind the FTL that are important: garbage collection and wear levelling.

2.1 Garbage Collection

Garbage collection is a process that takes place in the NAND Flash memory to prepare memory cells for new data when they have previously been used to store data. NAND flash has many limitations that must be addressed by the controller chip. Some of these limitations are:

- It is unable to overwrite original data at the byte level.
- The smallest writable area is a page.
- It is made up of blocks of data containing pages.
- It has a limitation that only allows the memory to write in pages and delete in blocks. For data to be overwritten, the entire block must first be cleared. There is one exception to this, where the data to be written is a strict subset of the data. This means that the data has the exact same zero values and can write ones to zeros. It cannot write a zero to a one. If you want to write a zero to a one, then the entire block needs to be cleared and reset to accept new data.

When a page needs to be cleared you are required to clear the entire block. The problem here is that some of the adjacent pages in the same block may still have allocated data. In this case the allocated pages must be moved to a new block, and then the entire block is deleted, i.e., garbage collection. This does not solely happen when the OS tries to overwrite previous data. If the SSD supports TRIM, the OS sends a TRIM command to the SSD when it deletes data notifying the SSD that the area is no longer needed. The SSD controller then uses this information along with garbage collection to prepare new areas ahead of the time when it will be needed [4, 5].

2.2 Wear Levelling

During the regular use of a computer, many files may be put on the device's storage and remain for the entire life of that computer. Typical users would also have many files that get updated regularly. This becomes a problem for the SSD as certain areas might be hitting the end of their usable life, while others may have just one write cycle and never been erased. The ideal scenario would be to have all the blocks fail at the exact same time. By doing this you allow the longest lifespan of the drive and the best user experience. To facilitate this behavior, the SSD controller moves data around, so that areas with low write/erase cycles are now used more frequently. This happens inside the SSD and behind the FTL and is not transparent to the OS and the end user.

There are three types of NAND flash memory and each type has a different lifespan:

- Single-Level Cell (SLC): These are high performance, enterprise grade devices. They perform up to 100,000 program/erase cycles per cell. They have lower power consumption, with faster write speeds and a much higher cost (up to three times higher than MLC) [8].
- Multi-Level Cell (MLC): This is average performance consumer grade storage. They perform up to 10,000 program/erase cycles per cell. They have higher density (two or more bits per cell), a lower endurance level than SLC, and a lower cost (up to 3 times lower than SLC). These are used in consumer goods and are not suggested for critical applications that have frequent updates of data [8].
- Three-Level Cell (TLC): These are the lower performance, lowest cost option. They perform up to 5,000 thousand program/erase cycles per cell. They have the highest density (three bits per cell), lower endurance level, and slower read/write speeds than MLC. They are a good fit for low end consumer products and are not recommended for critical applications that have frequent updates of data [6].

2.3 Data Behind the FTL

Since the data stored on SSDs is hidden behind the FTL, to directly examine it, the memory chips must be removed from the SSD circuit board. The NAND flash memory can now be directly read bypassing the controller. When we read each chip, we have no way of determining how the controller has stored the data and what it will take to put it back into a usable format. The details of the controller and the firmware are trade secrets of the manufacturer. The companies manufacturing these SSDs want to hide their technique for providing the best possible performance. To determine how SSDs store the data, visual storage representation software is used to display the data. This software also allows you to reassemble the data. Two companies that have designed products to recover this data in this way are ruSolute and ACE Labs [7].

2.4 TRIM

TRIM is a term (not an acronym) used to identify certain ATA commands that allow the OS to notify the SSD controller that data is no longer needed. The meaning of word TRIM is simply coming from the fact that the area of the drive is reduced or trimmed (made smaller). TRIM became necessary to allow the OS to tell the SSD that an area is no longer needed.

In the case of HDDs, when the OS deletes a file, the OS updates the file allocation table and marks the area as unallocated. The underlying data is not deleted from the HDD. This becomes a problem for SSDs since they need to prepare deleted areas before allowing any new data to be saved in this area. SSDs are required to write in pages (usually 512 bytes) and delete in blocks. This process works fine if the drive is not full and has available space to write its data, however when the drive starts to become full things change drastically. The drive now needs to find a page to store the data. This makes the controller work harder to try and find available space. To do this, it will start moving allocated pages from blocks with many unallocated pages to new blocks. It then clears the entire block, i.e., garbage collection. This results in a significant slowdown of the device. TRIM attempts to overcome this issue by providing a way for the OS to tell the SSD that it no longer needs certain areas. The SSD controller is now able to perform many of the functions needed to clear data well in advance of any need from the OS. These internal processes could also be done at times when the SSD is under minimal load causing the process to be hidden or masked from the user. For TRIM to be active, three things need to be present: the OS must support it, it must be supported by the SSD, and it must be supported by the file system that is used.

3   Related Work

NIST suggest that modern SSDs are subject to a process that is "self-corrosive" [2]. It suggests that these self-corrosive processes are done in the absence of computer instructions. Gubanov et al. [4] explain how the data destruction process is only triggered by the TRIM command, and the data destruction itself is carried out by the separate process of background garbage collection. The authors also explain why different outcomes are found as a result of analysis when TRIM is operating. In some cases, they found all zeros, and other times they find actual data. This is explained because some drives implement Deterministic Read After TRIM (DRAT) and Deterministic Zeroes After TRIM (DZAT). With DZAT the drive returns all-zeros immediately after the TRIM command releases a certain data block. In the case where a drive uses non-deterministic TRIM, each read command after TRIM may result in different data. In some cases, the data read can return different non-original data, not because the data has been cleaned, but because the SSD controller says that there is no valid data held in these areas. Some areas of logically corrupted data allow for recovery since the TRIM command is not issued over corrupted areas. A portion of the authors' conclusion is very important, where they note that many SSDs follow the DRAT approach, and therefore a simple format of the drive is likely to instantly render all the data inaccessible to standard read operations. Write blockers will have no effect to stop this process.

The comparison of reactions in SSD drives using different file systems and TRIM has been detailed in [8]. This is the first analysis over different file systems including NTFS, EXT4, and HFS+ that support TRIM on SSDs. This paper explains that when TRIM is enabled, the OS notifies the drive that data has been deleted from its location and then marks the location as invalid. In this paper, the authors determined that when TRIM was enabled, the deleted data was purged and unrecoverable within minutes. This was not the case in EXT4 as the commands are sent in batches and therefor may not be sent immediately. They also found that manual TRIM being used as an anti-forensics method was not very successful and suggested the use of the ATA Secure Erase standard built into most SSDs.

Bednar and Katos presented two challenges for digital forensics of SSDs [9]. The first is that data that has been deleted is not necessarily removed from the disk because the logical structures are not necessarily mapped to physical locations on the disk. Data is required to be processed through a complex algorithm that is known only to the manufacturer. The second is that the controller purges data on its own independently of the OS. This happens whenever the drive is powered on. The authors also suggested two options to overcome these issues. One being that the memory chips could be removed from the drive and read independently. The data could be put back together for analysis. The second option would be to remove the drive controller and replace it with one that is forensically safe to recover all the data. The later would be considered almost impossible due the many different variations available as well as the difficult requirement to tamper with the evidence. The authors suggested that hash functions cannot be used to determine the integrity of SSDs as they will inevitably change over time. This will result in potentially different hash values each time they are imaged. The use of write blockers is somewhat negated as they will not stop the writes made internally to the data on the memory chips. The write blockers are attached outside of the drive on the SATA cable; therefore potentially making the data not acceptable for use in court.

Shah et al. studied the forensic potentials of SSDs from different manufacturers and determined what data will be available after deletion from the SSD. It is suggested that data can be recovered from an SSD in a similar manner as a HDD if the SSD does not have background garbage collection and TRIM has been disabled. They also indicate that data can be recovered after the SSD has been formatted. The use of TRIM only functions when the drive is connected to the SATA or NVMe primary channel. In cases where the drive is connected via a secondary SATA channel or via a USB connection, TRIM does not function, and therefore the deleted data is entirely available for recovery.

With empirical analysis, King et al. [11] tries to show how much data is retained on 15 different SSDs. The authors listed drive models with details of how much data is recovered with and without TRIM enabled. The authors found that data recovery using TRIM-enabled disks was practically impossible for large disks, showing a near zero percent of data. For the small files, these results varied with the SSD manufacturer. Some reported 25–30%, while Intel reported zero percent. They suggested that different results were caused by Intel using a proprietary controller software, while the others used software licensed from Indilinx. They also found that without TRIM (using Windows XP), they could recover almost 100% of the data. This occurred for both large and small files. An important point was that they seemed to be able to recover higher percentage of data when dealing with high usage disks. They commented that this was likely due to garbage collection struggling to prepare disk space when dealing with high usage. They found that the TRIM command has made all data not recoverable. Without TRIM enabled, allows for nearly 100% of the data being recovered. They state that "as SSD adoption grows as well as use of Windows 7 and other TRIM-supported OS's, traditional data recovery will no longer be a viable option for Investigators."

4   Experiments and Findings

In order to answer the research questions raised in the introduction, this section describes several case studies with analysis.

4.1   Platforms

In this section, we describe the datasets and hardware we used in our experiments. The sample data needed to fill large a volume of drive space and needed to be a type of data that can be measured in free space after deletion. To do this, large text files were created with a repeating string value followed by a unique MD5 hash value. By using an alliteration multiple repeating values could be output to numerous text files thereby filling a folder to a pre-selected volume. The string and MD5 combination is then used to name the folder created to store all the data. Briefly, we have a folder named with the string and MD5 hash combination and numerous text files containing the sample data, as can be seen in Fig. 1. Each of these folders will be searched for the string-MD5 combination. A count of the number of hits will be recorded for comparison, shown in Fig. 2. This data will then be used to determine the percentage of recovered data in each case.

Fig. 1.   View of sample of repeating data inside the one of the text files.

Twelve drives (two of each model) were used in our experiments. These were brand new and had not been used for any other purpose. Ten of the drives were 250 GB and two were 500 GB. Each drive is attached to a Z87X-UDSH Gigabyte motherboard, Intel i7 4770 CPU @ 3.5 GHz computer, on the primary SATA channel. Windows 10, 64-bit Pro edition was installed on a NTFS partition. This is done to represent a real-life scenario where a laptop or desktop computer is encountered during a typical search warrant. The odd numbered drives were confirmed to have TRIM operating by using the command line entry `fsutil` behavior query `DisableDeleteNotify`. If the response received is `DisableDeleteNotify` = 0, then TRIM is turned on. The even numbered drives had the TRIM turned off using the `fsutil` behavior set

10GBDeletedPart11fb63b148136721 2c1855b3885e6b8c2	6/20/2017 1:35 PM	File folder
10GBDeletedPart39f9742c5e846923e5f5fb97f8ef8ce70	6/21/2017 6:49 AM	File folder
10GBDeletedPart239543f748d0f07ec971206310a4f2122	6/21/2017 6:25 AM	File folder
10GBDeletedPart464092f00c0b623d7b8334581d16d2c03	6/21/2017 10:17 PM	File folder
50GBAllocated757ccb014947e1129366093f02153fbc	6/20/2017 12:12 PM	File folder

Fig. 2. Sample data used in analysis.

`DisableDeleteNotify = 1`, and then confirmed using `fsutil` behavior query `DisableDeleteNotify`. If TRIM is turned off correctly the response received is `DisableDeleteNotify = 1`.

4.2   Experiment 1

Through this experiment, we aim to reply the research questions 1, 2, 3 and 4 raised in Sect. 3.

Four sets of data folders were copied to each drive. Each set represents approximately twenty-five percent of the 250 GB drive volume (in the case of the 500 GB drives, two sets are copied each time). These sets contain a 50 GB folder of allocated data that will be left on the drive and not deleted. The sets also contain an additional 10 GB of data that will be deleted immediately without going to the recycle bin (i.e., "shift delete" to emulate user behavior). Each of these 10 GB folders will be unique to the set. After each set is copied to the drive, the drive is imaged immediately using either a Tableau TD2 Forensic Imager, or a Tableau T35u Forensic SATA/IDE Bridge and FTK Imager software version 3.4.3.3. The drive is then left powered on idle for one hour and reimaged. After a further 8 h of being powered on idle, it is again imaged one final time. This entire process is completed three more times, each time after adding another set of data containing an additional twenty-five percent of data.

Each image is then opened in X-ways forensics Version 19.0 SR-4 x64 software and a text search is initiated for each of the combined string and MD5 values with the option selected to count the number of hits. These values will be compared to the original data that was added and then deleted to determine how much data can be recovered. This will be completed four times in total, once after each additional amount of data is added. Comparisons will be made and percentages will be calculated for each type of data, trying to determine how much is recoverable after each addition. In cases where the image hash of the one hour and eight hour images match the zero hour hash, then only one of the images will be searched as the data will be exactly the same. In any cases where the zero hour, one hour, or eight hour hashes do not match, then the different images will be compared in X-ways forensics to try and determine what has changed. These comparisons should be able to tell if any changes are taking place inside the SSD that are visible to the OS through the FTL.

First part of this experiment consisted of adding data to fill approximately 25% of the drive. The analysis of this experiment showed varying amounts of data available for recovery. These were found to be from a fraction of a percent to nearly all the data available for recovery after data deletion. What was clear from the results is that drives that had TRIM enabled on the OS, had significantly lower amounts of data available for recovery. The images taken at the 0 h, 1 h, and 8 h, as can be seen in Fig. 3, were all the same, i.e., their hashes matched.

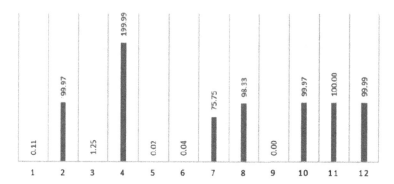

Fig. 3. Recovered data percent, first data set (even numbered drives had TRIM disabled, odd numbered drives had TRIM enabled). Note: Drives 3 and 4 were over twice the size of the others.

The second part of this experiment consisted of adding another 25% (50% full) of data to the drive. The analysis of this experiment again showed varying amounts of data available for recovery. These were found to be from a fraction of a percent to about 50% of the data was available for recovery after data deletion. What is again clear from the data is that drives that had TRIM enabled on the OS, had significantly lower amounts of data available for recovery. The images taken at the 0 h, 1 h, and 8 h, as outlined in Fig. 4, were again all the same, i.e., their hashes matched.

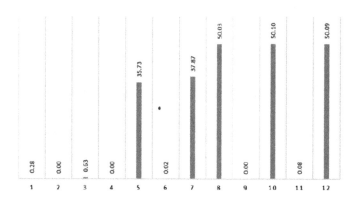

Fig. 4. Recovered data percent, second data set (even numbered drives had TRIM disabled, odd numbered drives had TRIM enabled).

The third part of this experiment consisted of adding another 25% (75% Full) of data to the drive. The analysis of this experiment again showed varying amounts of data available for recovery. These were found to be from a fraction of a percent to about 65% of the data was available for recovery after data deletion. What is again clear from the data was that drives that had TRIM enabled on the OS, had significantly lower amounts of data available for recovery. The images taken at the 0 h, 1 h, and 8 h, as shown in Fig. 5, were again all the same, i.e., their hashes matched.

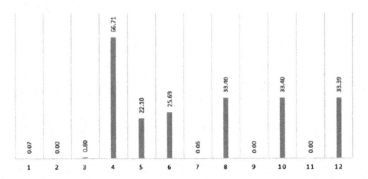

Fig. 5. Recovered data percent, third data set (even drives had TRIM disabled, odd drives had TRIM enabled).

The fourth part of this experiment consisted of adding another 25% (nearly 100% Full) of data to the drive. The analysis of this experiment again showed varying amounts of data available for recovery. These were found to be from a fraction of a percent to about 65% of the data was available for recovery after data deletion. What is again clear from the data was that drives that had TRIM enabled on the OS, had significantly lower amounts of data available for recovery. The images taken at the 0 h, 1 h, and 8 h, as outlined in Fig. 6, were again exact matches.

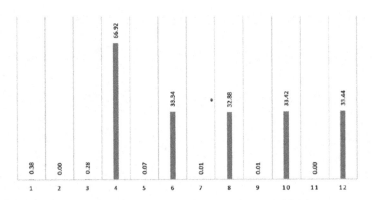

Fig. 6. Recovered data percent, fourth data set (even numbered drives had TRIM disabled, odd numbered drives had TRIM enabled).

The analysis of this data showed that data did not change over time and what seems to make the drive reduce the amount of previously deleted data from being recovered is the addition and deletion of data and not the time that the drive is powered on.

4.3   Experiment 2

In this experiment, we aim to find out "how much data is left after formatting a SSD drive with both TRIM enabled and disabled?". We are filling drives to near full capacity and formatting the drive.

The drives outlined in Experiment 1 are also used in Experiment 2. Drive 3 to 12 each have additional data added so that the free space is below 1 GB. Each of these drives is then imaged using the same process as Experiment 1. Drives 1 and 2 will not have any additional data added besides the operating system. These two drives will be used as bootable drives on the Primary SATA channel with Drives 3 to 12 being quick formatted on the secondary channel. Drive 1 is matched to Drives 3, 5, 7, 9, and 11, so that the odd drives are formatted with a TRIM enabled OS. Drive 2 is matched to Drives 4, 6, 8, 10, and 12, so that even drives are formatted with a TRIM disabled OS.

Once all the drives are formatted, they will be immediately shut down. All ten drives will be reimaged, and then again after being powered on and left idle for an additional 8 h.

Each image is then opened in X-ways Forensics Version 19.0 SR-4 x64 software and a text search is initiated for each of the combined string and MD5 values with the option selected to count the number of hits. The amount of recovered data from images taken before the formatting will be compared to the recovered data from images taken after the formatting. From this data an analysis of how formatting the drives will affect the data recovery.

The results showed that all the data was removed and set to zeros on eight of the drives, however two drives (Drives 5 and 6) had nearly all the data available for recovery. This abnormality is difficult to understand without knowledge of the inner workings of the devices' firmware. The TRIM version containing 99.63% and the Non-TRIM version containing 82,83%, as shown in Fig. 7.

	Before Format	After Format
Drive 1		
Drive 2		
Drive 3	10,000.334,198	0
Drive 4	10,000,078,637	0
Drive 5	4,444,480,004	4,428,146,536
Drive 6	4,444,492,854	3,681,448,761
Drive 7	4,444,481,343	0
Drive 8	4,444,480,371	0
Drive 9	4,444,483,675	0
Drive 10	4,444,480,004	0
Drive 11	4,444,483,170	0
Drive 12	4,444,524,993	0

Fig. 7. Amount of recovered data after a format on Drives 3 to 12 (Drive 1 and 2 were used as the base OS drives and therefore no data was gleamed from them).

4.4   Experiment 3

Experiment 3 tested if the SSD could be overwhelmed with garbage collection and if this could be seen somehow. Testing was conducted using the format command in Microsoft Windows 10 GUI file explorer. It used a new Samsung 500 Gb SSDs and measured the time to copy data to 500 GB of data to it until it reported being full. The drive would then be formatted, and another 500 GB of data would immediately be written to it. The hypothesis is that the measurement of time should significantly increase if the drive now suddenly needs to make room for the new data using garbage collection. The time of each write will be compared to see if background garbage collection will slow the data transfer after the format takes place. In this experiment no significant difference in time was found between the first and second writes. The action of background garbage collection could not be seen using this method.

4.5   Experiment 4

Experiment 4 tested if the SSD could be overwhelmed with garbage collection and if this could be seen somehow. Testing using deleting of data and rewriting.

It used a new Samsung 500 Gb SSDs and measured the time to copy data to 500 GB of data to it until it reported being full. The data on the drive was all deleted (shift delete) and another 500 GB of data would immediately be written to it. The hypothesis is that the measurement of time should significantly increase if the drive now suddenly needs to make room for the new data using garbage collection.

The time of each write will be compared to see if background garbage collection will slow the data transfer after the data is deleted. Experiment 4 was similar to Experiment 3, however instead of formatting the drive, the data was simply deleted. This was again performed on a new drive that had never been used. The fact that a similar time was required was the same as in Experiment 3.

4.6   Experiment 5

Experiment 5 was performed to see if the action of garbage collection could somehow be seen by monitoring the power requirements.

In this case, the SSD was connected to a separate power supply and attached in series to a meter that could measure the power consumption to 1/100th of a milliamp. The drive was filled with data and then deleted or formatted as in Experiments 3 and 4. The hypothesis is that the drive should draw a high-power level until garbage collection ends and then settle down to an idle value. The amount of current will be monitored to see if background garbage collection can be observed.

In all cases, after the data was deleted or the drive was formatted the drive drew between 250 and 300 mA initially then within 10–15 s settled to approximately 150 mA. This stayed constant and never reduced after two days. Again, this experiment was inconclusive in determining if garbage collection could somehow be observed working in the background.

4.7   Analysis

Forensic examiners have always been taught that data must be unchanging and that hashes are used to verify the integrity of all data. This was first applied to HDDs that were hashed before imaging. Once the image was complete, the new image was then hashed to confirm that it was an exact bit stream copy. The hash verified its integrity. At any point in the forensic process, the image could be rehashed to prove that it perfectly represented the original data as it was at the time of seizure.

With advancements in technology, things have begun to evolve. NAND flash memory and the use of mobile devices have caused a situation where it is now necessary to change data only slightly to be able to recover evidence. Every day criminals are convicted of crimes that depend on cellphone evidence to provide the smoking gun. But in nearly every case the extraction tools needed to recover the data must communicate with the operating phone. The phone needs to be charged, turned on, and just about ready to make a call. To have the phone operating means that it has changed data in the process. If companies like Cellebrite and Micro System Automation (XRY) could not change data, they would likely not be in business, and many crimes would go unsolved. It is the new norm to change data to allow an extraction to take place. Cellphones have an additional problem because they also use NAND flash memory that changes data behind the FTL, using garbage collection and wear levelling, as well as TRIM [2, 12].

SSDs contain NAND flash memory and behave in ways that have been compared to tampering when doing forensics on these devices [14]. It has been suggested that hashing these drives cannot confirm integrity since data changes over time [9].

Experiment 1 has found a very different conclusion. In every test of the drives being hashed found that over time the values did not change. This does not mean that the data behind the FTL was not changing, but just that what is presented to the OS does not change.

In Experiment 1, 144 images were made. These included three timed images, one immediately after the data was added and deleted, one after sitting idle for one hour, and a final completed eight hours after sitting idle. In each case, the zero hour, one hour, and eight-hour images all had their hashes match. This was opposite to what was discovered in Geier's paper. It should be noted that Geier's paper never mentioned whether they used a write blocker and that could easily explain why they saw hash changes [15].

Experiment 1 also found that data could be recovered after deletion on an SSD, however, it was not like what is expected from HDD. The amount of recovered data varied from model and manufacturer and was greatly reduced with the use of TRIM. This is opposite to what appears to be noted about TRIM by Joshi and Hubbard [14].

When data was added or deleted, it reduced the amount of recovered data from previous additions and deletions. It's changes being made to some data that may affect the recovery of other deleted data. This makes the use of forensic write blockers so important to help ensure that you recover the most evidence as well as ensuring the integrity of the original evidence. This is in opposition to some papers that comment that forensic write blockers are not suggested when imaging SSD drives [9].

Another finding in this experiment is the loss of recoverable data in SSDs where TRIM was disabled. Although much less recoverable data was available, significant reductions in data still happened. With the deletion of files in HDDs only the File Allocation Table (FAT) is updated. In SSDs without TRIM, nothing is telling SSD to clear data with garbage collection. Some information was found that suggests that Samsung is using specialized algorithms that are capable of reading the $BitMap NTFS file. [2] This is a file in the NTFS file system that keeps track of the available clusters and is updated by the OS. Since the OS updates, this file with every deletion and this file is stored on the SSD; it only makes sense that the SSD controller can control the clearing of data using this file. The analysis in Experiment 1 shows that all manufacturers are using a similar design to keep up with the clearing of available data areas with or without TRIM. TRIM, however, seems to do a much better job, by leaving less recoverable data than the non-TRIM testing. It should be noted that TRIM is not needed with the advancements in newer SSD firmware. This suggestion was also mentioned in [9].

The results of this experiment are practically useful in providing support to any cases that might be challenged in court regarding the integrity of the evidence. Using a forensic write blocker ensures that any reduction of recoverable evidence was caused by the suspect and not the forensic examiner. The integrity of the evidence can be proven from this point forward by simply rehashing the image.

The analysis in Experiment 1 is more comprehensive than many other papers as it used 12 different models of drives that were imaged a total of 148 times to gather the needed evidence. These were new drives and contained no prior data, as well they were operated on the primary SATA channel with an OS installed on each drive. Experiment 1 tried to replicate a standard laptop or desktop seized during a search warrant.

An interesting finding happened with Drive 9. This drive would not boot after the first set of data was added and then imaged. After the boot failure the drive was wiped, and then the experiment was started again. In all cases, no data was recovered from the drive during first three additions of data and imaging. This was unusual to see this happen with just one drive. It is likely possible that the memory was empty when first purchased, but the wiping process added scrambled data to all areas of the memory when the wiping program used a zero's in the filling process. This would actually mean that the drive was full when the experiment took place and would likely have different results than any of the other drives. It is possible that some of the experiments in other papers that had opposing results to the ones in this paper may have used drives that had been wiped and used previously. None of the papers reviewed in this paper noted buying new unused drives. This is another reason why the results of this paper are comprehensive. This specific issue could also be the basis for further investigations regarding the issue between new drives and wiped drives.

Experiment 2 tested whether data was available for recovery after being filled with data and then formatted. The drives had data added so that they were within 1 Gb of being full. The drive was imaged and then formatted. The drives were imaged immediately to create an after-format image. A subsequent image was again made after the drive sat idle and powered up for eight hours. In this case, the results were slightly mixed. Eight of the ten drives showed only the partition table and NTFS structure with the rest all being zeros. Drives 3 and 4 had nearly all the data recoverable. This shows that each of the drives have firmware that works differently. TRIM did not seem to affect any of the results in drive three and four. In every case, the eight-hour image matched the image that was done immediately after format. This further confirmed the results found in Experiment 1 where the data did not change over time.

Experiment 3 tested if the SSD could be overwhelmed with garbage collection, and whether it could be seen somehow. It used a new Samsung 500 Gb SSDs and measured the time it took to copy 500 GB of data until it reported being full. The drive would then be formatted, and another 500 GB of data would immediately be written to it. The hypothesis is that the measurement of time on the second write should significantly increase if the drive now suddenly needs to make room for the new data using garbage collection. The first write took approximately 18 min using a secondary SATA channel. The second write after formatting took about the same time. In fact, it may have been slightly faster. The results of this experiment were inconclusive. It did not help determine if garbage collection was working behind the FTL, making room for data in the background.

Experiment 5 was performed to see if the action of garbage collection could somehow be seen by monitoring the power requirements. In this case, a SSD was connected to a separate power supply and attached in series to a meter that could measure the power consumption to 1/100th of a milliamp. The drive was filled with data and then deleted or formatted as in Experiments 3 and 4. The hypothesis is that the drive should draw a high-power level until garbage collection ends and the drive settle's down to an idle value. In all cases, after the data was deleted or the drive was formatted the drive drew between 250 and 300 mA initially then within 10–15 s settled to approximately 150 mA. This stayed constant and never reduced after two days. Again, this experiment was inconclusive in determining if garbage collection could somehow be observed happening behind the FTL.

5   Conclusion and Future Work

The experiments in this paper have been successful in bringing forward an opposing view to some of the other papers [1, 15]. These experiments show that although things have changed in SSDs when compared to HDDs the way forensic examiners do forensics should stay practically the same. This comes with an understanding that NAND flash may hold deleted evidence that will not be shown to the OS. Currently, the standard practice is to image the SSD using a write blocker and the SATA/NVMe connection. In the future, forensic examiners will need to look at chip removal to bypass the FTL and be able to access all the possible deleted data. This comes with a cost where the labs will need to be able to remove the chips and correctly reconfigure the allocated data as well as recover additional deleted data. The experiments in this paper left many opportunities for further research regarding the data behind the flash translation layer and how to recover it for important cases.

References

1. Bell, B., Boddington, R.: Solid State Drives: The Beginning of the End for Current Practice in Digital Forensic Recovery? Perth (2010)
2. Guidelines on Mobile Device Forensics, from National Institute of Science and Technology. http://nvlpubs.nist.gov/nistpubs/SpecialPublications/NIST.SP.800-101r1.pdf. Accessed 8 July 2017
3. Sheremetov, S.: Chip–off digital forensics - data recovery after deletion in flash memory. In: Techno Security and Digital Forensics Conference, Myrtle Beach (2017)
4. Gubanov, Y., Afonin, O.: Recovering evidence from SSD drives: understanding TRIM, garbage collection and exclusions, Belkasoft, Menlo Park (2014)
5. Garbage Collection in Single-Level Cell NAND Flash Memory, by Micron. https://www.micron.com/∼/media/Documents/Products/Technical%2520Note/NAND%2520Flash/tn2960_garbage_collection_slc_nand.ashx+&cd=1&hl=en&ct=clnk&gl=ie&client=firefox-b
6. SLC, MLC or TLC NAND for Solid State Drives by Speed Guide.net. https://www.speedguide.net/faq/slc-mlc-or-tlc-Nand-for-solid-state-drives-406. Accessed 6 June 2017
7. NAND Bad Columns analysis and removal by ruSolute. http://rusolut.com/nand-bad-columns-analysis-and-removal/. Accessed 5 July 2017
8. Nisbit, A.: A forensic analysis and comparison of solid state drive data retention with trim enabled file systems. In: Australian Digital Forensics Conference, Auckland (2013)
9. Bednar, P., Katos, V.: SSD: New Challenges for Digital Forensics
10. Shah, Z., Mahmood, A.N., Slay, J.: Forensic potentials of solid state drives. In: Tian, J., Jing, J., Srivatsa, M. (eds.) SecureComm 2014. LNICST, vol. 153, pp. 113–126. Springer, Cham (2015). https://doi.org/10.1007/978-3-319-23802-9_11
11. King, C., Vidas, T.: Empirical analysis of solid state disk data retention when used with contemporary operating systems. In: The Digital Forensic Research Conference DFRWS 2011 USA, New Orleans (2011)
12. tn2919_nand_101 Nand Flash commands from Micron. https://www.micron.com/∼/media/documents/products/.../tn2919_nand_101.pdf
13. Guidelines on Mobile Device Forensics, from National Institute of Science and Technology. http://nvlpubs.nist.gov/nistpubs/SpecialPublications/NIST.SP.800-101r1.pdf. Accessed 8 July 2014
14. Joshi, B.R., Hubbard, R.: Forensics analysis of solid state drive (SSD). In: Proceedings of 2016 Universal Technology Management Conference, Omaha (2016)
15. Geier, F.: The differences between SSD and HDD technology regarding forensic investigations, Sweden (2015)

Associating Drives Based on Their Artifact and Metadata Distributions

Neil C. Rowe[(⊠)]

Computer Science, U.S. Naval Postgraduate School, Monterey, CA, USA
ncrowe@nps.edu

Abstract. Associations between drive images can be important in many forensic investigations, particularly those involving organizations, conspiracies, or contraband. This work investigated metrics for comparing drives based on the distributions of 18 types of clues. The clues were email addresses, phone numbers, personal names, street addresses, possible bank-card numbers, GPS data, files in zip archives, files in rar archives, IP addresses, keyword searches, hash values on files, words in file names, words in file names of Web sites, file extensions, immediate directories of files, file sizes, weeks of file creation times, and minutes within weeks of file creation. Using a large corpus of drives, we computed distributions of document association using the cosine similarity TF/IDF formula and Kullback-Leibler divergence formula. We provide significance criteria for similarity based on our tests that are well above those obtained from random distributions. We also compared similarity and divergence values, investigated the benefits of filtering and sampling the data before measuring association, examined the similarities of the same drive at different times, and developed useful visualization techniques for the associations.

Keywords: Drives · Forensics · Link analysis · Similarity · Divergence
Artifacts · Metadata

1 Introduction

Most investigations acquire a set of drives. It is often important to establish associations between the drives as they may indicate personal relationships and downloading patterns that can provide leads. Such link analysis has become an important tool in understanding social networks. Methods of digital forensics now allow us to do link analysis from drive features and artifacts. Knowing that two drives share many email addresses, files, or Web-page visits establishes a connection between them even before we know exactly what it is. Such associations are important in investigating criminal conspiracies and terrorists, intellectual-property theft, propagation of malware or contraband, social-science research on communities, and in finding good forensic test sets.

However, there are big challenges to forensic link analysis from drive data. One is the large amount of irrelevant data for most investigations, especially in files that support software [10]. A second problem is determining how best to establish associations between drives. Some clues are more helpful for further investigation (such as

© ICST Institute for Computer Sciences, Social Informatics and Telecommunications Engineering 2019
Published by Springer Nature Switzerland AG 2019. All Rights Reserved
F. Breitinger and I. Baggili (Eds.): ICDF2C 2018, LNICST 259, pp. 165–182, 2019.
https://doi.org/10.1007/978-3-030-05487-8_9

email addresses), some are harder to extract (such as all words in file names, or worse, all words within files), and some are harder to compare (such as personal-file names).

This work attempted to answer these challenges by investigating 18 kinds of relatively easily calculable clues that could relate drives. They include both forensic artifacts obtained by scanning tools, such as email addresses and phone numbers, and metadata obtained from file directories, such as file sizes and words in file names. Most are routinely collected by tools such as SleuthKit. Processing can be made faster by filtering out data unlikely to be of forensic interest or by sampling.

This work tested association methods on a large corpus of drives using cosine similarity and divergence, and tried to establish significance thresholds. Similarity or divergence do not prove causation or communication since two associated drives may have obtained data from a common source. However, associations suggest structure in a corpus and that can be interesting in its own right.

This work is empirical research. Empirical methods may be rare in digital forensics, but are common and accepted in other areas of science and engineering. Empirical research can justify methods and algorithms by tying them to careful observations in the real world.

This paper will first review previous work. It then introduces the corpori studied, the clues used to compare drives, and formulae used for comparison. It then presents several kinds of results and makes some recommendations for associating drives.

2 Previous Work

Comparing drive data was first explored in [8] under the term "cross-drive analysis". That work compared email addresses, bank-card numbers, and U.S. social-security numbers to relate drives. This work has not been much followed up although it has been integrated into a broader investigative context in [11], combined with timeline analysis in [14], and applied to malware detection in [6]. Hashes on regular partitions of drive images [22] can relate all the data on drives including unallocated storage, but they are sensitive to variations in placement of data and their computation is time-consuming. Scanning drives for particular keywords [7] is also time-consuming. It would thus seem useful to evaluate the original idea of cross-drive analysis with a systematic approach to possible features and methods for comparison.

Previous work has measured similarities between documents for aiding online searches. That work focused heavily on word and word-sequence [7] distributions of documents, with some attention to weighting of word values and measuring the "style" of a document [13]. Much of this work uses the cosine similarity and the Kullback-Leibler divergence to be discussed; some uses the Jaccard distance and its variants [12]; some uses latent semantic indexing; and some uses the Dirichlet mixture model [20]. Although we used the Jaccard formula previously, it is crude because it treats all words as equally important. Latent semantic indexing only works for words with a rich semantics. The Dirichlet mixture model assumes the data is a superposition of distinct processes, something not often true for digital-forensic data. Document-comparison methods have been generalized to other kinds of data as in measuring similarity of files to known malware [21]. Generalization is important for digital forensics because many distinctive features of drive images such as IP addresses and file sizes are not words.

Similarity can also be based on semantic connections, but that is mainly useful for natural-language processing and we do not address it here. Note that similarity of drives is different from the similarity between artifacts on the same drive suggested by colocation and format similarity, a lower-granularity problem addressed elsewhere [18].

Usually the goal of analysis of forensic links is to build models of social networks [5, 25, 26]. Degree of association can be thresholded to create a graph, or the inverse of similarity can be used as an approximate distance and the points fitted to a metric space as we will discuss. Associated data can also be aggregated in a forensic integration architecture [15] to enable easier systematic comparison.

3   Data Used in Experiments

This work used five corpori. The main one was images of 3203 non-mobile drives of the Real Data Corpus (RDC) [9], a collection obtained from used equipment purchased in 32 non-US countries around world over 20 years, of which 95% ran the Windows operating system. A second corpus was the 411 mobile devices from the RDC, research sponsors, and our school. A third corpus was 236 randomly selected classroom and laboratory computers at our school (metadata and hash values only). In total we had 3850 images of which 977 had no identifiable operating system though possibly artifacts. Artifact data was obtained for the RDC with the Bulk Extractor open-source tool [4] for email, phone, bank-card, GPS, IP-address, URL, keyword-search, zip-file, and rar-file information.

The Mexican subcorpus of the RDC, 177 drives in eight batches purchased in Mexico, was analyzed to provide the more easily visualized results shown later in this paper. Also studied was the separate M57 patent corpus [24], a collection of 83 image "snapshots" over time for a set of machines with scripted usage. Its snapshots on different days provide a good test of high-similarity situations. All five corpori are publicly available under some access restrictions.

4   Measuring Drive Associations

4.1   Clues to Associations

The experiments described below focused on clues from artifacts and metadata that are often routinely calculated in forensic investigations and do not require additional processing. Artifact clues (the first 11 below) were obtained with Bulk Extractor tool, and metadata clues (the remaining 7) were obtained with the Fiwalk open-source tool now included with SleuthKit (www.sleuthkit.org). Experiments were done both with the raw set of clues and with the subset after filtering to eliminate the likely uninteresting ones. Filtering methods are described below. In general, filtering of artifacts tried to eliminate vendor and organization contact data, fictional data, artificial data, and ambiguous data (such as "mark field" as a personal name). Filtering of metadata tried to eliminate software-associated files not containing personal information. These filtering criteria are appropriate for criminal and intelligence (but not malware) investigations. The clues were:

- Em: Email addresses, found by Bulk Extractor's "email" plugin. Filtering was done using a stoplist (exclusion list) of 500,000 addresses found by NIST in their National Software Reference Library, plus filtering of clues whose rating was under a threshold by our Bayesian rating scheme [18] using factors such as the appearance of known personal names, type of domain, and number of drives on which the name was found. Bayesian parameters were calculated from a manually labeled training set.

- Ph: Phone numbers, found by Bulk Extractor's "phone" plugin. Bayesian filtering [17] excluded candidates based on factors such as informational area codes, artificiality of the numbers, and number of drives having that number.

- Pn: Personal names, found by our methods using dictionary lookup of known personal names and regular expressions applied to Bulk Extractor's "context" output [17]. Bayesian filtering eliminated candidates based on factors such as delimiters, use of dictionary words, and adjacency to email addresses.

- Sa: Street addresses, found using regular expressions on Bulk Extractor's "context" argument. Bayesian filtering used factors of the number of words, position in the argument, suitability of the numbers for addresses, capitalization of the words, length of the longest word, number of digits in the numbers, use of known personal names, use of words frequently associated with streets like "Main", "street", and "rd", use of "#", and membership in a stoplist of 2974 adverbs, conjunctions, prepositions, and common computer terms.

- Bn: Numeric strings that could be bank-account numbers, found using Bulk Extractor's "ccn" plugin. Error rates were high. Filtering excluded numbers not well delimited.

- Gp: Formatted GPS data found by Bulk Extractor's "gps" plugin. There were only a few instances in our corpori.

- Zi: Zip-compressed files found by Bulk Extractor. They are a weak clue to drive similarity since there are many frequently-seen zip archives. Filtering excluded those on 10 or more drives.

- Ra: Rar-compressed files found by Bulk Extractor, handled similarly to zip-compressed files.

- Uw: Words in the file names of Web links found by Bulk Extractor's "url" plugin. We did not consider numbers and words of directory names because they usually indicate infrastructure. Filtering excluded words in the Sa-clue stoplist.

- Ks: Keywords in searches found by Bulk Extractor's "url_searches" plugin (26% of which were from the browser cache). Filtering excluded those occurring on 10 or more drives.

- Ip: Internet IP addresses [2]. Filtering excluded addresses on ten or more drives. However, they have more to do with software and local configurations than URLs do, and thus do not help as much to identify the similar user activity which matters more in most forensic investigations.

- Ha: MD5 hash values computed on files. Filtering excluded files based on ten factors described below.

- Fn: Words in the file names on drives. Filtering used the ten factors.
- Ex: File extensions on the drive including the null extension. Filtering used the ten factors.
- Di: Immediate (lowest-level) directory names on the drive (with the null value at top level). Filtering used the ten factors.
- Fs: Logarithm of the file size rounded to the nearest hundredth. Comparing these suggests possible similar usage. Filtering used the ten factors.
- We: Week of the creation time on the drive. Its distribution describes the long-term usage pattern of the drive; [1] and [14] argue for the importance of timestamps in relating forensic data. Filtering used the ten factors.
- Ti: Minute within the week of the creation time. This shows weekly activity patterns. Filtering used the ten factors.

U.S. social-security numbers and other personal identification numbers were not included because our corpus was primarily non-US and the formats varied. Sector or block hashes [22] were not included because obtaining them is very time-consuming and results in large distributions. As it was, comparing of hash values on full files took considerably more time than analysis of any other clues.

Filtering of the metadata clues used ten negative criteria developed and tested in [16]: hash occurrence in the National Software Reference Library (NSRL), occurrence on five or more drives, occurrence of the file path on 20 or more drives, occurrence of the file name and immediate directory on 20 or more drives, creation of the file during minutes having many creations for the drive, creation of the file during weeks with many creations for the corpus, occurrence of an unusually common file size, occurrence in a directory whose other files are mostly identified as uninteresting by other methods, occurrence in a known uninteresting directory, and occurrence of a known uninteresting file extension. Filtering also used six overriding positive criteria indicating interestingness of a file: a hash value that occurs only once for a frequent file path, a file name that occurs only once for a frequent hash value, creation in an atypical week for its drive, an extension inconsistent with header analysis, hashes with inconsistent size metadata, and file paths including words explicitly tagged as interesting such as those related to secure file erasure. Files were filtered out if either they matched NSRL hashes or matched at least two negative criteria and none of the positive criteria. Applying the criteria provided a 77.4% reduction in number of files from the RDC (with only 23.8% due to using NSRL) with only a 0.18% error rate in failure to identify potentially interesting files, as estimated by manual investigation of a random sample [16].

Table 1 gives counts of the clues found in our main corpus of the RDC, mobile, and school drives. The first column gives the raw count of the clue, the second column the count after the filtering described, and the third column the number of drives with at least 10 different values of the clue (our threshold for sufficient data for comparison). The fourth column counts the sum of the number of distinct clue values per drive, meaning that it counts twice a clue on two drives but once a clue twice on a single drive.

Table 1. Counts of clues found on drives in our main corpus of 3850 drives.

Clue type	Count in our full corpus	Filtered count in our corpus	Number of drives having $\geq$ 10 values	Sum of distinct values over all drives in our filtered corpus
Email addresses (Em)	23,928,083	8,861,907	2,063	7,646,278
Phone numbers (Ph)	2,686,169	1,641,406	1,310	1,393,584
Personal names (Pn)	11,821,200	5,270,736	2,008	2,972,767
Street addresses (Sa)	206,506	135,586	782	88,109
Bank-card numbers (Bn)	6,169,026	5,716,530	671	332,390
GPS data (Gp)	159	159	4	121
Zip-compressed files (Zi)	11,993,769	4,218,231	1,302	3,886,774
Rar-compressed files (Ra)	574,907	506,722	654	382,367
Words in file names of Web links (Uw)	1,248,356	204,485	981	7,631
Keyword searches (Ks)	849,894	769,520	830	661,130
IP addresses (Ip)	51,349	50,197	168	45,682
File hashes (Ha)	154,817,659	8,182,659	2,477	2,091,954
Words in file names (Fn)	19,095,838	6,178,511	2,567	759,859
File extensions (Ex)	1,003,609	422,638	2,288	27,810
Immediate directories (Di)	3,332,261	653,212	2,094	107,808
File size ranges (Fs)	2,275,412	1,671,392	2,731	2,003
File creation week (We)	577,035	254,158	1,906	1,749
File creation minute within week (Ti)	252,786	195,585	2,080	169

4.2 Measuring Similarities and Divergences

Document comparison methods use a variety of association formulae. This work tested two of the best-known, the term-frequency inverse-document-frequency (TF-IDF) cosine similarity and the Kullback-Leibler divergence. We interpret a "document" as the set of clues on a drive of a particular type, e.g. the set of email addresses on a drive, so to compare drives we compare clue distributions (histograms) per drive. If s_{ij} means the similarity of drives i and j, k is a clue-value number out of M possible clue values, c_{ki} is the count of clue value k on drive i, n_k is the number of drives on which clue value k appears, and $w_k = \ln\left(\frac{D}{n_k}\right)$ is the classic inverse document-frequency weight for D drives total ([8] used a rarely-used logarithm-free formula), the cosine-similarity formula is:

$$s_{ij} = \left[\sum_{k=1}^{M}\left(c_{ki}c_{kj}w_k^2\right)\right] \Big/ \left[\sqrt{\sum_{k=1}^{M}\left(c_{ki}^2 w_k^2\right)}\right]\left[\sqrt{\sum_{k=1}^{M}\left(c_{kj}^2 w_k^2\right)}\right]$$

This ranges between 0 and 1 for nonnegative data such as counts. Drives have considerably diversity on most of the clues investigated, so cosine similarities close to 0 are common for random pairs of drives. An average similarity between two drives can be computed over all their similarities on clues. However, similarities on different clues do mean different things and it can important to distinguish them.

Hash values on files are the most time-consuming of the clues on which to compute similarity since there are so many. Computation time can be reduced by removing the hash values that occur on only one drive, about 61.2% of our main corpus, after counting them. This count should be included in the denominator of the formula, but does not affect the numerator.

[23] notes that cosine similarity despite its popularity does not satisfy intuitive notions of similarity in many cases since it is symmetric. Asymmetric similarity would make sense for a drive having many downloads from a larger drive so a larger fraction of the smaller drive is shared. So this work calculated an asymmetric measure of entropy-based Kullback-Leibler divergence on the clue distributions per drive, defined where N_i is is the total count of the first distribution and N_j is the total count of the second distribution as:

$$d_{ij} = \sum_{k=1}^{M}(c_{ki}/N_i)\log_2 \frac{\left(\frac{c_{ki}}{N_i}\right)}{\left(\frac{c_{kj}}{N_j}\right)}$$

Divergence is smaller for larger similarities in a rough inverse relationship. The formula is only meaningful when comparing clue values that the two distributions share, as we are computing for each value on drive j the similarity of its count to the count on drive i. Thus N_i should be defined as the total count on drive i of items also on drive j.

Since divergence is directional, the minimum of the divergences in the two directions provides a single consensus value of association since the smaller divergence indicates the stronger association. Also note that similarity and divergence are only meaningful with sufficient data, so at least 10 distinct clue values on each drive were required to compare two drives in our experiments.

5   Results

5.1   Comparing Similarity and Divergence

A large cosine similarity generally means a low divergence, and vice versa, so a question is to what degree they measure different things. However, attempts to fit a formula from one to the other were unsuccessful with our data for the weighted average similarity and the weighted average divergence of the clues. We tried the simplest possible formulae that could apply to an inverse relationship: $s = -c_1 d + c_2$, $s = c_1/(d + c_2)$, $s = c_1/\left((d + c_2)^2 + c_3\right)$, $s = \frac{c_1}{\left(\sqrt{d + c_2} + c_3\right)}$, and $s = \frac{c_1}{(\log(d + c_2) + c_3)}$; in each case a better least-square fit was obtained from $s = c_1$. We interepret this as meaning that similarity and divergence in general measure different things for our data, and it is useful to compute both. However, the fit did vary with clue. On the filtered data, the Pearson correlation coefficient between similarities and divergences was 0.744 for phone numbers, 0.679 for street addresses, and 0.659 for email addresses, but 0.451 for personal names and 0.332 for hash values. The last makes sense because divergence rates highly the strong subsetting relationships between drive files whereas similarity does not.

5.2   Clue Counts Per Drive

Histograms can be computed on the number of clue values per drive. Many of these histograms approximated normal curves when the logarithm of clue count was plotted against the logarithm of the number of drives, but with an additional peak on the left side representing drives mostly lacking the clue. Exceptions were for street addresses (uniform decrease with no peak) and time within the week (two peaks at ends of the range), the latter probably reflecting the difference between servers and other machines.

5.3   Significance Tests of Clue Similarity

An important question is the significance of values of cosine similarity. Figure 1 shows average similarities for the 10 artifact clues and Fig. 2 shows average similarities for the 8 metadata clues, broken down by corpus. The filtering was described in Sect. 4.1; GPS data was insufficient and was excluded. Two controls were obtained by taking 5000 random samples from the distribution of each of the clue values over all drives with sample sizes approximating the distribution of clue counts over all drives. Thus the controls represent similarity values of completely uncorrelated random drives of the same total sizes as our corpus. Results were similar for divergences but inverted.

The corpori show significantly more correlation than the controls, especially the school computers since they are centrally managed. The average observed similarities in our corpori are so far above the controls that they are definitely significant even lacking ground truth about drive associations. Note also that unfiltered data shows more similarities than the filtered data, most noticeably for file size (Fs) and file name (Fn), likely due to its larger number of spurious correlations. Note also that filtering does not affect all clues equally.

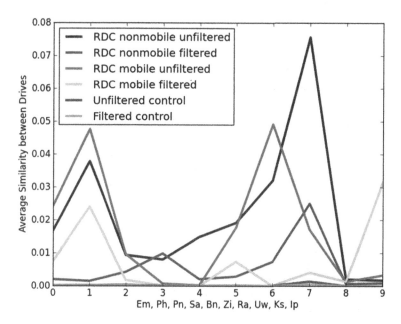

Fig. 1. Average similarities for artifact clues.

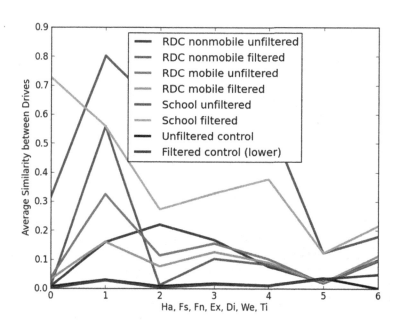

Fig. 2. Average similarities for metadata clues.

The variances of the average similarities were significantly larger than the means, due to the large number of random pairs that had zero similarity. Thus the similarity distributions are not Poisson. Nonetheless, we can provide significance thresholds for similarity for each of the 18 clues by taking three standard deviations above the mean (Table 2), a standard statistical significance threshold. This table is based on the RDC data, which should be a good model for many broad corpori because of its diversity. The first two rows give thresholds for unfiltered distributions, and the last two for filtered distributions.

Table 2. Recommended thresholds of significance for similarity between drives, for abbreviations defined in Sect. 4; "UF" means unfiltered data and "F" means filtered data.

EmUF	PhUF	PnUF	SaUF	BnUF	GpUF	ZiUF	RaUF	UwUF
.213	.331	.161	.163	.322	1	.259	.423	.639
KsUF	IpUF	HaUF	FnUF	ExUF	DiUF	FsUF	WeUF	TiUF
.062	.033	.173	.300	.756	.522	.763	.301	.429
EmF	PhF	PnF	SaF	BnF	GpF 1	ZiF	RaF	UwF
.106	.081	.148	.194	.121		.121	.226	.332
KsF	IpF	HaF	FnF	ExF	DiF	FsF	WeF	TiF
.043	.031	.166	.170	.539	.614	.521	.189	.416

Table 3 shows average similarity by country code over all clues, a useful inverse measure of the diversity of our acquired drives by country. Ratios of average similarities of metadata clues for undeleted versus deleted files were 1.304 for Fn, 1.471 for Ex, 1.202 for Di, 1.121 for Fs, 0.454 for We, and 0.860 for Ti. So file deletion status mattered too for metadata clues; artifact clues were rarely within files.

Table 3. Average similarities as a function of the most common country codes.

	AE	AT	BD	BS	CN	IL	IN	MX	MY	PK	PS	SG	TH	UK
Count	124	48	77	34	807	336	716	176	78	93	139	206	188	33
Av. sim.	.213	.042	.009	.051	.006	.025	.066	.031	.088	.024	.115	.007	.043	.065

5.4   The Effects of Sampling on Similarities

When the primary goal is to find drive pairs with high similarities, processing time can be reduced by comparing random samples of the clues on the drives. Table 4 shows the average effects over five random samples, each with sampling rates of 0.3, 0.1, and 0.03, on the similarities of our filtered RDC corpus for three artifact clues and three metadata clues. Sampling generally decreased the similarities of drives and effects showed little variation between samples. The artifact clues and file name words were more sensitive to sampling rates due to the smaller counts in their distributions. Judging by this table, a 0.3 sampling rate will obtain 80% of the original similarity for many clues and should be adequate; file extensions, however, could be accurately sampled at a much lower rate.

Table 4. Average effects of random sampling on similarities of particular clues.

Clue	Sampling rate	Mean original similarity	Mean similarity of samples	Standard deviation of samples
Email address (Em)	0.3	0.00063	0.00047	0.00002
	0.1		0.00034	0.00002
	0.03		0.00024	0.00001
Phone number (Ph)	0.3	0.00070	0.00053	0.00001
	0.1		0.00040	0.00002
	0.03		0.00033	0.00003
Personal name (Pn)	0.3	0.00444	0.00380	0.00005
	0.1		0.00321	0.00007
	0.03		0.00256	0.00005
File extension (Ex)	0.3	0.13435	0.14290	0.00051
	0.1		0.14812	0.00069
	0.03		0.14856	0.00083
File name (Fn)	0.3	0.02394	0.02127	0.00007
	0.1		0.01684	0.00009
	0.03		0.01191	0.00008
File size (Fs)	0.3	0.19609	0.19098	0.00068
	0.1		0.16597	0.00049
	0.03		0.13258	0.00091

5.5   Correlations Between Clue Similarities

Pearson correlations were measured between the similarities of different clues as a measure of clue redundancy. Table 5 shows the results for main corpus without filtering, excluding GPS, bank-card, and rar files which did not occur frequently enough to be reliable in this comparison, and excluding drives for which there was no data for the clue. The metadata clues (the last seven) were more strongly inter-associated than the artifact clues, though there was a cluster for email addresses (Em), phone number (Ph), personal names (Pn), and (interestingly) zip files (Zi). The redundancy between the metadata clues suggests if we had to choose one, we should compare file extensions since they are easiest to extract and require little space to store. Similarly, the weaker redundancy between the artifact clues suggests we compare email distributions because they are frequent artifacts, are easy to collect with few errors, and require little space to store. Of course, each investigation can assign its own importance to clues, as for instance an investigation of a crime in a business might assign higher importance to phone numbers. Note that IP addresses were uncorrelated with the other clues, suggesting that using them for link analysis [2] rarely reveals anything for unsystematically collected corpori like the RDC, and this is likely true for the closely associated MAC addresses as well. As for processing times for clues, the times in minutes on a Gnu Linux 3.10.0 64-bit X86 mainframe for the total of extraction and comparison using Python programs were Em 726, Ph 1010, Pn 556, Sa 8, Zi 1, Uw 15, Ks 54, Ip 1, Ha 1150, Fn 108, Ex 112, Di 1501, Fs 355, We 41, and Ti 54.

Table 5. Pearson correlations for similarities of pairs of major clues over the unfiltered RDC and school data. Abbreviations are defined in Sect. 4.1.

	Em	Ph	Pn	Sa	Zi	Uw	Ks	Ip	Ha	Fn	Ex	Di	Fs	We	Ti
Em	1	.29	.63	.06	.18	.03	−.01	.00	.07	.06	.02	.05	−.01	−.08	−.22
Ph		1	.35	.09	.35	.13	−.02	−.01	.10	.10	.10	.12	.06	.09	.03
Pn			1	.11	.24	.05	−.01	.00	.09	.07	.04	.07	.02	.09	.03
Sa				1	.03	−.01	−.01	−.02	.05	.05	.03	.04	.02	.02	.03
Zi					1	.18	−.02	−.01	.05	.06	.07	.09	.04	.06	.01
Uw						1	−.03	−.01	.03	.04	.04	.07	.02	.02	−.03
Ks							1	.00	−.01	−.01	−.03	−.02	−.03	−.01	−.03
Ip								1	.00	.00	−.01	−.01	−.01	−.01	−.01
Ha									1	.67	.35	.49	.31	.53	.31
Fn										1	.50	.64	.45	.36	.23
Ex											1	.71	.67	.26	.24
Di												1	.54	.36	.25
Fs													1	.18	.19
We														1	.44
Ti															1

5.6 Comparing Drive Snapshots Over Time

The M57 corpus [24] was studied to see how clues change over time. M57 data is from a managed experiment simulating four employees in a scenario in a patent office over a month, one image per day except for weekends and holidays. Figures 3 and 4 show the average similarity of unfiltered clues over all drive-image pairs as a function of number of days between them (forward or backward) on the same drive. Using unfiltered data was important because these images had many initial similarities and frequent occurrence of a clue is a reason for filtering it out. Street-address, GPS, Zip, and Rar data are omitted because of low occurrence rates. Clue similarities decreased over time (especially artifact clue similarities), though they still remained larger than those for the random drives shown in Sect. 5.3. By contrast, data from different drives in the M57 corpus on successive days showed no trends over time, despite the efforts of the scenario to make them relate. We infer that artifact self-similarity decays significantly over days because of frequent overwriting of caches which are the source of many artifacts. However, note these drives had little user data beyond experimental data, and likely show a stronger decay rate than the RDC drives obtained over a 20-year period yet having much stronger similarities than random control comparisons.

5.7 Visualizing Drive Similarities and Divergences

Investigators find it helpful to visualize associations of drives. To do this, we optimized locations in a two-dimensional space to fit distances computed from the similarities and divergences, ignoring similarities under a threshold and divergences over a threshold. This is an instance of the "embedding problem" in applied mathematics [19] which

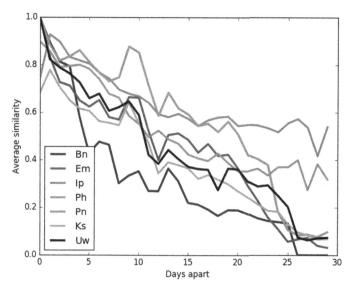

Fig. 3. Average similarity of artifact clues in the M57 corpus on the same drive a specified number of days apart in either direction.

tries to map a highly dimensional space to fewer dimensions. The formula with lowest error of fit from similarity to distance from systematic testing on the filtered data in our main corpus was $D = (-\ln(s))^{0.2 + (10*T)}$ where D is distance, s is similarity, T is the threshold, and (by experiment) T = 0.4. Similarly, the best formula found for relating divergences to distances was $D = d^{0.5T}$ where d is the divergence for T < 3. Distance errors averaged around 0.4 for both similarities and divergences. Optimization assigned random locations to start, used an attraction-repulsion algorithm to move locations repeatedly to improve ratios of calculated distances to target distances, then plotted the final locations. Specifically, the algorithm sought (x_i, y_i) pairs to minimize this formula over N drives where D_{ij} is the desired distance between locations i and j:

$$\sum_{i=1}^{N} \sum_{\substack{j\,where \\ D_{ij} < D_{min}}}^{N} \left| log \left[\frac{\sqrt{(x_i - x_j)^2 + (y_i - y_j)^2}}{D_{ij}} \right] \right|$$

Location optimization used a version of the familiar delta rule for machine learning where changes to the coordinates were proportional to a learning factor (0.1 worked well in these experiments), the distance between the points, and the log ratios shown above. 20 rounds of optimization were done, followed by rerandomization of the drive locations whose error exceeded a threshold (averaging about 11% of the locations), followed by another 20 rounds of optimization. Rerandomization gave a second chance to drives that were assigned poor initial locations. A minimum-similarity or maximum-divergence threshold can improve optimization speed by excluding weakly associated

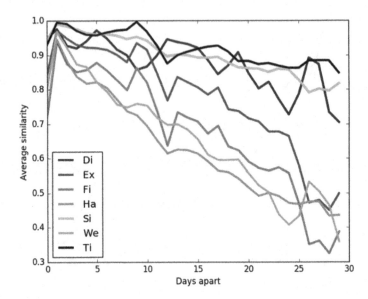

Fig. 4. Average similarity of metadata clues in the M57 corpus on the same drive a specified number of days apart.

drive pairs from this optimization. For instance, setting a threshold of greater than 0.1 for the average clue similarity for a drive reduced the number of drive pairs considered from 177*176/2 = 15,576 to 818 on our Mexican subcorpus.

Figure 5 shows an example visualization of the similarities of the unfiltered hash-value distributions of the 177 Mexican drives, and Fig. 6 shows their divergences. Colors and shapes represent the eight batches in which drives were acquired, which are only weakly correlated with distances though there are several closely related pairs. A stronger cluster emerges with the divergences. Since random starting locations are chosen, the display may appear rotated or inverted between two runs on the same input.

Figure 7 visualizes the similarities of the distributions of the hash values for the unfiltered M57 files. Colors and shapes indicate the users here, and their drives are well separated, with some spread involving the early snapshots and two kinds of usage by the user indicated with the green diamonds.

Our estimated distances can be used for clustering directly [3]. Graphs can also be built from this data by drawing edges between nodes closer than a threshold distance. Then a variety of algorithms can analyze the graphs. For instance, if we set a threshold of 0.5 on the hash-value similarity for the filtered Mexican drives, our software identifies a clique of 24 drives. Checking the data manually did confirm this was a likely clique and found many similarities between its drives. Our software also checks for commonalities in each clique; for that example, it noted that the drives in that 24-drive clique are all Windows NT with a hash-value count after filtering from 603 to 1205.

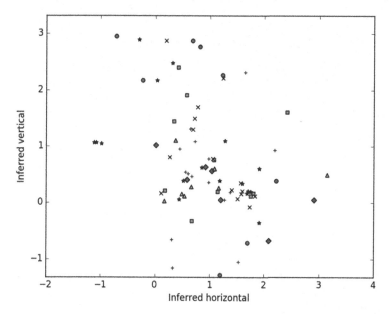

Fig. 5. Visualization of the unfiltered Mexican drives based on similarities of the hash-value distributions after optimization; color and shape code the batch out of 8.

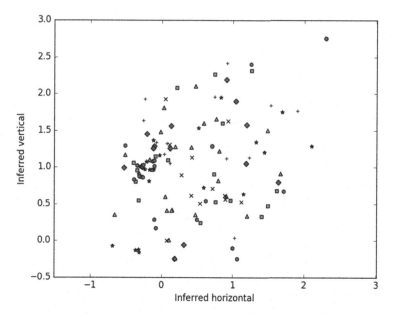

Fig. 6. Visualization of the unfiltered Mexican drives based on divergences of the hash-value distributions after optimization; color and shape code the batch out of 8.

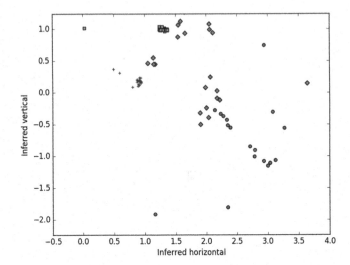

Fig. 7. Visualization of the M57 drives based on similarities of the hash-value distributions after optimization; color and shape code the simulated users out of 4.

6 Conclusions

This work has shown how computing a few characteristics of drives can be used to infer associations, even if the clues are quite subtle and the drive owners are not aware of it. Both the cosine similarity and the Kullback-Leibler divergence showed useful results with some differences between them. Thresholds of significance for similarity were provided on 18 clues for a large corpus. The clues differ in computational requirements, accuracy, redundancy, and investigative value, however, so we have provided some data to enable an intelligent choice of clues for investigators. If a quick comparison of drives is desired, comparing email artifacts (sampled at a 0.3 rate) as an indicator of contacts and file extensions (sampled at a 0.03 rate) as an indicator of usage type were adequate. Hash-value comparisons were time-consuming with few benefits over faster clues, and are thus not recommended.

We also showed the effects of filtering of data before computing similarity, which tended to decrease spurious similarities. We also discussed the effects of the passage of time on the similarity of images from the same drive, and provided a visualization technique in two dimensions for overall similarities and divergences. As drive data is increasingly erased or encrypted before forensic analysis, this kind of broad survey will become increasingly difficult to accomplish, so it is valuable to do now. Our results reflect general principles of what software and people store on drives, and will continue to be valid for a number of years.

Acknowledgements. This work was supported by the Naval Research Program at the Naval Postgraduate School under JON W7B27. The views expressed are those of the author and do not represent the U.S. Government. Edith Gonzalez-Reynoso and Sandra Falgout helped.

References

1. Abe, H., Tsumoto, S.: Text categorization with considering temporal patterns of term usages. In: Proceedings of IEEE International Conference on Data Mining Workshops, pp. 800–807 (2010)
2. Beverly, R., Garfinkel, S., Cardwell, G.: Forensic caving of network packets and associated data structures. Digital Invest. **8**, S78–S89 (2011)
3. Borgatti, S., Everett, M.: Models of core/periphery structures. Soc. Netw. **21**(4), 375–395 (2000)
4. Bulk Extractor 1.5: Digital Corpora: Bulk Extractor [software] (2013). digitalcorpora.org/downloads/bulk_extractor. 6 Feb 2015
5. Catanese, S., Fiumara, G., A visual tool for forensic analysis of mobile phone traffic. In: Proceedings ACM Workshop on Multimedia in Forensics, Security, and Intelligence, Firenze, Italy, October 2010, pp. 71–76 (2010)
6. Flaglien, Anders, Franke, Katrin, Arnes, Andre: Identifying Malware Using Cross-Evidence Correlation. In: Peterson, Gilbert, Shenoi, Sujeet (eds.) DigitalForensics 2011. IAICT, vol. 361, pp. 169–182. Springer, Heidelberg (2011). https://doi.org/10.1007/978-3-642-24212-0_13
7. Forman, G., Eshghi, K., Chiocchetti, S.: Finding similar files in large document repositories. In: Proceedings of 11th ACM SIGKDD International Conference on Knowledge Discovery in Data Mining, Chicago, IL, US, August 2005, pp. 394–400 (2005)
8. Garfinkel, S.: Forensic feature extraction and cross-drive analysis. Digital Invest. **3S**, S71–S81 (2006)
9. Garfinkel, S., Farrell, P., Roussev, V., Dinolt, G.: Bringing science to digital forensics with standardized forensic corpora. Digital Invest. **6**, S2–S11 (2009)
10. Jones, A., Valli, C., Dardick, C., Sutherland, I., Dabibi, G., Davies, G.: The 2009 analysis of information remaining on disks offered for sale on the second hand market. J. Digital Forensics Secur. Law **5**(4) (2010). Article 3
11. Mohammed, H., Clarke, N., Li, F.: An automated approach for digital forensic analysis of heterogeneous big data. J. Digital Forensics, Secur. Law **11**(2) (2016). Article 9
12. Nassif, L., Hruschka, E.: Document clustering for forensic analysis: an approach for improving computer inspection. IEEE Trans. Inf. Forensics Secur. **8**(1), 46–54 (2013)
13. Pateriya, P., Lakshmi, Raj, G.: A pragmatic validation of stylometric techniques using BPA. In: Proceedings of International Conference on The Next Generation Information Technology: Confluence, pp. 124–131 (2014)
14. Patterson, J., Hargreaves, C.: The potential for cross-drive analysis using automated digital forensic timelines. In: Proceedings of 6th International Conference on Cybercrime Forensics and Training, Canterbury, NZ, October 2012 (2012)
15. Raghavan, S., Clark, A., Mohay, G.: FIA: an open forensic integration architecture for composing digital evidence. In: Proceedings of International Conference of Forensics in Telecommunications, Information and Multimedia, pp. 83–94 (2009)
16. Rowe, N.: Identifying forensically uninteresting files in a large corpus. EAI Endorsed Trans. Secur. Safety **16**(7) (2016). Article e2
17. Rowe, N.: Finding and rating personal names on drives for forensic needs. In: Proceedings of 9th EAI International Conference on Digital Forensics and Computer Crime, Prague, Czech Republic, October 2017
18. Rowe, N., Schwamm, R., McCarrin, M., Gera, R.: Making sense of email addresses on drives. J. Digital Forensics Secur. Law **11**(2), 153–173 (2016)

19. Sippl, M., Scheraga, H.: Solution of the embedding problem and decomposition of symmetric matrices. In: Proceedings of National Academy of Sciences, USA, vol. 82, pp. 2197–2201, April 1985
20. Sun, M., Xu, G., Zhang, J., Kim, D.: Tracking you through DNS traffic: Linking user sessions by clustering with Dirichlet mixture model. In: Proceedings of 20th ACM International Conference on Modeling, Analysis, and Simulation of Wireless and Mobile Systems, Miami, FL, US, November 2017, pp. 303–310 (2017)
21. Tabish, S., Shafiq, M., Farooq, M., Malware detection using statistical analysis of byte-level file content. In: Proceedings of ACM Workshop on Cybersecurity and Intelligence, Paris, France, June 2009, pp. 23–31 (2009)
22. Van Bruaene, J.: Large scale cross-drive correlation of digital media. M.S. thesis, U.S. Naval Postgraduate School, March 2016
23. Whissell, J., Clarke, C.: Effective measures for inter-document similarity. In: Proceedings of 22nd ACM International Conference on Information and Knowledge Management, pp. 1361–1370 (2013)
24. Woods, K., Lee, C., Garfinkel, S., Dittrich, D., Russell, A., Kearton, K.: Creating realistic corpora for security and forensic education. In: Proceedings of ADFSL Conference on Digital Forensics, Security, and Law, pp. 123–134 (2011)
25. Zhao, S., Yu, L., Cheng, B.: Probabilistic community using link and content for social networks. IEEE. Access **PP**(99), 27189–27202 (2017)
26. Zhou, D., Manavoglu, E., Li, J., Giles, C., Zha, H.: Probabilistic models for discovering e-communities. In: Proceedings of WWW Conference, 23–26 May 2006, Edinburgh, Scotland, pp. 173–182 (2006)

Artefact Correlation

Digital Forensics Event Graph Reconstruction

Daniel J. Schelkoph$^{(\boxtimes)}$, Gilbert L. Peterson, and James S. Okolica

Air Force Institute of Technology (AFIT), 2950 Hobson Way,
Wright-Patterson AFB, OH 45433, USA
{daniel.schelkoph,gilbert.peterson,james.okolica}@afit.edu

Abstract. Ontological data representation and data normalization can provide a structured way to correlate digital artifacts and reduce the amount of data that a forensics investigator needs to process in order to understand the sequence of events that happened on a system. However, ontology processing suffers from large disk consumption and a high computational cost. This paper presents Property Graph Event Reconstruction (PGER), a data normalization and event correlation system that utilizes a native graph database to store event data. This storage method leverages zero index traversals. PGER reduces the processing time of event correlation grammars by up to a factor of 9.9 times over a system that uses a relational database based approach.

Keywords: Graph database · Digital forensics · Property graph
Ontology · Event reconstruction

1 Introduction

With society's ever-increasing reliance on technology, the demand for digital forensics has risen significantly. This is noted in the 2017 Bureau of Labor Statistics ten-year job outlook figures for the related fields of Forensic Technicians (up 17%) [2] and Information Security Analysts (up 28%) [3]. Part of this need is driven by the time-consuming task of manual data correlation required for digital forensics investigations [7].

One potential approach for automating data correlation is to leverage an ontology [5]. An ontology creates standardized data structures for events, allowing for relationships between heterogeneous data sources and creates data that is highly connected, representing a graph-like structure. Using expert rules, certain patterns (or subgraphs) can be identified to combine data into higher-level events [7]. Current approaches leverage the Resource Description Framework (RDF) from the Ontological Web Language (OWL) as a storage medium [6]. OWL formatted data is stored as tables in a relational database. However, identifying patterns in a graph using a relational database can be slow; finding an adjacent node in the graph representation of an ontology is an $O(log_2 n)$ problem [17].

© ICST Institute for Computer Sciences, Social Informatics and Telecommunications Engineering 2019
Published by Springer Nature Switzerland AG 2019. All Rights Reserved
F. Breitinger and I. Baggili (Eds.): ICDF2C 2018, LNICST 259, pp. 185–203, 2019.
https://doi.org/10.1007/978-3-030-05487-8_10

The presented Property Graph Event Reconstruction (PGER) tool provides fast correlations by leveraging a property graph database to speed graph traversals. Utilizing the native graph property of zero-index traversal, finding an adjacent node can be accomplished in constant time. This provides a substantial speed increase. PGER has been programmed to abstract forensics events from expert generated inference rules or machine generated rules provided by the Temporal Event Abstraction and Reconstruction (TEAR) tool [16].

In testing, PGER was able to correctly identify 65/67 startup and shutdown events based on an 8 statement expert ruleset. Additionally, PGER automated the correlation of web history and downloaded data (18 statements) to determine the entry point of the file on the system and any activity involving the file on the host system. Finally, PGER was compared to a relational database approach by testing much longer (86 statements) machine generated ruleset that detect the opening of Microsoft Word. In this test, PGER performed 9.98 times faster.

2   Related Work

2.1   Event Reconstruction Techniques

Due to the ever-increasing amounts of data forensic examiners have to analyze, a focus of digital forensics research is to try and create an automated way to consolidate data and reconstruct events [15]. In addition, many forensic investigations are for legal proceedings with strict rules regarding evidence, so it is desirable that event reconstruction be the result of a formal theory [9]. Previous research has tried different methods to establish such a theory: finite state machines [9], machine learning [14], and inference rules [12, 19].

Finite State Machines. Finite state machines provide a mathematical foundation for forensic events, providing rigor to findings [9]. Finite state machines are constructed by working backwards from the final state and using expert knowledge to make transitions and states, eventually ending with the events that need to happen before the final state can be accomplished [13]. Unfortunately, the number of possible variations from each final state produce very large finite state machines and are hard to create by experts [6]. At times, the finite state machines may be shrunk by previous events or other evidential information [13]; however, this is currently a manual task and limits the usefulness of this process [6].

Machine Learning. Expert-created event patterns can be complex and time-consuming to create. Some researchers have tried using machine learning to automatically find patterns in data. In 2006, researchers proposed a neural network that found the execution of various sequences in Internet Explorer [14]. This neural network was able to reconstruct events with an accuracy of 90%. However, neural network techniques do not show how low-level actions are associated with other events to infer a high-level activity [6]. Since examiners were not able to explain why the neural network created a certain series of events, this technique is hard to use in evidential situations [7].

Temporal Event Abstraction and Reconstruction (TEAR) is another attempt at using machine learning [16]. Unlike neural networks, this method of pattern matching allows humans to confirm the identified patterns and trace the high-level events to the individual low-level events. Its algorithms create a hierarchy of events using pattern matching in order to represent a high-level event (See Fig. 1) [16]. At the lowest level are terms which represent an atomic event such as a registry key modification. Each term has an action, a type, and a regular expression to determine what events get a specific term label. A term representing a created file in a user's document directory would have an action of 'Created', a 'file' type, and a regular expression of '^.*/Documents/.*$'. The next level on the hierarchy is strings. Strings are composed of other strings and/or terms. Next, production rules consist of both terms and strings, and provide a successful pattern for a high-level event. This helps represent multiple paths to the same high-level event. If a production rule with no parent finds a match in the data, then the high-level event occurred.

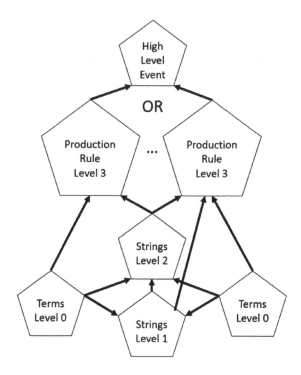

Fig. 1. Temporal event abstraction & reconstruction hierarchy.

2.2   Inference Rules

Inference rules allow forensic tools to reconstruct events by applying rules to existing information from the device image. This method performs similarly to Expert Systems; some tools even use an Expert System directly [19]. The rules are used to find patterns in existing data and, if a rule matches a pattern, a reconstructed event is created. For instance, an inference rule could look for events that contributed to the insertion of a USB device [12]. If the rule triggers on the appropriate registry entries, it could create a new reconstructed event stating that the USB device was inserted. This technique requires well-structured ontological data because the applied rules rely on the semantics of the data [6]. In research, the FORE tool uses the expert system in the Jena Apache Framework [19]. The Semantic Analysis of Digital Forensic Cases (SADFC) uses the ORD2I ontology and queries on the dataset as its rule set. If a query matches a set of data, they are combined to form a reconstructed event [6]. A tool called Parallax Forensics (ParFor) uses its own tool to query data and functions similarly to SADFC [20]. PGER utilizes inference rules for its expertly generated ruleset.

2.3   Graph Databases

A graph database allows the user to interact with data as nodes and edges. This is much different from a traditional relational database that represents data as tables. Using a graph representation can result in performance benefits for connected data, but it is highly dependent on how the graph database model is constructed [17]. Each graph database model is on two spectrums: the data format and the processing method [17].

Although all graph databases represent a graph, each graph model has a data format on a spectrum between non-native and native [17]. Non-native storage converts nodes and edges to relational database tables or another format (e.g. document-based). This can be useful if the database is large, allowing for a straightforward way to shard the data over multiple servers [17]. For native storage, the graph is the storage mechanism. This can provide performance benefits for certain queries, as the database does not have to construct the graph before processing [17].

Graph databases are also distinguished by their processing method on the spectrum between non-native and native. This is how the graph handles all Create, Read, Update, Delete (CRUD) operations [17]. Non-native processing does not use a graph to conduct an operation. Instead, it deals directly with how the data is stored. This style can utilize performance benefits like indexes from relational or document databases [17]. Native processing utilizes a graph to perform CRUD operations, providing performance benefits unique to graph databases [18]. However, not all query operations are faster in a native graph database. Care must be taken to ensure that queries take advantage of the performance benefits.

One of the biggest performance benefits for native graph processing is the ability to perform an index free traversal [18]. In highly connected data, it is often useful to examine the relationships between different nodes. To determine if two pieces of data share a relationship, a traditional database (non-native processing) would need to perform a join on multiple tables. This would require at least two index-based searches with a runtime of $O(\log_2 n)$ [18]. To determine more complex relationships, like finding if a particular walk on a graph exists, the queries become even more complex and time-consuming. Native graph processing allows a search on related data (data incident to another piece of data) in constant time, otherwise known as an index free traversal [18]. Searching a graph for a particular walk (subgraph) can be much faster by processing in a native format.

Most ontological digital forensics research uses RDF and OWL to store event data. Forensic of Rich Events (FORE) [19], Digital Forensics Analysis Expression (DFAX) [5], and Ontology for the Representation of Digital Incidents and Investigations (ORD2I) [7] are all stored using these standards. OWL is typically stored as a non-native storage model; the previous examples use relational database tables to store all triples. This means that these databases do not have the ability for index-free traversal, making queries regarding graph structure time consuming [18].

neo4j is a labeled property graph that is stored in a native graph format [8]. One major difference between this model and RDF is the ability to store data in nodes, allowing for more compact graphs in certain instances [1]. neo4j also allows for index-free traversal of the graph, allowing queries to take advantage of relationships between nodes for rapid queries [18]. In fact, the main use of labeled property graphs is for rapid transactions [17].

3   Property Graph Event Reconstruction (PGER)

Property Graph Event Reconstruction (PGER) performs abstraction of user actions from digital media. It utilizes a labeled property graph to store ontological event data, leveraging the speed of index free traversals. Events are represented in terms of artifacts and relationships, making queries easier to understand and create. It also allows users to leverage quick path searching to quickly find subgraph patterns in event data. PGER is a combination of several tools, some were created specifically for PGER and others were re-purposed for PGER as shown in Table 1.

PGER accomplishes event reconstruction in four processing layers (Fig. 2). The first layer takes a device image and extracts events. The second layer converts the extracted events into ontological subgraphs stored in neo4j. The normalization layer ensures identical objects are represented by the same object. Finally, the abstraction layer uses either expert rules or a machine generated ruleset to extract higher-level events.

Each layer is designed as an atomic entity, allowing for independent operation. This design isolates versions of a database during testing or multiple cases so they can be processed in a pipeline-like fashion. Each forensics image is represented by a separate neo4j database and is run in a separate instance of a docker container. The next sections discuss the details of each processing layer.

Table 1. PGER Tool Origins.

PGER Step	Tool Name	Existing Tool	Created
Data Extraction	PLASO	X	
	TEAR Event Extractor	X	
Graph Conversion	Logstash	X	
	Logstash Parsers		X
	Python Script		X
Normalization	Normalizer		X
Abstraction	Expert Rules		X
	Application of TEAR Ruleset		X
	TEAR Ruleset	X	

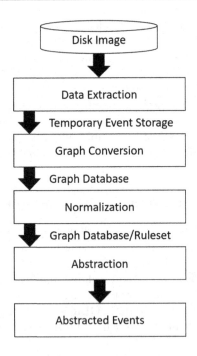

Fig. 2. PGER processing layers.

3.1 Data Extraction

The first processing layer takes a device image and converts it into an intermediate format. This format can then be converted to a graph database in another processing layer. There are two ways PGER can create this intermediate format: PLASO and TEAR event extraction.

PLASO (Plaso Langar Að Safna Öllu) converts a device image into a supertimeline and outputs the resulting data to an elastic database [11]. The other method of data extraction is utilizing the TEAR event extraction. It is a C++ program that takes the device image and creates a series of event files. File table, registry, and Windows events are among the data sources that are stored as CSV files. A Sqlite file for each browser is also extracted for web history.

3.2 Graph Conversion

Different event artifacts, such as registry keys or prefetch information, contain unique details that provide additional insight on the forensics image. Examples include the values of a registry key or the time an executable was run. The processing steps required are specific for each type of artifact.

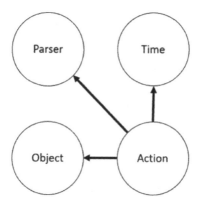

Fig. 3. Core subgraph.

The main purpose of the graph conversion processing layer is to convert heterogeneous event artifacts into a semantic, graph-based format. The base of the semantic format is the core subgraph (Fig. 3). This is based on the standard format found in SOSLA [16]. Every artifact is converted into a core subgraph and contains an action, an object, a parser, and a time. The time is a Unix timestamp and is unique in the database. This represents the time that an action occurred. Multiple artifacts that occur simultaneously are linked to the same time node. The action contains a description of an action that affects a digital object. The object is the digital object that is affected by the action and contains an identifying name of an object such as a URL, registry key, or file path. The identifying name is unique in the database. Since objects are unique, they are also indexed by neo4j, providing speed improvements during queries. If there are different objects with the same name, such as registry keys in user hives, the username is appended to the beginning of the identifying name. Each artifact subgraph is combined with the existing subgraphs in the neo4j database.

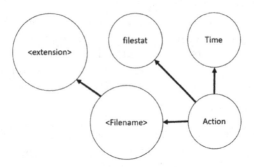

Fig. 4. File table subgraph.

File Table. The File Table parser produces at least one subgraph for each item in a system's file table. This subgraph adds an additional node to the core subgraph that represents the extension of the file object. The extension node is unique in the database. To help reduce congestion in the database, file table times (created, changed, modified, accessed) are combined into the same action if they occurred at the same time. The action description lists all the times that have changed during that timestamp ('Modified, Created Time Altered') and a new field is added to the action where each changed time type is an item in a list ("['Modified', 'Created']").

Web History. Each web browser has its own parser due to differences in history recording. In general, a parser records three different events: history, downloads, and keyword searches. Figure 5 details subgraph examples. History events add a visit ID to the core subgraph. Visit IDs link to other visit IDs to indicate a sequence of events in a browser. Downloaded events show the location of the downloaded object and the URL source. Keyword search subgraphs add a field in the action node that indicates the words used in a search.

Registry Keys. All parsed registry keys that are unique for each user (user-class.dat and ntuser.dat files) contain the core subgraph with the key value as the object and a node with an edge to the key indicating the owner. All other registry keys omit the user node in their subgraph. The action node contains a field that holds the value of the registry key. Registry keys that provide more information have an expanded subgraph.

Recent Apps (SOFTWARE/Microsoft/Windows/CurrentVersion/Search/RecentApps/) and User Assist (SOFTWARE/Microsoft/Windows/CurrentVersion/Explorer/UserAssist) registry keys help provide evidence of program execution [4]. Both keys are updated when a program is run to populate recently used programs lists in Windows. These entries use the registry subgraph but add an additional object node with an edge to the action, indicating the program specific program that was executed.

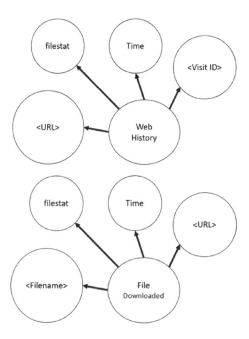

Fig. 5. Web history and download subgraphs.

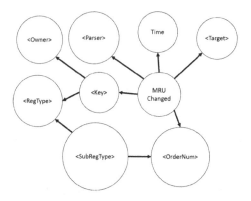

Fig. 6. MRU registry subgraph.

Most Recently Used (MRU) registry entries (SOFTWARE/Microsoft/Windows/CurrentVersion/Explorer/RecentDocs/) retain a list of recently used files for each extension (.doc, .jpg, etc) [4]. The recently used files for each extension are listed in ascending numerical order where 0 represents the most recently used file. The MRU subgraph (Fig. 6) captures this data by creating a sub-registry type node that represents the most recently used files of a particular extension. In Fig. 6, this is .ppt. The numerical order of an extension's MRU files are created as separate nodes to allow easy traversal of the files in order of use. There is also an additional object attached to the action node that was extracted from the value of the correct registry key and indicates the used file. The rest of the subgraph follows the standard registry subgraph.

Additional registry entries that can be processed are appcompatcache and shellbag keys. Like recent apps and users assist entries, appcompatcache helps provide evidence of program execution, updating registry values when a program is executed [4]. Shellbag entries maintain UI information for folders viewed in the Windows File Explorer [4]. These values can remain in the registry if the original directory is deleted, possibly providing additional information on the file system.

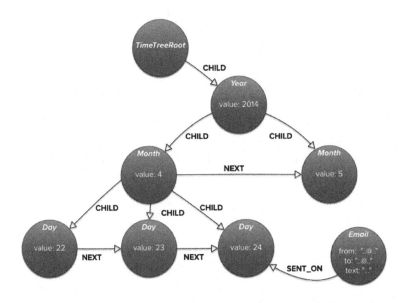

Fig. 7. Time tree format [10].

After an artifact has been transformed into a subgraph, neo4j performs a transformation of the subgraph centered on the time node. Using the timetree plugin from GraphAware, these time events are converted into a time tree (Fig. 7) [10]. The timestamp is divided into year, month, day, hour, minute, and second levels, and all actions are attached to the second nodes. This transformation allows queries to search for temporally adjacent events by following the next relationship.

3.3 Normalization

The next processing layer normalizes the neo4j database by combining objects that are the same but have a different identifying name. For example, MRU Registry Values only list the filename of the used file

(Snowball_Fighting(1).doc) in an object node where the file table entry for the same file will be listed in an object node using the whole path (C:/Users/user/Downloads/Snowball_Fighting(1).doc). In order to properly see all the actions that happen on an object, these nodes need to be combined. The normalization processing layer combines nodes if there is only one match. If there are multiple matches, the node is linked to the possible matches with the relationship called 'POSSIBLE_REAL_PATH'.

3.4   Abstraction

Abstracting low-level event data into higher-level events is the final processing layer. Abstraction in PGER uses two different sources: expert rules and data mined rulesets.

Expert Rules. Expert forensics knowledge rules extract high-level events from a sequence of low-level events. For example, if there is evidence of a program execution, and a file is accessed with an extension associated with the executable within a certain time window, it is likely that the two actions are related. These known sequences can be quantified into rules to find specific subgraphs. Examples of these patterns can be found in the subsequent paragraphs.

History of a File. A simple example of extracting information from the graph database is determining a file's history. Since every file is unique in the database, the specific node can be expanded to list all the actions that affect the file. This can be done with the following query:

```
1  MATCH (obj:object)
2  WHERE obj.filename = "<filename>"
3  MATCH (sec:Second)<-[:AT_TIME]-(act:action)--(obj)
4  OPTIONAL MATCH (obj)<-[:LINK_TARGET]-(lnkObj)--(
      lnkAct:action)
5  RETURN sec.time, collect(act.action), collect(lnkAct
      .action)
```

The first two lines find the desired object. The third line finds all the actions and times that affect the desired object. Line four gives the history of link files that are associated with the desired object.

Power Events. Using a combination of objects from the Windows event logs, power events can be determined (shutdown, startup, sleep). If enabled, the Windows Customer Experience Improvement (CEI) service will start and stop just before power events. The Windows Event Log service does the same. The Event Log also records the Windows Version and uptime when Windows powers on. Each of these events appear at every power event and serves as the baseline for power events for a given time window. Additional events may appear in the shutdown/startup process: Microsoft Windows Power Troubleshooter - System

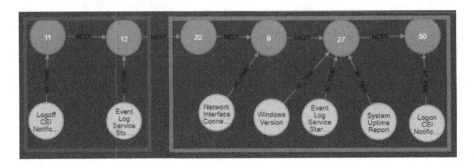

Fig. 8. Shutdown event (Left Box), startup event (Right Box).

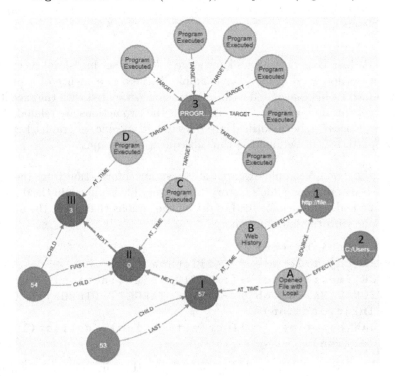

Fig. 9. Download/File system integration.

Returned from a Low Power State; Network Interface Connected/Disconnected; Microsoft Windows RestartManager - Starting/Ending Session. These optional events help increase the likelihood of a power event occurring.

Web History. Combining web history entries can show complex activities. As mentioned previously, there are three main types of data recorded in the graph: history, downloaded files, and keyword values. By chaining consecutive web visits using the visit IDs and time, a sequence of visits can be obtained. Furthermore, downloaded files can be tracked to the destination on the host file system where file history can be obtained (Fig. 9). This figure shows the web history entry (1) and the downloaded location of the file (2). The subgraph also shows that Microsoft Word opened using a prefetch file (3).

Combining Expert Rules. The previous abstractions can also combine together to create new layers of abstraction. Figure 9 is a basic concept of this idea. Both web history and file table information are combined to enrich an examiner's understanding of events that occurred. All actions nodes (A-D) describe the action the user took on artifacts 1–3: opened a file directly from the Firefox browser (A) from a specific URL (B), executing a program (C-D). The graph database is a great way to structure abstraction using a tree-like structure as a new node could be created, linking all actions A-D to this narrative.

3.5 Data Mined Ruleset

The second method of abstraction is to use machine generated rulesets created by Temporal Event Abstraction and Reconstruction (TEAR). These rulesets are much larger and more detailed than the rules generated by experts. For example, TEAR found 86 distinct patterns for the various ways Microsoft Word opens as accessing the program through a jump list or from a web browser affects different artifacts. While possible for an expert to categorize and detail every variation, it is extremely time consuming. To utilize a TEAR rulset, PGER performs a conversion of the strings and terms from TEAR relational database into a tree structure (See Fig. 1) that can then be converted into expert rules. These rules are then applied to the graph in order to produce the same results as TEAR.

4 Results

PGER provides a speedup for digital forensics artifact correlation and event reconstruction. The following tests compare PGER's ability to find events based on expert and machine generated rules compared to truth data and a performance comparison of PGER and a relational database implementation using a machine generated ruleset to find when Microsoft Word opens.

The test image was a 65 GB Window 10 image with sample activities that included: Web Browsing/Downloading Files from Microsoft Edge, Mozilla Firefox, and Google Chrome; Microsoft Office: Creation/Manipulation of Word, Excel and PowerPoint Files; Viewing Downloaded PDFs; Sleep, Startup, and Shutdown Sequences; Viewing image files; Manipulating files in Windows Explorer.

All tests were conducted on a machine with the following specifications: CPU - i3-6100U (2 Cores, 4 Threads), RAM - 12 GB, HDD - 250 GB Samsung 840 EVO SSD, OS - Ubuntu 16.04 LTS, Docker Version - 17.09, Python Version - 3.6, Elastic Stack Version - 5.5.2, neo4j Version - 3.2.2, PLASO Version - 1.5.1.

Table 2 lists details on the size of the resultant PGER graph.

Table 2. neo4j Database Parameters After Graph Conversion.

neo4j Database Size	656.18 MB
Node Count	1,069,671
Relationship Count	2,587,503
Processing Time	00:16:28

4.1 Expert Rule Results

The following tests evaluate PGER's ability to accurately abstract events using expert generated rules compared to the known activity on the device image. The first test finds all startup/shutdown events and the second test finds all files downloaded from a web browser.

Power Events. A power event represents a shutdown or startup on the forensics machine. To find the power events on the device image, a power event is primarily determined by the status of the CEI and Windows Log Services. If they are shutdown, it indicates a shutdown event; the opposite is also true. Startup also can contain optional Windows log entries to further bolster the evidence of a startup event.

Table 3. Power Event Sequence (UNIX Timestamps).

Start Time	End Time	Event
1491971379	1491971414	Startup
1491972643	1491972656	Shutdown
1491972859	1491972888	Startup
1492112687	1492112712	Startup
1492113771	1492114425	Shutdown

After applying rules to the dataset, a total of 65 shutdown events and 67 startup events were detected. There was apparently an error in the rules as two shutdown events were missing. After examination, there were two sequences that contained consecutive startup events. One such sequence is in Table 3.

After reviewing the actions between the two consecutive startup events using the query below, a Windows Update seemed to occur.

```
1  MATCH (sec:Second {time: 1491972888})
2  MATCH p = (sec)-[:NEXT*..500]->(:Second {time:
      1492112687})
3  UNWIND nodes(p) as secNode
4  MATCH (secNode)<-[:AT_TIME]-(act:action)-[:EFFECTS
      ]->(obj:object)
```

```
5  RETURN secNode.time, collect(act.action), collect(
     obj.filename)
```

Of the 5706 objects that had altered timestamps, 4830 matched the pattern C:/ Windows/WinSxS/*; these files are known to be related to Windows updates. The shutdown sequence during Windows updates differs from other shutdowns and do not include additions to the event logs.

Updates might also explain the large gap in the start and end times for some shutdown events. For example, the last event in the table has a difference of 654 s between its start and end times. Upon examination, several files are changed 361 s after the start of the event. These files match the pattern C:/Windows/WinSxS/ amd64_windows-defender-am-sigs or C:/ProgramData/Microsoft/Windows Defender /Definition Updates/. As a result, it appears that Windows Defender Definitions are updated before a shutdown. In future iterations, this needs to be captured as additions to the expert rules.

Table 4. Downloaded File Expert Rule Result.

Download Information	
Username	user
Download Time	1497574737
Filename	C:/Users/user/Downloads/Snowball_Fighting(2).doc
Shortened URL	http://files.geekdo.com/geekfile_download.php?

Web History	
Time	URL
1497574730	/filepage/28906/snowball-fighting-rules-word-doc
1497574732	/file/download/2hkk77tped/Snowball_Fighting.doc
All URLs start with https://www.boardgamegeek.com	

File History	
Time	Action
1497574765	Accessed, Created Time Altered
1497574767	Modified Time Altered
1497574768	Changed Time Altered
1499350036	Recent .doc Changed
1499350036	Recent Docs Changed

Combined Expert Rules. The downloaded files expert rule is a great example of utilizing many different low-level event types to create a complex abstraction. The expert rules combine the following: previous web history, URL source for the downloaded file, location of the download file on the forensics image, file history of the downloaded file and username responsible for modified registry keys. The desired subgraph is similar to Fig. 9.

Firefox history shows nine files were download from the browser in the image and that the rules found all nine entries. One example entry is contained in Table 4.

These tables highlight the insights gained through connected data and provides multiple corroborating artifacts. An examiner can see recent web history, the URL source, the file system destination for the downloaded file, and what actions took place on the downloaded file. PGER was able to perform this relationship-heavy query for all nine objects in 18 ms.

4.2   Machine Generated Application Results

Applying expert rules, as evidenced by the results above, can be an effective way to abstract data. However, the rules in the previous section are short, only matching 8–18 different events in a time window. Some user actions are incredibly hard to capture using expert knowledge alone due to the immense number of objects and events that affect the outcome. TEAR tackles this problem by using a machine to generate patterns for complex events. For example, TEAR extracted a combination of 86 different artifacts that can occur when Microsoft Word opens. Incorporating the TEAR method of finding high-level events into PGER is important to evaluate PGER's ability to abstract complex events.

The final evaluation tested PGER's ability to replicate the results produced by TEAR, which uses a relational database on the same dataset. Both processing time and accuracy in replicating TEAR's results were the criteria for evaluating PGERs performance.

Testing for both PGER and TEAR used the same device image, event extractor, and pre-processed ruleset. The ruleset was limited to opening Microsoft Word as the lone top-level rule. Terms that represented accessed prefetch files appeared in all term sequences. Since both tools used the same data extraction method, this step was ignored in both testing categories. Timing results were an average of three runs.

Processing Time. Performance of PGER is compared to the processing time of TEAR due to their differing storage methods for their ontologies; TEAR uses a relational database and PGER utilizes a property graph database. This test shows how a property graph database can have a significant effect on performance on forensics queries. To help further understand the comparison, the processing steps of TEAR and PGER are compared in next paragraph.

TEAR matches high-level events utilizing following steps:

1. Load event data from a SQLite database to memory
2. Apply terms to events, abstract terms to strings
3. Process the generated term list in chronological order. Find high-level events by matching a variant with the term list of the current time window.

To accomplish the same feat, PGER uses the graph conversion, normalization, and abstraction processing layers. Graph conversion and normalization

Table 5. PGER and TEAR Runtime Comparison (h:mm:ss).

TEAR Step	TEAR Time	PGER Step	PGER Time
1	0:29:52	Graph Conversion	0:16:28
		Normalization	
2	3:02:06	Build Ruleset Tree/Apply Terms	0:04:32
		Create Time Windows	
3	0:09:34	Find High-Level Events	0:01:12
Total Time	3:41:32		0:22:12

matches with TEAR's first step. PGER's abstraction layer accomplishes both steps 2 and 3. To provide a direct comparison, the PGER abstraction layer splits into two categories to better match TEAR's steps. The first group, corresponding to TEAR's second processing step, contains building the ruleset tree, term application, and time window creation. Finding high-level events corresponds with TEAR's third processing step. In both programs, steps 1 and 2 are only accomplished once per image as long as the same ruleset is applied. Table 5 compares TEAR and PGER runtimes.

Both PGER and TEAR found 12 instances of the event. PGER applies the machine generated ruleset to a forensics image in less time than TEAR. This advantage is shown the best in step 2 where the TEAR ruleset is constructed into a tree and used to find the objects that apply to each term. One significant factor in the processing time difference is that PGER does not abstract sets of terms into strings; PGER finds all high-level rules only as different compositions of terms. This results in longer comparisons between time windows and rulesets, but PGER filters time windows in step 3 that do not include terms that are in every variant. In this case, the difference is significant, eliminating nearly 80% of all time windows (From 10,178 to 2,444). If there were rules that did not filter out as many time windows, the PGER runtime to find high-level events (TEAR step 3) could increase by a factor of five. However, PGER would still provide a performance advantage over TEAR.

5   Conclusion and Future Work

PGER reduces the processing time of event correlation grammars by up to a factor of 9.98 over a relational database based approach by using a native graph processing and storage format. This allows users to leverage the advantages of a graph database without the cost of just-in-time assembly of a graph or the completion of many join statements. Utilizing a graph database also allows for more natural queries of ontological data, affording users the ability to find subgraphs by searching for path patterns. If an ontological language uses a non-native processing method, it may be beneficial to convert into a native graph before analysis. PGER can also match the accuracy of TEAR and provide an increase in processing speed by filtering time windows and not abstracting terms into strings. Finally, expert rules were applied to the database, providing useful information for the examiner. However, longer rules might be better created by machine pattern matching, like TEAR, due to the difficulty in codifying the execution of a large set of events and objects.

Future work includes evaluating PGER performance compared to a RDF datastore, test PGER at scale on larger device images, expanding the expert ruleset, and applying curation rules to TEAR rulesets.

Acknowledgments. The views expressed in this document are those of the author and do not reflect the official policy or position of the United States Air Force, the United States Department of Defense or the United States Government. This material is declared a work of the U.S. Government and is not subject to copyright protection in the United States.

References

1. Angles, R.: A comparison of current graph database models. In: Proceedings of IEEE 28th International Conference on Data Engineering Workshops, ICDEW 2012, pp. 171–177. IEEE (2012). https://doi.org/10.1109/ICDEW.2012.31
2. Bureau of Labor Statistics: Occupational Outlook Handbook: Forensic Science Technicians (2017). https://www.bls.gov/ooh/life-physical-and-social-science/forensic-science-technicians.htm
3. Bureau of Labor Statistics: Occupational Outlook Handbook: Information Security Analysts (2017). https://www.bls.gov/ooh/computer-and-information-technology/information-security-analysts.htm
4. Carvey, H., Hull, D.: Windows Registry Forensics, 2nd edn. Elsevier, Cambridge (2016). https://doi.org/10.1016/C2009-0-63856-3
5. Casey, E., Back, G., Barnum, S.: Leveraging CybOX^{TM} to standardize representation and exchange of digital forensic information. Digit. Investig. **12**(S1), S102–S110 (2015). https://doi.org/10.1016/j.diin.2015.01.014
6. Chabot, Y., Bertaux, A., Nicolle, C., Kechadi, M.T.: A complete formalized knowledge representation model for advanced digital forensics timeline analysis. Digit. Investig. **11**, S95–S105 (2014). https://doi.org/10.1016/j.diin.2014.05.009. http://www.sciencedirect.com/science/article/pii/S1742287614000528
7. Chabot, Y., Bertaux, A., Nicolle, C., Kechadi, T.: An ontology-based approach for the reconstruction and analysis of digital incidents timelines. Digit. Investig. **15**, 83–100 (2015). https://doi.org/10.1016/j.diin.2015.07.005
8. Chao, J., Graphista, N.: Graph Databases for Beginners: Native vs. Non-Native Graph Technology (2016). https://neo4j.com/blog/native-vs-non-native-graph-technology/
9. Gladyshev, P., Patel, A.: Finite state machine approach to digital event reconstruction. Digit. Investig. **1**(2), 130–149 (2004). https://doi.org/10.1016/j.diin.2004.03.001
10. GraphAware: GraphAware Neo4j TimeTree (2018). https://github.com/graphaware/neo4j-timetree
11. Guðjonssón, K.: Mastering the Super Timeline With log2timeline (2010). https://www.sans.org/reading-room/whitepapers/logging/mastering-super-timeline-log2timeline-33438

12. Hargreaves, C., Patterson, J.: An automated timeline reconstruction approach for digital forensic investigations. Digit. Investig. **9(Suppl.)**, S69–S79 (2012). https://doi.org/10.1016/j.diin.2012.05.006

13. James, J., Gladyshev, P., Abdullah, M., Zhu, Y.: Analysis of evidence using formal event reconstruction. Digit. Forensics Cyber Crime **31**, 85–98 (2010). https://doi.org/10.1007/978-3-642-11534-9

14. Khan, M.N., Mnakhansussexacuk, E., Wakeman, I.: Machine Learning for Post-Event Timeline Reconstruction. PGnet (January 2006), 1–4 (2006)

15. Marrington, A., Mohay, G., Clark, A., Morarji, H.: Event-based computer profiling for the forensic reconstruction of computer activity. AusCERT2007 R&D Stream **71**, 71–87 (2007). http://eprints.qut.edu.au/15579

16. Okolica, J.S.: Temporal Event Abstraction and Reconstruction. Ph.D. thesis, AFIT (2017)

17. Robinson, I., Webber, J., Eifrem, E.: Graph Databases, 2nd edn. O'Reilly Media Inc., Sebastopol (2015)

18. Rodriguez, M.A., Neubauer, P.: The graph traversal pattern. Computing Re-search Repository, pp. 1–18 (2010). https://doi.org/10.4018/978-1-61350-053-8, http://arxiv.org/abs/1004.1001

19. Schatz, B., Mohay, G., Clark, A.: Rich Event Representation for Computer Forensics. In: Asia Pacific Industrial Engineering and Management Systems APIEMS 2004, pp. 1–16 (2004)

20. Turnbull, B., Randhawa, S.: Automated event and social network extraction from digital evidence sources with ontological mapping. Digit. Investig. **13**, 94–106 (2015). https://doi.org/10.1016/j.diin.2015.04.004

Multi-item Passphrases: A Self-adaptive Approach Against Offline Guessing Attacks

Jaryn Shen[1], Kim-Kwang Raymond Choo[2], and Qingkai Zeng[1(✉)]

[1] State Key Laboratory for Novel Software Technology, Nanjing University, Nanjing, Jiangsu 210023, China
jarynshen@gmail.com, zqk@nju.edu.cn
[2] Department of Information Systems and Cyber Security, University of Texas at San Antonio, San Antonio, TX 78249-0631, USA
raymond.choo@fulbrightmail.org

Abstract. While authentication has been widely studied, designing secure and efficient authentication schemes for various applications remains challenging. In this paper, we propose a self-adaptive authentication mechanism, Multi-item Passphrases, which is designed to mitigate offline password-guessing attacks. For example, "11th July 2018, Nanjing, China, San Antonio, Texas, research" is a multi-item passphrase. It dynamically monitors items and identifies frequently used items. Users will then be alerted when there is need to change their passphrases based on the observed trend (*e.g.*, when a term used in the passphrase consists of a popular item). We demonstrate the security and effectiveness of the proposed scheme in resisting offline guessing attacks, and in particular using simulations to show that schemes based on multi-item passphrases achieve higher security and better usability than those using passwords and diceware passphrases.

Keywords: Offline guessing attacks · Self-adaptive · Authentication Passphrases

1 Introduction

Access control schemes, such as those based on biometrics, graphical passwords, and hardware tokens [1,11], are fundamental in ensuring the security of systems and data. Due to the associated benefits of using (textual) passwords (*e.g.*, low cost, and ease of use and implementation), the latter is the most commonly used form of authentication and likely to remain popular in real-world applications.

There have been a number of incidents where hashed passwords were exfiltrated or leaked due to the servers being compromised (*e.g.*, by exploiting existing vulnerability(ies) in the servers) [4,8]. As most user passwords are human-memorable with low entropy [14,24], it would also be easy to brute-force

© ICST Institute for Computer Sciences, Social Informatics and Telecommunications Engineering 2019
Published by Springer Nature Switzerland AG 2019. All Rights Reserved
F. Breitinger and I. Baggili (Eds.): ICDF2C 2018, LNICST 259, pp. 204–221, 2019.
https://doi.org/10.1007/978-3-030-05487-8_11

such passwords offline, particularly using advanced probabilistic password guessing/cracking techniques [13,15,17]. In other words, organizations can no longer rely on only *salt* and hashing to protect user passwords.

In this paper, we propose a self-adaptive approach, Multi-item Passphrases. A multi-item passphrase is a sequence of multiple items. For example, "3rd August 2005, Jack, wife, holiday, Maldives" is a multi-item passphrase. Bonneau *et al.* [3] explained that passphrases are vulnerable to guessing attacks in practice, because users select popular words in natural language. Our approach is designed to mitigate this limitation because Multi-item Passphrases can self-adaptively remove popular words. In other words, our approach builds on existing password-based authentication and hence, will be significantly less expensive for e-commerce organizations to adopt this approach (rather than one that requires a complete overhaul of the entire system).

Our approach monitors items that are being used and flags frequently used words in a self-adaptive way. The items in a multi-item passphrase can be input in a different order than initially enrolled. The proposed Multi-item Passphrases approach includes our self-adaptive algorithm, which is designed to recognize and remove popular items dynamically. To demonstrate the potential of this approach, we build three text password-based authentication systems for evaluation. Findings from the quantitative experiment show that multi-item passphrases achieve higher security and better usability than passwords and diceware passphrases. The participants also rated multi-item passphrases higher. We also evaluate participants' attitude towards frequent passphrase changes and summarize their remarks.

In the next section, we will describe the relevant background materials.

2   Background

Offline attackers are able to guess user private passwords correctly from the files of hashed passwords, mainly due to advances in computing technologies and the low entropy of the passwords (*e.g.*, users selecting easy-to-remember passwords and the set that comprises these passwords is small).

For simplicity, we consider a setting with two users, Alice and Bob. All the possible passwords in the password space constitute the set P. In theory, Alice can choose any password in P. In fact, Alice only selects those that are easy to remember in P, say set A. In other words, passwords in $\bar{A}$ (*i.e.*, $P - A$) are hard to remember for Alice, and hence Alice does not choose passwords in $\bar{A}$. The same can be said for Bob, where Bob does not choose passwords in $\bar{B} = P - B$, where B is the set of easy-to-remember passwords for Bob.

In reality, there are passwords that are deemed to be easy to remember by both Alice and Bob. Thus, Alice's password set overlaps Bob's: $A \cap B \neq \emptyset$, which is illustrated in Fig. 1a. If there are three users: Alice, Bob and Charlie, then these three users' password sets contain certain common passwords (see Fig. 1b). If there are more users, they are most likely to share common passwords (see Fig. 1c). This is evident from several real-world incidents [15,24]. The implication of this is that these commonly used passwords (the central dark circle in Fig. 1c) can then be used to facilitate password guessing, and this is also leveraged in password cracking tools such as John the Ripper.

Therefore, in this paper, we seek to remove the overlapping user password sets, such as the central dark circle in Fig. 1c.

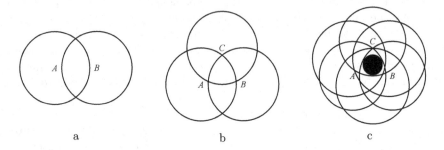

a   b   c

Fig. 1. (a) The area of circle A represents all potential passwords that Alice may choose, the area of circle B represents those that Bob may choose. Alice's password set overlaps Bob's: $A \cap B \neq \emptyset$. (b) Alice, Bob and Charlie's password sets contain common passwords: $A \cap B \cap C \neq \emptyset$. (c) Users' password sets contain common passwords. The central dark circle are the common passwords for all users.

Our proposed Multi-item Passphrases approach is based on the premise that if both Alice and Bob construct their passwords independently and in a way that both their potential password sets are different (*i.e.*, $A \cap B = \emptyset$), then the adversary will have no leverage in the password guessing. We will present the proposed approach in the next section.

3   Proposed Multi-item Passphrases Approach

Our approach seeks to identify and remove popular passwords from the password space.

3.1   Passphrase

There are a number of questions we need to consider. First, if a specific password is popular, should we remove the whole password or some characters in this password? If we do the former, how do we address other passwords that similar to this one and how do we define this kind of similarity? If the latter, which characters in this password should be removed? Additionally, there are only 95 printable characters in total, if we remove some characters, then the password space shrinks fast. Hence, we utilize passphrases instead of passwords.

A passphrase composes of items, and these are mainly English words. Common English words include nouns and noun phrases, such as "sun", "flower",

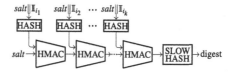

Fig. 2. The process from a user's passphrase to the final digital digest. The items in a passphrase are sorted in this process.

"Romeo and Juliet". As there are significantly more numerals and some numbers are private to users (*e.g.*, concatenation of user's and user next of kin's birthdays), attackers will take a longer time to correctly guess the numerals. Verbs and nouns can form sentences, and sentences may be clues to the attackers. Hence, we do not suggest users select a verb as an item. Adjectives and nouns always constitute frequently-used set structures, which decrease the attackers' guessing difficulty. Hence, we also do not suggest users select an adjective as an item. In order to enrich the item space, characters (including English letters, digits and symbols) and their arbitrary combinations are also considered as items in passphrases.

3.2   Modeling

The noun space is $\mathbb{N}_1$, the noun-phrase space is $\mathbb{N}_2$, the numeral space is $\mathbb{N}_3$, and the character space is $\mathbb{N}_4$. $\mathbb{N} = \mathbb{N}_1 \bigcup \mathbb{N}_2 \bigcup \mathbb{N}_3 \bigcup \mathbb{N}_4$. The total number of nouns, noun phrases, numerals, character combinations in $\mathbb{N}$ is $n = |\mathbb{N}|$. Each noun, noun-phrase, numeral, or character combination is an item, and each item belongs to $\mathbb{N}$. $\mathbb{N}$ is the item space. A passphrase $\mathcal{P}$ consists of k items: $\mathcal{P} = \{\mathbb{I}_{i_1}, \mathbb{I}_{i_2}, \mathbb{I}_{i_3}, ..., \mathbb{I}_{i_k}\}$. Each item is sorted by alphanumeric order in $\mathbb{N}$. For example, if $r < s$, $\mathbb{I}_r < \mathbb{I}_s$. Each passphrase $\mathcal{P}$ is just a set of items whose order does not matter. For example, if $\mathcal{P}_1 = \{\mathbb{I}_r, \mathbb{I}_s\}$ and $\mathcal{P}_2 = \{\mathbb{I}_s, \mathbb{I}_r\}$, then $\mathcal{P}_1 = \mathcal{P}_2$. Here, r, s, k, i_1, i_2, i_3, ..., i_k are all natural numbers.

When a user creates an account and specifies a passphrase $\mathcal{P} = \{\mathbb{I}_{i_1}, \mathbb{I}_{i_2}, \mathbb{I}_{i_3}, ..., \mathbb{I}_{i_k}\}$, the authentication system of the server computes the digital digest of this passphrase $\mathcal{P}$. The authentication system needs to sort the items in the passphrase $\mathcal{P}$ because the user can input these items in any order. Without loss of generality, we assume $i_1 < i_2 < i_3 < ... < i_k$. First, the authentication system generates a random *salt* value for this passphrase. Then, it computes the hash value for each item attached this *salt* with a hash function HASH: $H_1 = \text{HASH}(salt\|\mathbb{I}_{i_1})$, $H_2 = \text{HASH}(salt\|\mathbb{I}_{i_2})$, $H_3 = \text{HASH}(salt\|\mathbb{I}_{i_3})$, ..., $H_k = \text{HASH}(salt\|\mathbb{I}_{i_k})$. After that, the authentication system iteratively computes HMAC values with an HMAC function HMAC: $hmac_1 = \text{HMAC}(salt, H_1)$, $hmac_2 = \text{HMAC}(hmac_1, H_2)$, $hmac_3 = \text{HMAC}(hmac_2, H_3)$, ..., $hmac_k = \text{HMAC}(hmac_{k-1}, H_k)$. Finally, it computes the digest with a slow hash function SLOWHASH: $digest = \text{SLOWHASH}(hmac_k)$. These procedures are illustrated in Fig. 2.

Prior to computing the final digital digest with the slow hash function, we use *salt*, a hash function and an HMAC function to preprocess each item. *salt* is used to prevent offline attackers from building potential rainbow tables in advance. We use the hash function to avoid the need to keep plaintext items of passphrases in the memory. We use the HMAC function to turn each passphrase and its corresponding *salt* into the final digital digest. The SLOWHASH function is used to increase the time required for offline guessing attacks. In other words, the model is designed to increase the difficulty of offline attacks.

The authentication system stores the final digital digest with the account name and the *salt* value in a disk file, which is used for verifying the account information when a user logs on each time.

3.3   Usage

When a user creates an account, the authentication system will prompt the user to select passphrases. The user may select some nouns, noun phrases, numerals or character combinations to form the passphrase. A user can, for example, choose the items for the passphrase based on something that only the user knows (*e.g.*, a particular event such as a meeting) and can remember easily. For instance, a user selects "11th July 2018, Nanjing, China, San Antonio, Texas, research" to form the passphrase associated with the research collaboration between teams from Nanjing, China and San Antonio, Texas, and the kickoff meeting was held on July 11th, 2018. In other words, passphrases can be personalized and private to the users. Other example multi-item passphrases include "smile:-), @_@, '_', *_*, (-:elims" and "M_08032005, M_Jack, M_wife, M_holiday, M_Maldives". After specifying the passphrase, the user can then log on the system using the passphrase. The input order of the items in a passphrase is irrelevant.

4   Self-adaptive Algorithm

4.1   Definitions and Assumptions

Definition 1. *δ denotes the least upper bound of the total number of times needed to correctly guess a secure cryptographic secret key. If the least upper bound of the total number of times to correctly guess a password is no less than δ, then the password is secure.*

A cryptographic key is randomly generated. If the b-bit key is the shortest secure key, then $\delta = 2^b$. A password is selected by a user. Given a password, if the number of guesses to break this password is at least 2^b, then this password is secure and cannot be brute forced by the attackers in a reasonable amount of time. We give the following assumption.

Assumption 1. $\delta = 2^{128}$.

Here, $\delta = 2^{128}$ means that a 128-bit cryptographic key is currently secure. With advances in hardware and software, we need to increase the value of δ accordingly. Multi-item Passphrases is robust, and it is not affected by the exact value of δ. $\delta = 2^{128}$ in Assumption 1 is for demonstration purpose only.

Definition 2. ϵ denotes a maximal negligible probability of occurrence. If the probability of an event is not greater than ϵ, then this event is negligible and unlikely to happen. However, if the probability of an event is greater than ϵ, then this event is non-negligible and likely to happen.

Assumption 2. $\epsilon = 2^{-80}$.

For example, consider an event: p users select the same item ($p \geq 2$). Assume that each item is selected with equal probability in the item space $\mathbb{N}$, we can obtain P, the probability that p users select the same item: $P = |\mathbb{N}|^{-p}$. If $P > \epsilon$, this event is likely to happen; otherwise (*i.e.*, $P \leq \epsilon$), this event is unlikely to happen.

4.2 Algorithm

In order to explain the self-adaptive algorithm, we start with the simplest case and work our way up to the general case. Consider the simplest case: there are only two users, Alice and Bob. Alice chooses a passphrase $\mathcal{P}_A$, which consists of $|\mathcal{P}_A|$ items, and Bob chooses $\mathcal{P}_B$ comprising $|\mathcal{P}_B|$ items. $\mathcal{P}_A$ and $\mathcal{P}_B$ have q identical item(s): $|\mathcal{P}_A \cap \mathcal{P}_B| = q$, $q \geq 1$. $P_{|\mathcal{P}_A \cap \mathcal{P}_B|=q}$ denotes the probability that q item(s) are identical in $\mathcal{P}_A$ and $\mathcal{P}_B$. Assume each item is selected with equal probability in the item space $\mathbb{N}$, and $n = |\mathbb{N}|$, we obtain the following equation:

$$P_{|\mathcal{P}_A \cap \mathcal{P}_B|=q} = \frac{\binom{n}{|\mathcal{P}_A|}\binom{|\mathcal{P}_A|}{q}\binom{n-|\mathcal{P}_A|}{|\mathcal{P}_B|-q}}{\binom{n}{|\mathcal{P}_A|}\binom{n}{|\mathcal{P}_B|}} \qquad (1)$$

If $P_{|\mathcal{P}_A \cap \mathcal{P}_B|=q} \leq \epsilon$, then $\mathcal{P}_A \cap \mathcal{P}_B$ are popular item(s). Reasons are as follows: It is unlikely that both $P_{|\mathcal{P}_A \cap \mathcal{P}_B|=q} \leq \epsilon$ and $|\mathcal{P}_A \cap \mathcal{P}_B| = q \geq 1$ are true according to Definition 2. Because it is the established fact that $|\mathcal{P}_A \cap \mathcal{P}_B| = q \geq 1$, which must be true, it is false that $P_{|\mathcal{P}_A \cap \mathcal{P}_B|=q} \leq \epsilon$. Therefore, $P_{|\mathcal{P}_A \cap \mathcal{P}_B|=q} > \epsilon$. This means that Alice and Bob select these q item(s) with a higher probability in $\mathbb{N}$. Hence, $\mathcal{P}_A \cap \mathcal{P}_B$ are popular item(s).

Thus, if the value of Eq. 1 is not greater than ϵ, then the self-adaptive algorithm should remove $\mathcal{P}_A \cap \mathcal{P}_B$ from $\mathbb{N}$ and Alice and Bob should change their passphrases.

Consider the general case: there are u users in the system and $n = |\mathbb{N}|$. $P_{|\bigcap_{i=1}^{p} \mathcal{P}_i|=q}$ denotes the chance of $|\bigcap_{i=1}^{p} \mathcal{P}_i| = q$, where $2 \leq p \leq u, 1 \leq q \leq \min_{i=1}^{p} |\mathcal{P}_i|$:

$$P_{|\bigcap_{i=1}^{p} \mathcal{P}_i|=q} = \frac{\binom{n}{q}\binom{n-q}{|\mathcal{P}_1|-q}\prod_{i=2}^{p}\binom{n-q-\sum_{j=1}^{i-1}(|\mathcal{P}_j|-q)}{|\mathcal{P}_i|-q}}{\prod_{i=1}^{p}\binom{n}{|\mathcal{P}_i|}} \qquad (2)$$

Similarly to Eq. 1, when both $P_{|\bigcap_{i=1}^{p} \mathcal{P}_i|=q} \le \epsilon$ and $|\bigcap_{i=1}^{p} \mathcal{P}_i| = q$, one of the two must be false. Since $|\bigcap_{i=1}^{p} \mathcal{P}_i| = q$ is the established fact, $P_{|\bigcap_{i=1}^{p} \mathcal{P}_i|=q} \le \epsilon$ is false. Therefore, $P_{|\bigcap_{i=1}^{p} \mathcal{P}_i|=q} > \epsilon$ and $\bigcap_{i=1}^{p} \mathcal{P}_i$ are popular items. The self-adaptive algorithm removes $\bigcap_{i=1}^{p} \mathcal{P}_i$ from $\mathbb{N}$, and these p users should change their passphrases.

When a new passphrase $\mathcal{P}^*$ is submitted to the system, we need not compute Eq. 2 with all the passphrases $\bigcup_{i=1}^{u} \{\mathcal{P}_i\}$ because those passphrases $\bigcup_{i=1}^{u} \{\mathcal{P}_i\} - \{\mathcal{P}^*\}$ have been handled before $\mathcal{P}^*$ joins in. Hence, the self-adaptive algorithm for the general case (see Algorithm 1) is efficient.

Algorithm 1. Self-Adaptive Algorithm for the general case

Input: $\mathcal{P}^*, \bigcup_{i=1}^{u} \{\mathcal{P}_i\}$ //Input the passphrases, $\mathcal{P}^* \in \bigcup_{i=1}^{u} \{\mathcal{P}_i\}$.

Output: $\hat{\mathcal{P}}, \overline{\mathbb{N}}$ //Output the popular items, $\hat{\mathcal{P}} \subseteq \overline{\mathbb{N}}$.

1: $\mathbb{S} \leftarrow \bigcup_{i=1}^{u} \{\mathcal{P}_i\} - \{\mathcal{P}^*\}$ //$\mathbb{S}$ contains what are handled, $\mathcal{P}^*$ is a fresh one.

2: Compare $\mathcal{P}^*$ to every element in $\mathbb{S}$ //To see whether there are identical item(s).

3: Find all distinct groups that p passphrases from $\mathbb{S}$ which have the same q item(s) as $\mathcal{P}^*$ //That is, $|(\bigcap_{i=1}^{p} \mathcal{P}_i) \bigcap \mathcal{P}^*| = q \ge 1$.

4: **if** There is no passphrase from $\mathbb{S}$ that has the same item as $\mathcal{P}^*$ **then**

5:     Exit the algorithm   //Find no identical item(s), so exit.

6: **end if**

7: **for** each group that $p \ge 1$ **do**   //If no such group, do Line 4 to Line 6.

8:     $\hat{\mathcal{P}} \leftarrow (\bigcap_{i=1}^{p} \mathcal{P}_i) \bigcap \mathcal{P}^*$ //For convenience, let $\hat{\mathcal{P}}$ denote $(\bigcap_{i=1}^{p} \mathcal{P}_i) \bigcap \mathcal{P}^*$.

9:     **if** $P_{|\hat{\mathcal{P}}|=q} \le \epsilon$ **and** $|\hat{\mathcal{P}}| = q$ **then**   //$P_{|\hat{\mathcal{P}}|=q} \le \epsilon$ is false; $|\hat{\mathcal{P}}| = q$ is the established fact.

10:         $\overline{\mathbb{N}} \leftarrow \overline{\mathbb{N}} + \hat{\mathcal{P}}$ //$\hat{\mathcal{P}}$ are q popular item(s), which are added to $\overline{\mathbb{N}}$.

11:         Set these $p + 1$ users' *PassphraseStatus* fields to "1"

12:     **end if**

13: **end for**

Once a user registers or changes a passphrase, the self-adaptive algorithm executes. If the self-adaptive algorithm asks some users to change their passphrases, then these requests will be recorded in the disk file that stores the account information. The main structure of this disk file is as below:

$$|UserName|salt|DigitalDigest|PassphraseStatus|$$

The *PassphraseStatus* field stores the status of the corresponding user's passphrase. The default value of this field is "0". If the self-adaptive algorithm asks a user to change the passphrase, then this user's *PassphraseStatus* field is set to "1". When a user logs on with success, if the value of this user's *PassphraseStatus* field is "1", this user is asked to change the passphrase at once. If this user changes the passphrase successfully, then the value of this field is reset to "0"; otherwise, the system rejects this user's further access until this user changes the passphrase successfully.

It is noteworthy that the self-adaptive algorithm does not directly compare the plaintext items of different passphrases other than the hash values of the items. All hash values of the items for every users' passphrase are kept in memory. The plaintext passphrases are discarded. For the purpose of resisting the rainbow table, we hash every item with the attached *salt* of the corresponding passphrase. This is performed to prevent a malicious insider from dumping the contents of memory and learning all the passphrases. The item comparison of different passphrases incurs little cost.

We do not employ the slow hash function to protect the items in memory just because slow hashing is time-consuming and Eq. 2 (see Line 9 in Algorithm 1) needs to compare each hashed item with attached *salt*. As each user's *salt* is generally different, it will need a lot of time if slow hashing is employed in the items in memory especially when there are millions of users in the system.

The digital digests of every passphrase are stored in the disk file. When rebooting the server, all the hash values of the items of every passphrase in memory will disappear. However, it does not matter since the system can recognize users because the disk file records the digests of user passphrases. The removal of the hash values in the memory results in $\mathbb{S} = \emptyset$ in Algorithm 1. If the rebooting is intentional, then all the hashed items in memory can be dumped before rebooting and restored after rebooting. If the rebooting is accidental, as users log on successively, $\mathbb{S}$ is filled up again. The accidental rebooting does not affect the registered user passphrases, but newly registering user passphrases may be under the influence of the accidental rebooting because $\mathbb{S}$ will not become full swiftly after the accidental rebooting. The solution to the accidental rebooting is simple: rerun Algorithm 1 for these newly registering user passphrases as long as $\mathbb{S}$ is changed by those registered user passphrases. The rebooting of the server does not destroy the self-adaptive algorithm (*i.e.*, Multi-item Passphrases is reliable).

Scaling up is also not a concern, although Algorithm 1 might be time-consuming. For example, according to the *PassphraseStatus* field of the disk file, users can change their passphrases in a timely fashion. Without the slow hash operation, the system can protect user passphrases ahead of offline attackers. Moreover, we can obtain the value of Eq. 2 by a look-up table, so as to avoid unnecessary repetitive computation.

4.3 Item Space Construction

There are two methods to construct the item space: the direct method and the indirect method. The direct method is to set a large table representing $\mathbb{N}$, all the potential items are contained in this table. When need to remove some popular items selected by users, just remove them from this large table. The indirect method is to set a table representing $\overline{\mathbb{N}}$. The items outside this table are all feasible items that users can select. Once need to remove some popular items chosen by users, just add them into this table.

We adopt the latter indirect method. Users are not allowed to select items in the table $\overline{\mathbb{N}}$. All of the elements in $\overline{\mathbb{N}}$ are generated dynamically by the self-adaptive algorithm (see the 10th line in Algorithm 1). As a supplement, we can also add popular words to $\overline{\mathbb{N}}$ in advance so as to stop users choosing these popular items.

The most main reason we do not employ the former but the latter is that a direct item space table $\mathbb{N}$ exposes users' password sets and is equivalent to a word list of a password cracking tool, which helps attackers. Instead, the table $\overline{\mathbb{N}}$ can include word lists of existing password cracking tools in advance, which resists password guessing attacks.

4.4   Size of Item Space

Because we take numerals and character combinations into account, the actual size of the item space is infinite. For maximum convenience of users, we manage to make our approach easy to use on the condition that only English words belong to the item space.

Given a k-item passphrase $\mathcal{P}$, according to Definition 1, for security, the number of guesses to certainly crack $\mathcal{P}$ should be at least δ. δ is made up of two parts: $\delta = \delta_1 \times \delta_2$. Part 1, δ_1, derives from the traversal of $\binom{n}{k}$ distinct passphrases. Part 2, δ_2, is the number of cycles for slow hash, which stems from the slow hash function in the model of Multi-item Passphrases.

A frequently-used slow hash function is $bcrypt$ [18]. We take $bcrypt$ as an example of the slow hash function in this paper. In $bcrypt$, $\delta_2 = 2^{cost}$, $cost$ is an adjustable parameter. According to Assumption 1, $2^{128} = \binom{n}{k} \times 2^{cost}$. We assign 88 to $cost$ and evaluate n with different k. The detailed results are listed in Table 1.

Table 1. Size of item space

k	n ($\delta_1 = 2^{128}, \delta_2 = 1$)	n ($\delta_1 = 2^{40}, \delta_2 = 2^{88}$)
2	$>2.6 \times 10^{19}$	1,482,911
3	$>1.2 \times 10^{13}$	18,756
4	9,506,325,306	2,268
5	132,496,421	669
6	7,910,346	307
7	1,080,111	181

When the slow hash function is out of use, $\delta_2 = 1$, $\delta_1 = 2^{128}$, and n exceeds one million even though $k = 7$. Because there are not so many nouns in English, the slow hash function is necessary to our approach in consideration of usability.

When $cost = 88$, $\delta_2 = 2^{88}$ and $\delta_1 = 2^{40}$. Assume the hash time of the slow hash function is 1 ms when $cost = 88$. The average time that attackers crack a passphrase equals 1 ms times 2^{39}, which means a large time span for more than 17 years. It is a time span long enough that we believe the passphrase is secure. In order to ensure this level of security of a passphrase, if $k = 7$, the item space needs only 181 items; if $k = 3$, the item space needs no more than 20,000 items. At the same time, there are 218,632 words inside the Second Edition of the *Oxford English Dictionary*, over half of them (more than 100,000 entries) are nouns, and noun phrases are much more [6,16]. Hence, provided the slow hash function comes into use, the item space is big enough to actualize our approach Multi-item Passphrases.

4.5   Relationship Between δ and $\delta_2 = 2^{cost}$

When hardware computing speed increases, δ and $\delta_2 = 2^{cost}$ should be augmented correspondingly. Thus, δ_1 need not be changed because $\delta = \delta_1 \times 2^{cost}$, as explained using the following example:

Assume the hash time of the slow hash function is 1 ms when $cost = 20$, and $\delta_1 = 2^{40}$, then $\delta = 2^{60}$ means a large time span for more than 34 years. If hardware computation speeds up 1000 times, the iterative times of the slow hash function $\delta_2 = 2^{20}$ is reduced from 1 ms to 1 microsecond. Then, we adjust $cost$ from 20 to 30, remain $\delta_1 = 2^{40}$, and $\delta = 2^{70}$ still means a large time span for more than 34 years.

Hence, we do not need to expand the passphrase space as hardware computing speed improves. Multi-item Passphrases is a stable approach.

We assume $\delta = 2^{128}$ in Assumption 1 and assign 88 to $cost$ in Table 1. They are just examples for demonstration purposes. In fact, because $\delta = \delta_1 \times \delta_2 = \delta_1 \times 2^{cost}$, we can always obtain an appropriate value of δ through adjusting the value of $cost$ as long as δ_1 is large enough such as $\delta_1 = 2^{40}$.

4.6   Parameter Values

n can be assigned $\epsilon^{-0.5}$ in the self-adaptive algorithm although the actual item space is boundless. In Eq. 2, when n is assigned no less than $\epsilon^{-0.5}$, different users are restricted from selecting the same item; when n is assigned less than $\epsilon^{-0.5}$, the smaller n is, more of the same items can be selected by different users. We may decrease the value of n in order to reduce users' frequency of changing their passphrases due to popular items.

In Assumption 2, we set $\epsilon = 2^{-80}$, which is a widely used value in the cryptographic literature.

k is a small integer between 3 and 20 generally, which is used to strike a balance between security and the usability of passphrases. In general, given an item space, the larger k is, the more secure passphrases are. The smaller k is, the more usable passphrases are.

$$\delta_1 = \sum_k \binom{n}{k}.$$

5   Experiments

We performed a series of experiments to evaluate the multi-item passphrases, using an online website we built. There were four experiments on this website. These experiments contained three text password-based authentication systems: passwords, multi-item passphrases, and diceware passphrases [19]. For the experiments, we recruited a total of 372 undergraduate students, aged between 18 and 23, from the school of management. There were 189 female and 183 male participants. Our experiments were approved by Nanjing University's IRB.

We randomly grouped these 372 participants into four groups by their student numbers, in order to obtain four independent samples at random: Group 1: 86 persons for Experiment 1; Group 2: 81 persons for Experiment 2; Group 3: 86 persons for Experiment 3; and Group 4: 119 persons for Experiment 4.

The experiments were divided into two phases: day one and day four (*i.e.*, three days after they had started the experiment). In the second phase (*i.e.*, day four), only 293 participants (149 females and 144 males) returned to complete the experiments.

- Group 1: 68 persons
- Group 2: 74 persons
- Group 3: 73 persons
- Group 4: 78 persons

The experiment setup is now explained below.

Experiment 1: Passwords. We asked the recruited participants to visit our website on a certain day. They were asked to register and log on to their accounts using their user credentials. Their account names were arbitrary, and the passwords they specified must include at least three of the following four character types: lowercase English letters, uppercase English letters, numbers, and symbols, and the passwords were at least 16 characters long.

Three days later, we asked them to access our web site again and log on to their accounts. On this occasion, however, they were presented with their account names and they only needed to input their passwords. Participants were allowed to try as many times as possible, if they had entered an incorrect password. Then, we asked the participants to comment on the usability of this authentication system.

Experiment 2: Multi-item Passphrases. In this experiment, we assigned $\epsilon^{-0.5}$ to n in Eq. 2. Participants were asked to register and log on to their accounts using their chosen multi-item passphrases on our web site on a certain day. The passphrases must include five or more than five unpopular items and the order of these items was irrelevant. If an item they specified was popular, then they were asked to change their passphrases. Similar to Experiment 1, the participants returned three days later to enter their passphrases. However, if an item in their passphrases had become popular during these three days, then they would be asked to change their passphrases when they logged on.

We asked for their comments on the usability of this authentication system, and particularly the following questions:

Q(1) How do you feel about the need to change your passphrase (repeatedly) when you select a popular item during account registration?
Q(2) How do you feel about the need to change your passphrase because others selected the same item(s) as you?

To these two questions above, we provided the following four options for the participants:

(A) It is good, because now I know which item is popular and can avoid using such item(s) from now on.
(B) I can accept it in order to ensure that my account is secure.
(C) It annoys me a little as I have to think of a different passphrase.
(D) It is absolutely unacceptable!

Experiment 3: Diceware Passphrases. Participants were told to register and log on accounts using diceware passphrases, which include five ordered diceware words selected at random from the diceware item list [19]. Three days later, they were asked to log on to their accounts on our website and comment on the usability of this authentication system.

Experiment 4: Rating. Participants were asked to finish all of the experiments in Experiments 1, 2 and 3. After that, based on usability and security, they were asked to rate these three password-based authentication systems where 1 is the lowest (worst) and 3 is the highest (best). They had to also provide a reason for the ratings.

5.1   Findings I: Multi-item Passphrases vs. Passwords

Quantitative Results. The findings are as follows: after creating their accounts, 28 of the 68 participants remembered their passwords and logged on to their accounts successfully three days later in Experiment 1; 40 of the 74 participants remembered their multi-item passphrases and logged on to their accounts successfully three days later in Experiment 2.

Strength. In Experiment 1, we asked participants to specify a 16-character-long password although most passwords were only 8 characters long, and the password space of a 16-character-long password is 95^{16}.

In Experiment 2, without even considering the numerical and character combinations, the total number of nouns and noun phrases is significantly larger than 669 based on what we obtained from the *Oxford English Dictionary* [6,16]. Thus, according to Table 1, $n \gg 669$ and $k \geq 5$, so $\delta_1 \gg 2^{40}$ and $\delta \gg 2^{128}$ when

$\delta_2 = 2^{88}$. Because $\delta \gg 2^{128} \gg 95^{16}$, considering only English words, the multi-item passphrases' space is significantly larger than that of passwords. Hence, taking the numerical and character combinations into account, the strength of multi-item passphrases in Experiment 2 is very much greater than that of passwords in Experiment 1.

Recall. Let p_1 and p_2 be the true proportion of users who can recall successfully their multi-item passphrases and passwords, respectively.

$H_0 : p_1 = p_2$.
$H_1 : p_1 > p_2$.
$\alpha = 0.1$.

The null hypothesis of H_0 is that multi-item passphrases and passwords are both equally hard to remember, and the alternative hypothesis H_1 indicates that multi-item passphrases are easier to remember than passwords. For the hypothesis testing, we use *"Two Samples: Tests on Two Proportions"* [23]:

$$z = \frac{\hat{p}_1 - \hat{p}_2}{\sqrt{(\frac{1}{n_1} + \frac{1}{n_2})(\hat{p}(1 - \hat{p}))}} \tag{3}$$

In Eq. 3, the sizes of the two independent samples are n_1 and n_2, respectively: $n_1 = 74, n_2 = 68$. The point estimates of p_1 and p_2 are $\hat{p}_1$ and $\hat{p}_2$ for the two samples respectively, and they are computed as $\hat{p}_1 = \frac{40}{74}$ and $\hat{p}_2 = \frac{28}{68}$. The pooled estimate of the proportion is $\hat{p} = \frac{40+28}{74+68}$. Thus, $z = 1.53$. Therefore, $P = P(Z > 1.53) = 0.0630$. Hence, we reject H_0 ($\alpha = 0.1$ and $p = .0630$) and accept H_1. In other words, multi-item passphrases are easier to remember than passwords.

5.2 Findings II: Multi-item Passphrases vs. Diceware Passphrases

Quantitative Results. The findings are as follows: after creating their accounts, 19 of the 73 participants remembered their diceware passphrases and logged on to their accounts successfully three days later in Experiment 3; 40 of the 74 participants remembered their multi-item passphrases and logged on to their accounts successfully three days later in Experiment 2.

Strength. In Experiment 2, there are a large number of non-popular items (*e.g.*, numeric and arbitrary combinations of characters). Since the diceware list only contains 7776 items, the diceware passphrase space is $P_5^{7776} = 5!\binom{7776}{5} = 120\binom{7776}{5}$ in Experiment 3. Hence, the strength of multi-item passphrases is much greater than that of diceware passphrases.

Recall. The findings here echoed those of Findings I, in the sense that multi-item passphrases are much easier to remember than diceware passphrases ($p < .0001$).

5.3   Findings III: Usability Under Frequent Passphrase Changes

The breakdown to the questions is as follows: Question (1): 41 participants chose (A), 68 participants chose (B), 42 participants chose (C), and one chose (D); and Question (2): 19 participants chose (A), 67 participants chose (B), 46 participants chose (C), and 20 participants chose (D). The findings are also reported in Fig. 3.

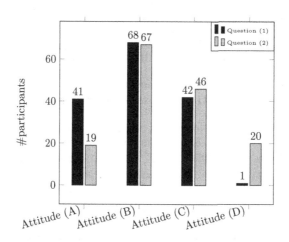

Fig. 3. Attitudes to frequent passphrase changes.

From the findings, we observe that the majority of the participants were positive towards Question (1), since they might be used to frequently changing their passwords due to stringent password composition policies (although they might not enjoy doing so, and this is beyond the scope of this study).

Participants were generally more negative towards Question (2) because they were new to the fact that they had to change the passphrase for their existing account just because it comprised a popular item. This is a mindset that will require some adjusting. Users could, for example, be educated on why they need to avoid popular passwords/passphrases (*e.g.*, the overlapping parts in Fig. 1c).

5.4   Findings IV: Rate Three Authentication Systems

In Experiment 4, 78 participants scored the three systems and the findings are shown in Table 2.

From Table 2, we observe that multi-item passphrases system has the highest score of 2.58, followed by passwords (score 1.87) and diceware passphrases (score 1.55). The average score of multi-item passphrases is much higher than those of the other two (Kruskal-Wallis test, $p < .0001$). The highest rating score suggests that the participants strongly believe that Multi-item Passphrases is a better password-based authentication system than passwords and diceware passphrases.

Table 2. Ratings for the three authentication systems

Systems	#Score			Average score
	#1	#2	#3	
Multi-item passphrases	4	25	49	2.58
Passwords	26	36	16	1.87
Diceware passphrases	48	17	13	1.55

5.5   Findings V: Qualitative Results from Participants' Remarks

Participants in Groups 1, 2, and 3 commented on the respective authentication systems, and participants in Group 4 explained their ratings. Some interesting findings are as follows:

(1) Although the space for passwords is much greater than the space for diceware passphrases (*i.e.*, $95^{16} \gg P_5^{7776}$), many participants believed that "*diceware passphrases were more secure than passwords*". They did not trust the security of passwords, which is perhaps because several participants "*had the experience of having the passwords stolen*".

(2) Many participants commented that "*diceware passphrases were secure*", but at the same time, they also said they "*would never consider making use of it because it was too difficult to remember*".

(3) Participants' security awareness was strong, which is not surprising consider the age group of these participants (*i.e.*, digital natives) and their educational background. Some participants even commented that they hoped to see the next release of our research.

We now present a snapshot of the participants' remarks on the three password-based authentication systems:

Passwords. "*A 16-character password was too long.*" Although it was the most commonly used, "*it was somewhat difficult to recall*" as it must contain three of the following four character types: lowercase English letters, uppercase English letters, numbers, and symbols. Hence, "*A shorter or simpler password was better*" for using but was easy to crack.

Multi-item Passphrases. "*It was the best of the three.*" "*It was a good tradeoff between user experience and security.*" "*The order of items in a passphrase was indifferent, which was humanized.*" "*The system could find popular items, which was good.*" However, "*five items were a bit too many*".

Diceware Passphrases. It was picked randomly, so "*it was very hard to remember*" although "*it was secure*" because of its randomness. "*It was a painful and difficult experience*" for users.

6 Related Work

Passwords have been used for decades, and one known limitation is password-guessing attacks such as offline guessing attacks [2,5,7,15]. Passphrases may be a slightly better option than passwords because passphrases are generally harder to guess, with minimal implementation changes or disruption to user experience [22].

A closely related work is Diceware [19], which comprises a Diceware list. In order to pick passphrases, Diceware selects items at random from the Diceware list. Although Diceware is simple and straightforward, participants rated our approach to be better than Diceware in terms of usability and security (see Findings II).

Another similar related work is Telepathwords [10]. Telepathwords predicts users' passwords with several fixed patterns to prevent users from creating weak passwords. These patterns include common character sequences, keyboard movements, repeated strings, and interleaved strings. This particular approach relies on the pattern of a password, while Multi-item Passphrases focuses on concrete elements (popular items) in passphrases. It is not sufficient to make use of finite fixed patterns to avoid weak passwords. For example, Telepathwords can detect "abcdefg", but cannot detect the weak password "gfedcba" because Telepathwords does not consider reverse character sequences. The constructive patterns of passphrases are much more complicated than those of passwords. Hence, Multi-item Passphrases does not employ fixed patterns to avoid weak passphrases. Instead, our approach prevents the use of popular items in user passphrases.

In the Bloom filter-based approach proposed by Schechter et $al.$ [20], a key limitation is a high false positive ($i.e.$, unpopular passwords being wrongly flagged as popular). Moreover, their approach cannot resist offline attacks due to the inherent weakness of the Bloom filter.

Segreti et $al.$ [21] undertook a user study, focusing on the approaches of Schechter et $al.$ [20] and PathWell [12]. PathWell is similar to Telepathwords. Key differences between the study of Segreti et $al.$ and ours are: the former focuses on passwords and does not include any qualitative study.

When constructing the item space, we construct a complement of the item space: $\overline{\mathbb{N}}$. The concept "a complement of the item space" is similar to the password blacklist studied by Habib et $al.$ [9]. A key difference between them is that the complement of the item space is automatically generated and dynamically added in our approach.

7 Conclusion

It may not be realistic to expect that password-based systems will fade away in the near future, and hence we need to design sufficiently robust password-based authentication systems to mitigate existing known limitations ($e.g.$, users selecting weak and easy-to-guess passwords). Thus, this motivated the design of our proposed Multi-item Passphrases approach. We demonstrated the security of the proposed approach, as well as evaluated its performance.

Acknowledgement. We thank the anonymous reviewers for their constructive feedback. This work has been partly supported by National NSF of China under Grant No. 61772266, 61572248, 61431008.

References

1. Biddle, R., Chiasson, S., Van Oorschot, P.C.: Graphical passwords: learning from the first twelve years. ACM Comput. Surv. (CSUR) **44**(4), 19 (2012)
2. Bonneau, J., Herley, C., van Oorschot, P.C., Stajano, F.: Passwords and the evolution of imperfect authentication. Commun. ACM **58**(7), 78–87 (2015)
3. Bonneau, J., Shutova, E.: Linguistic properties of multi-word passphrases. In: Blyth, J., Dietrich, S., Camp, L.J. (eds.) FC 2012. LNCS, vol. 7398, pp. 1–12. Springer, Heidelberg (2012). https://doi.org/10.1007/978-3-642-34638-5_1
4. Burnett, M.: Today I am releasing ten million passwords, February 2015. https://xato.net/passwords/tenmillion-passwords/
5. Chatterjee, R., Athayle, A., Akhawe, D., Juels, A., Ristenpart, T.: pASSWORD tYPOS and how to correct them securely. In: IEEE Symposium on Security and Privacy, pp. 799–818 (2016)
6. Oxford Living Dictionaries: How many words are there in the English language? (2018). https://en.oxforddictionaries.com/explore/how-many-words-are-there-in-the-english-language/
7. Wang, D., Cheng, H., Wang, P., Yan, J., Huang, X.: A security analysis of honeywords. In: Proceedings of the 25th Annual Network and Distributed System Security Symposium (2018)
8. D'Orazio, C., Choo, K.K.R., Yang, L.T.: Data exfiltration from Internet of Things devices: iOS devices as case studies. IEEE Internet Things J. **4**(2), 524–535 (2017)
9. Habib, H., et al.: Password creation in the presence of blacklists. In: Proceedings of USEC (2017)
10. Komanduri, S., Shay, R., Cranor, L.F., Herley, C., Schechter, S.E.: Telepathwords: preventing weak passwords by reading users' minds. In: USENIX Security Symposium, pp. 591–606 (2014)
11. Krol, K., Philippou, E., De Cristofaro, E., Sasse, M.A.: "they brought in the horrible key ring thing!" analysing the usability of two-factor authentication in UK online banking. In: Symposium on NDSS Workshop on Usable Security (2015)
12. Leininger, H.: Libpathwell 0.6.1 released, 2015 (2015). https://blog.korelogic.com/blog/2015/07/31/libpathwell-0_6_1
13. Li, Z., Han, W., Xu, W.: A large-scale empirical analysis of Chinese web passwords. In: Proceedings of 23rd USENIX Security Symposium, USENIX Security, August 2014
14. Mazurek, M.L., et al.: Measuring password guessability for an entire university. In: Proceedings of the 20th ACM SIGSAC Conference on Computer and Communications Security, pp. 173–186. ACM (2013)
15. Morris, R., Thompson, K.: Password security: a case history. Commun. ACM **22**(11), 594–597 (1979)
16. OED: Dictionary milestones: a chronology of events relevant to the history of the OED (2017). http://public.oed.com/history-of-the-oed/dictionary-milestones/
17. Paul: New 25 GPU monster devours passwords in seconds, December 2012. https://securityledger.com/2012/12/new-25-gpu-monster-devours-passwords-in-seconds/
18. Provos, N., Mazieres, D.: A future-adaptable password scheme. In: USENIX Annual Technical Conference, FREENIX Track, pp. 81–91 (1999)

19. Reinhold, A.G.: The diceware passphrase home page, October 2017. http://world.std.com/~reinhold/diceware.html
20. Schechter, S., Herley, C., Mitzenmacher, M.: Popularity is everything: a new approach to protecting passwords from statistical-guessing attacks. In: USENIX Conference on Hot Topics in Security, pp. 1–8 (2010)
21. Segreti, S.M., et al.: Diversify to survive: making passwords stronger with adaptive policies. In: Symposium on Usable Privacy and Security (SOUPS) (2017)
22. Tazawa, H., Katoh, T., Bista, B.B., Takata, T.: A user authenticaion scheme using multiple passphrases and its arrangement. In: International Symposium on Information Theory and Its Applications (ISITA), pp. 554–559. IEEE (2010)
23. Walpole, R.E.: One- and two-sample tests of hypotheses. In: Probability and Statistics for Engineers and Scientists, 7 edn. Pearson (2001). Chapter 10
24. Wang, D., Cheng, H., Wang, P., Huang, X., Jian, G.: Zipf's law in passwords. IEEE Trans. Inf. Forensics Secur. **12**(11), 2776–2791 (2017)

Short Paper

Hybrid Intrusion Detection System for Worm Attacks Based on Their Network Behavior

Hassan Hadi Latheeth AL-Maksousy$^{(\boxtimes)}$ and Michele C. Weigle

Department of Computer Science, Old Dominion University, Norfolk, VA 23529, USA
{halma002,mweigle}@odu.edu

Abstract. Computer worms are characterized by rapid propagation and intrusive network disruption. In this work, we analyze the network behavior of five Internet worms: Sasser, Slammer, Eternal Rocks, WannaCry, and Petya. Through this analysis, we use a deep neural network to successfully classify network traces of these worms along with normal traffic. Our hybrid approach includes a visualization that allows for further analysis and tracing of the network behavior of detected worms.

Keywords: Deep learning · Worm traffic · Internet worms · Sasser
Slammer · NotPetya · WannaCry · EternalRocks · Visualization

1 Introduction

Computer worms are small self-duplicating code that can rapidly infect hundreds of thousands of systems. The Slammer worm spread to 90% of its target systems in just 10 min [1]. In 2017, the NotPetya and WannaCry worms created a global panic [2]. A great deal of research based on different frameworks and numerous case studies are available for the analysis of the spread of worms across networks [3–6]. Worms' detrimental influence on computer systems has been significant over the last several decades. The worms propagate from one machine to the next and are detected using different methods. Therefore, it has become important to develop intrusion detection systems and prevention mechanisms to counter them.

The main goal of this work is to detect and visualize worms by understanding their network behavior. Our approach is a hybrid system that consists of machine learning intrusion detection and a visualization tool in order to classify and detect worms based on their network behavior. Our hybrid approach is meant to confront and deal with anomaly and network behavior aspects of worms through the use of machine learning and a visualization tool. This study implements a network traffic generator using the NS3 simulator, a packet analysis tool for examining PCAP files, a deep neural network approach to classify and detect worms, and a visualization tool based on D3 for analyzing network traces.

F. Breitinger and I. Baggili (Eds.): ICDF2C 2018, LNICST 259, pp. 225–234, 2019.
https://doi.org/10.1007/978-3-030-05487-8_12

2   Related Work

Signature-based detection uses a database of signatures containing known worms [7–9]. The detection algorithm uses this database to determine if a packet is infected, i.e., if it contains a known signature of a worm in the database. The main drawback of this method is that it relies upon knowing these signatures, therefore new worms will go undetected until they are discovered and added to the database. Due to the limitations of signature-based detection, anomaly or behavior-based detection was introduced. This approach looks for anomalous behavior of a worm by distinguishing it from what is normal behavior [10,11]. This function and purpose of a worm characterizes its behavior and provides a profile for this method.

Several recent works have analyzed network behavior for worm detection and classification. Sarnsuwan et al. [12] use network-based Internet worm detection utilizing thirteen packet features. Data mining algorithms such as Bayesian Network, Decision Tree, and Random Forest are used for classification of Internet worms, normal data, or network attack data. Barhoom et al. [13] propose a model that makes use of data mining techniques by combining different classifiers with an adaptive approach for detecting known or unknown worms. Another technique proposed by Rasheed et al. [14] focuses on detecting polymorphic worms. However, only a single worm MSblaster was used for testing. Tang et al. [15] proposed an intrusion detection system using the Deep Neural Network (DNN) model. A visualization of the computer system state during a worm attack requiring manual intervention by the user is presented by Axelsson et al. [16]. It was observed that the worm request clusters were noticeably different from the clusters formed by normal traffic.

3   Analyzed Worms

We analyze and develop a Finite State Machine (FSM) model for the following worms: Sasser, Slammer, Petya, WannaCry, and EternalRocks.

3.1   Sasser Worm

The Sasser worm targets computers running Microsoft Windows XP and Windows 2000. It has the capability of spreading rapidly over vulnerable computers via TCP port numbers 445 or 139 to infect other computers without any human interaction. This worm belongs to self-replicating worms from the W32.Sasser family [17] and exploits a vulnerable LSASS.EXE to infect the system, allowing the attacker to gain full control of the system [18].

3.2   Slammer Worm

The Slammer worm exploits a buffer overrun in the Microsoft SQL service. The worm's payload is small enough to fit inside a single packet. It spreads very rapidly [19] infecting unpatched SQL servers. It propagates by transmitting the same message to other SQL servers rapidly using random IP addresses. This attack can only be mitigated by taking the server offline. There is no additional malicious content included in the worm payload. However, because of the behavior and the speed with which it attacks systems, it executes an effective DoS attack as the network's resources are drained [20].

3.3   EternalRocks, WannaCry and Petya

EternalRocks, WannaCry and Petya utilize the EternalBlue exploit which was leaked as part of the EternalRocks Shadow Brokers dataset[1]. EternalBlue exploits a flaw in the SMBv1 service's NT Transaction request handler by sending a large NT Transaction Request, making it necessary for the target to accept one or more Trans2 Secondary requests. By sending malformed Trans2 Secondary requests, EternalBlue exploits a flaw in the protocol that allows shellcode to be delivered and executed on the target machine [2].

4   Approach

The machine learning approach is employed to classify and detect predefined worms and undefined worms with similar network behavior. Once the machine learning tool detects suspicious activity, then the visualization tool will be used to further analyze the network traffic. In analyzing the traffic, the visualization tool displays suspicious worm activity, traces the attack, and displays the affected nodes.

Our system architecture is shown in Fig. 1. Using a PCAP file as an input to the ipsumdump utility [21], we extract features as a CSV file. The preprocessor converts the features into a numerical array and normalizes the data. The data is passed to the deep neural network (DNN) for detection of worms. If the machine learning tool detects suspicious activity, the visualization tool is used to display the suspicious worm activity, trace the attacks, and display the affected nodes.

We use the following features from ipsumdump:

- wire-length: Overall length of captured packet, including headers
- length: IP packet length
- protocol: IP protocol
- ip-id: IP-ID field
- ip-sum: IP checksum
- ip-ttl: IP time to live field
- ip-tos: IP type of service field
- ip-hl: IP header length
- capture-length: Length of IP data
- sport: Source TCP or UDP port
- dport: Destination TCP or UDP port

---

[1] http://www.ericconrad.com/2017/04/shadowbrokers-pcaps-etc.html.

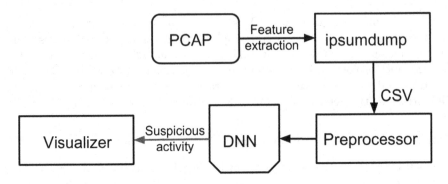

Fig. 1. System architecture

- payload-md5-hex: MD5 checksum of payload
- tcp-seq: TCP sequence number
- tcp-ack: TCP acknowledgement number
- tcp-window: TCP receive window
- udp-length: UDP length, reported in the header
- icmp-type: ICMP type
- icmp-code: ICMP code

4.1   Machine Learning

Deep neural network is a machine learning model that is trained using the dataset. DNNs are used to solve complex problems and possess the ability for unsupervised learning, a key component for automatically detecting worm variants and mutations.

We used the framework of Keras [22] to build a fully connected DNN. As a proof of concept, we trained the DNN model with five real time PCAP capture files from online sources [23–25] containing captures of worm traffic. In addition to the worm traffic, we also captured normal network traffic generated by our machine. The overall size of the processed dataset for training was 11.2 MB of malicious traffic and 85.1 MB of normal traffic. The test dataset was 10% of the entire dataset.

4.2   Worm Visualization

One of the main contributions of this work is building the visualizer IDS with D3. D3[2] is a JavaScript library that is used to create data visualizations. The data generated by computer networks is considerably large and visualization methods such as D3 are necessary to interpret and process this overwhelming data. The visualization tool is designed to help interpret the large amount of data and display this data on the screen in a visually appealing format.

---

[2] https://d3js.org.

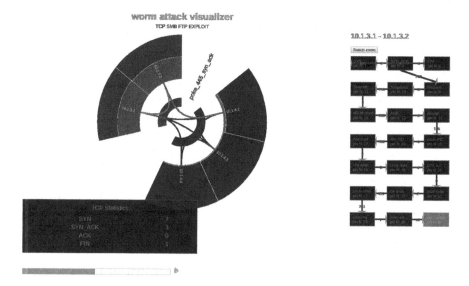

Fig. 2. Worm visualization. The FSM of the detected worm is shown on the right.

The worm visualization analysis tool presented in this paper uses the Finite State Machine (FSM) model, which defines the expected behavior of worm network traffic. When the behavior deviates from this expectation, the FSM will not display the new states, however, we will still be able to detect the worm attack using machine learning. Our packet analysis tool processes one or more captured network PCAP files and produces a JSON file. The JSON file is provided to the visualization tool to be interpreted. We use our FSM model to divide the packets into four categories: TCP, SMB, FTP, and Exploit. Packets in the Exploit category are various worm states of attack. Four colors have been assigned to these categories in order to visually determine the kind of packet. Exploit packets are red, and any red activity in the display can be associated with potential or actual worm attacks.

An example of the visualization tool can be seen in Fig. 2. The visualization tool displays each node represented by a wedge shape. Nodes are grouped based on their IP address and a specific color is assigned based on the network the node belongs to. The wedge shape is then filled depending on the overall percentage of the defined packet activity. This makes it easier to observe the overall activity distribution on the nodes during an analysis session. However, if a worm attack is detected, the activity area will be displayed as red. Packet transmissions between any two nodes are depicted by an arc made in the color of the packet category. Since the visualizer shows the network traffic over time, these interconnecting arcs will change and fade color as other categorized packets are transmitted. The complete PCAP session, whether from one or multiple files, is combined into a single timeline. We can navigate from the beginning to the end and to any point along the timeline of the session. The visualizer will update to show all activity up to the current index. Along with the pictorial representation of inter-connectivity and packet activity, the visualization tool displays packet statistics. At the center of the main graph the current packet type is always displayed. This text continuously and quickly updates based on the current timeline position. There is an overview of general TCP statistics, showing different TCP packet types and counts for each type. This is also dynamically updated with the position of the timeline. When a node is clicked, detailed statistics for that node is displayed, as seen in Fig. 2. When clicking on the connection between two nodes, we can see detailed FSM information. As with all parts of this tool, these statistics update dynamically based upon the current timeline position. This detail helps us determine in which direction the infection is occurring. From this view, we can click on a specific packet and see even more detail about its state. By changing the index on the timeline, it is easy to determine which node gets infected first by seeing the first node turn red, we can then determine the source of the attack.

5   Evaluation

5.1   Worm Traffic Generator Using NS3 Simulator

NS-3[3] is an open-source discrete event network simulator. Using Wireshark, a packet capture and analysis tool, we gather information about a particular worm. This information is fed into the simulator to simulate an attack from the worm. We simulate an attack because it is very difficult to get all attack data from online sources as many companies hide details of the attack for security reasons. Due to the hiding of the data, we cannot see the propagation of the worm throughout the network. Using a test network and the simulator allows us to simulate an attack and provides us with complete data about the attack giving a clear picture of the network behavior of the worm. In addition, by using the traffic generator we can change the network topology and simulate multiple worm attacks, capturing the attacks to PCAP files.

The network simulator configuration consist of six nodes in total as shown in Fig. 3. Nodes 0 and 1 are in Subnet 1. Nodes 3, 4, and 5 are in Subnet 2. Node 2 is a router that exists in both subnets and routes the traffic through them.

The generated traffic consists of normal traffic, SMB, FTP, and multiple packets containing the behavior of the Sasser and Slammer worms.

5.2   Experiment

We performed four experiments to demonstrate the ability of our method to analyze network traffic.

In the first experiment, we analyze the performance of our DNN to classify network traffic as being part of Sasser, Slammer, Eternal Rocks, Wannacry, or Petya worm attacks or as being normal traffic. Recall that our dataset, described

---

[3] https://nsnam.org.

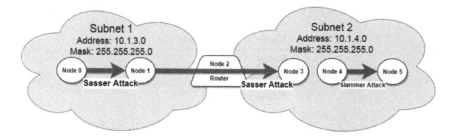

Fig. 3. Simulated evaluation network

Table 1. Performance of the DNN on classifying worm and normal traffic with known worms.

Name	Precision	Recall	F1
Sasser	0.8387	0.8125	0.8254
Slammer	1.0000	1.0000	1.0000
EternalRocks	0.9650	0.8894	0.9257
Wannacry	0.9581	0.9970	0.9772
Petya	0.9444	0.3119	0.4690
Normal	0.9985	0.9998	0.9991

in Sect. 4.1, had 11.2 MB of worm traffic and 85.1 MB of normal traffic. We used 90% of the dataset for training and 10% of the dataset for testing. Table 1 shows the precision, recall, and F1 score for the classification task on the test dataset. Our DNN achieved high precision in most cases. The precision for Sasser was lower, likely due to its high similarities to other worms. We observed low recall for the Petya worm, likely because its sample included normal traffic packets. We note that our classification of normal traffic was at 99%, which indicates that our system would have relatively low false alarms.

In the second experiment, we tested the system using a PCAP file containing both Sasser and Slammer worm traffic, which was generated using our NS-3 worm traffic generator tool. The PCAP file was applied as the input to the detection system and yields the results shown in Table 2. Our system uses packet by packet analysis to detect worms. The probability is calculated as:

$$P_n = \frac{\Sigma V[n]}{N},\qquad(1)$$

where $V[n]$ is the vector of probabilities generated by DNN and N is the number of vectors. In cases where the worm consists only of a single packet, the probability is low. In other cases where the worm attack consists of multiple packets, the probability is high. Despite the Slammer attack consisting of only one packet and having low probability, our system was still able to detect it.

Table 2. DNN classification probabilities on the simulated Sasser and Slammer worms.

Name	Probability
Sasser	0.7679
Normal	0.2030
Slammer	0.0012

Table 3. DNN classification probabilities on the unknown NotPetya sample.

Name	Probability
Petya	0.6046
Normal	0.2275
WannaCry	0.1206

In the third experiment, we wanted to test the system on a previously unseen, but similar worm. The main advantage of a DNN-based analyzer is the possibility to detect worms that may not be explicitly present in its training dataset. We obtained a sample of the NotPetya worm from CTU captures [26] and tested it with our classifier. NotPetya has similar, but not exactly the same, network behavior as the Petya worm. Table 3 shows that the DNN reported a 60% probability that the NotPetya trace was the Petya worm, which shows that the DNN can detect worms with similar network behavior.

Finally to further validate our DNN, we classified a sample of normal traffic obtained from Netresec[4]. Our DNN reported that the traffic was normal with a 99.996% probability, successfully classifying the normal traffic.

6   Conclusion

In this work, we have presented a hybrid worm detection and analysis approach. We trained a DNN classifier on the network traffic produced by several worms and normal network traffic. On the five worms tested, our classifier had an average precision of 94.1%. We also successfully classified a set of normal traffic with a 99.99% probability. In addition, we used our trained classifier to detect worm traffic that was unknown to the classifier but had network traffic similar to one of the known worms. The second part in our hybrid approach was the development of a visualizer based on D3 to observe the network and infection behavior of identified worms and to trace the attacks. The proposed hybrid approach provides better insight on worm activities and better detection of worms that have similar network behavior.

---

[4] https://www.netresec.com/?page=PCAP4SICS.

References

1. Moore, D., Paxson, V., Savage, S., Shannon, C., Staniford, S., Weaver, N.: Inside the slammer worm. IEEE Secur. Priv. **1**(4), 33–39 (2003)
2. Islam, A., Oppenheim, N., Thomas, W.: EternalBlue SMB protocol exploit (2017). https://www.fireeye.com/blog/threatresearch/2017/05/smb-exploited-wannacry-useof-eternalblue.html
3. Mishra, B.K., Jha, N.: SEIQRS model for the transmission of malicious objects in computer network. Appl. Math. Model. **34**(3), 710–715 (2010)
4. Mishra, B., Pandey, S.: Fuzzy epidemic model for the transmission of worms in computer network. Nonlinear Anal. R. World Appl. **11**(5), 4335–4341 (2010)
5. Toutonji, O.A., Yoo, S.-M.: Stability analysis of VEISV propagation modeling for network worm attack. Appl. Math. Model. **36**(6), 2751–2761 (2012)
6. Li, P., Salour, M., Xiao, S.: A survey of internet worm detection and containment. IEEE Commun. Surv. Tutor. **10**, 20–35 (2008)
7. Tang, Y., Chen, S.: Defending against internet worms: a signature-based approach. In: Proceedings of IEEE INFOCOM, vol. 2, pp. 1384–1394, March 2005
8. Kim, H.A., Karp, B.: Autograph: toward automated, distributed worm signature detection. In: Proceedings of the USENIX Security Symposium (2004)
9. Al-Hammadi, Y., Leckie, C.: Anomaly detection for internet worms. In: Proceedings of the 9th IFIP/IEEE International Symposium on Integrated Network Management, pp. 133–146, May 2005
10. Lakhina, A., Crovella, M., Diot, C.: Mining anomalies using traffic feature distributions. In: Proceedings of ACM SIGCOMM, pp. 217–228 (2005)
11. Chen, X., Heidemann, J.: Detecting early worm propagation through packet matching. Technical report, University of Southern California, Information Sciences Institute (2004)
12. Sarnsuwan, N., Charnsripinyo, C., Wattanapongsakorn, N.: A new approach for internet worm detection and classification. In: INC2010: 6th International Conference on Networked Computing, pp. 1–4, May 2010
13. Barhoom, T.S., Qeshta, H.A.: Adaptive worm detection model based on multi classifiers. In: Palestinian International Conference on Information and Communication Technology, pp. 57–65, April 2013
14. Rasheed, M.M., Badrawi, S., Faaeq, M.K., Faieq, A.K.: Detecting and optimizing internet worm traffic signature. In: 8th International Conference on Information Technology (ICIT), pp. 870–874, May 2017
15. Tang, T.A., Mhamdi, L., McLernon, D., Zaidi, S.A.R., Ghogho, M.: Deep learning approach for network intrusion detection in software defined networking. In: International Conference on Wireless Networks and Mobile Communications (WINCOM), pp. 258–263, October 2016
16. Axelsson, S.: Visualization for intrusion detection-hooking the worm. In: 8th European Symposium on Research in Computer Security ESORICS 2003 (2003)
17. Malaspinas, S.: Getting Sassy with Microsoft - An in depth analysis of the LSASRV.dll vulnerability. Global Information Assurance Certification Paper, pp. 1–56 (2004)
18. Abrams, T.: Microsoft LSASS buffer overflow from exploit to worm. SANS Network Security (2004)
19. Zheng, H., Lifa, W., Huabo, L., Fan, P.: Worm detection and containment in local networks. In: International Conference on Computer Science and Information Processing (CSIP), pp. 595–598 (2012)

234 H. H. L. AL-Maksousy and M. C. Weigle

20. Dübendorfer, T., Wagner, A., Hossmann, T., Plattner, B.: Flow-level traffic analysis of the blaster and sobig worm outbreaks in an internet backbone. In: Julisch, K., Kruegel, C. (eds.) DIMVA 2005. LNCS, vol. 3548, pp. 103–122. Springer, Heidelberg (2005). https://doi.org/10.1007/11506881_7
21. IPSumDump (2004). http://read.seas.harvard.edu/~kohler/ipsumdump
22. Francois Chollet. Keras (2015). https://keras.io/
23. Sasser (2017). https://wiki.wireshark.org/SampleCaptures
24. Wannacry (2017). https://precisionsec.com/wannacry-pcap-smb-445/
25. EternalRocks (2017). https://github.com/stamparm/EternalRocks/blob/master/misc/exploitation.pcap
26. CTU Malware Capture Botnet (2017). https://mcfp.felk.cvut.cz/publicDatasets/CTU-Malware-Capture-Botnet-288-1/

Author Index

Printed in the United States
By Bookmasters